A[illegible]AN Weather Book

To Margaret, Mary and Stephanie Colls

To Jan, Sarah and Matthew Whitaker

THE AUSTRALIAN Weather Book

Keith Colls, Supervising Meteorologist,
and Richard Whitaker, Senior Forecaster,
from the NSW Bureau of Meteorology

NATIONAL
BOOK DISTRIBUTORS AND PUBLISHERS

Photograph Acknowledgements

The authors and publisher would like to thank the following people and organisations for permission to reproduce their photographs.

Ineke Bardin: page 145.
Bureau of Meteorology: pages 9, 20, 23, 24, 26, 27, 28, 51, 68, 69, 83, 107, 111 above, 118, 120, 121, 122, 124, 128, 129, 130, 135, 147 above.
CSIRO: page 111 below.
Dominie Educational Press: pages 10 above, 12, 21, 148, 150.
Mr T. Donald: page 112 below.
Geoff Higgins: front and back covers; pages 10 below, 14, 16, 22, 39, 40, 57, 58, 75, 76, 93, 94, 149, 167, 168.
Dr Ness McVie: page 112 above.
Melbourne *Age*: page 143 above.
Queensland Newspapers: page 143 below.
Weldon Trannies: page 11.
Mr A. N. Whitaker: page 138.

Published by National Book Distributors and Publishers
3/2 Aquatic Drive
Frenchs Forest, NSW, 2086, Australia
This book has been edited, designed
and typeset in Australia by the publisher
First edition 1990
Reprinted 1993, 1995, 1996

Printed in Singapore by Kyodo Printing Co (S'pore) Pte Ltd
Typesetting processed by Deblaere Typesetting Pty Ltd

National Library of Australia
Cataloguing-in-Publication data

Colls, Keith.
The Australian weather book.

Bibliography.
Includes index.
ISBN 1 86302 287 2.

1. Meteorology — Australia. 2. Weather. 3. Australia — Climate. I. Whitaker, Richard. II. Title.

551.6994

Foreword

Meteorology and climate change are today topics of general discussion and of considerable media coverage. Everyone, it seems, suddenly wants to understand how Australia's climate relates to the global warming predicted to be a likely consequence of humankind's addition of greenhouse gases to the atmosphere. Even without potential changes to the climate, Australia enjoys (or suffers) perhaps the most highly variable climate of any continent on earth. Perhaps this is the reason why our culture reflects aspects of day-to-day and seasonal changes in the weather and climate. Australia is, in truth, a land 'of droughts and flooding rains' (Dorothea Mackellar, 1911).

In this book, Keith Colls and Richard Whitaker have aimed to describe atmospheric science in a way that we can all understand. They lead us gently from the early Greek and Roman fascination with weather as a gift and a threat from the gods through other aboriginal customs and folklore to the present-day science of meteorology. In describing how and why the atmosphere works, the authors give us a colourful overview of the climate of Australia, of atmospheric dynamics, and of weather phenomena which we can all observe as we go about our daily life.

At least as importantly, they put this comprehensive description of the weather patterns of Australia into the context of the general circulation of the atmosphere and of modern practices of meteorological observation including the type of satellite data display to which we have all become accustomed through television weather forecasts.

Weather and climate affect day-to-day living in many different ways: the economic impact of drought can be devastating for agriculture, but a 'shot in the arm' for breweries and ice-cream manufacturers. The authors detail these and the impacts of extreme weather events in the concluding chapters of the book. The final chapter focuses on climatic change and includes an overview of some of the current theories of climatic variation, concluding with a discussion of the greenhouse effect and of the ozone hole phenomenon.

There are two terrific advantages of this text: it is written by Australians for Australians and it is aimed specifically at members of the general public who have an interest in weather and climate and who wish to understand how these vital processes of the natural environment operate and the resultant atmospheric phenomena affect our lives. Without any doubt this book will gain a very wide readership and will serve to encourage many young people, and perhaps the not so young too, to observe the atmosphere more effectively and to understand its workings.

Professor Ann Henderson-Sellers
(Professor of Physical Geography)
Macquarie University
Sydney

Contents

The geostationary meteorological satellite (GMS). (See Chapter 7.)

Small cumulus clouds. The base of cumulus cloud is usually fairly flat. (See Chapter 6.)

Cumulus banks over historic church, Silverton, NSW. (See Chapter 6.)

Spectacular lightning over Brisbane, Qld. *(See Chapter 2.)*

Large cumulus clouds. These clouds can tower up to 7 or 8 kilometres into the atmosphere. (See Chapter 6.)

Altocumulus cloud is often mixed with altostratus cloud. (See Chapter 6.)

Introduction

The weather is possibly humanity's most discussed topic; it is talked about in all circles, from stockbrokers in Wall Street to Zulu tribesmen in Africa. It affects all of us in some way or another, either directly as in the cases of drought, flood or tempest, or in more subtle ways such as our moods, and our general day-to-day morale.

We live at the bottom of an ocean of air which, like the sea, is in constant restless motion, having breaking waves, spinning eddies and atmospheric tides, all of which go under the general title of 'the weather'. For thousands of years, humanity has felt a need to try to understand the causes of the weather and, through an understanding of them, has tried to manipulate those causes in order to control the weather.

Throughout history theories have been developed which attempt to explain the weather but it has been only in the present century that our understanding of the physical processes involved has advanced to the extent where the main features of atmospheric systems are understood sufficiently well to allow reasonably accurate weather predictions up to a few days ahead and broad seasonal outlooks up to a few months ahead.

These achievements would not have been possible without the advancements in technology which have allowed the state of the atmosphere to be sensed and described in a systematic fashion and on a global scale. It is only in recent times that we have been able to rise above our 'atmospheric sea' and look down on it from the vastness of space. Not only has this increased our understanding of the weather in motion, but it has also shown us the great beauty of our planet and awakened people to the need for protecting our atmosphere—the essential life support system of all living creatures on earth—which is now in danger of being drastically changed through the activities of humanity.

It is this knowledge of the significant atmospheric processes which has enabled reasonably reliable predictions of the climatic effects of the continued release of pollutants into the atmosphere to be made. The two most significant predictions are the enhancement of the greenhouse effect, resulting in a significant warming of the atmosphere, and the depletion of the ozone layer, leading to an increase in ultraviolet radiation reaching the earth's surface. If unchecked in the coming decades, both of these effects will have far-reaching and, for some forms of life, devastating consequences.

There is still a great deal to be discovered about the processes which drive the atmosphere and, irrespective of the technologies we develop, the weather will continue to be of prime importance to the human race for the foreseeable future.

The purpose of this book is not only to explain the essential features of the atmosphere and describe how these manifest as weather and climate but also to communicate to the reader some of the beauty of its phenomena and some of the awe and wonder which it has engendered in countless generations of humanity.

Overleaf: Banks of Cumulus clouds near Hay, NSW.

1. In the Beginning

The weather has long been a subject of fascination to the human race. From the earliest times the weather was believed to play a major role in the determination of an individual's happiness, security and well-being. Even in the modern urban environment, weather exerts an influence in such areas as increased food prices after drought or flood, or increased insurance premiums to cover weather-related disasters. Despite the invention of watertight shelter, air-conditioning and a reliable food-providing mechanism, humanity cannot ever divorce itself from the weather. It affects each of us, whether directly or indirectly, and will always play a role in our lives.

The study of the weather (meteorology—from the Greek *meteoros*, meaning 'high in the air', and *logos*, meaning 'discourse') has ancient roots in several different societies and has evolved over three broad eras; namely Divine (–1200), Folkloric (1200–1800) and Scientific (1800–).

Divine Era

Early ideas of the weather usually attributed the various states of the sky to the mood of the gods in control of that area of creation. The ancient Greeks believed that Zeus was the controller of the sky while storms at sea were caused by the activities of Neptune. Ancient Egyptians believed that Ra, the sun-god, determined the weather as he conducted his daily voyage across the sky, while the Romans paid allegiance to their god of the sky, Jupiter. Thor was the famous Teutonic god of thunder, and his Lithuanian counterpart was the god Perkunas. The Aborigines of northern Australia hold similar beliefs to explain the phenomena of thunder and lightning. The Arnhem Land Aborigines, for example, believe that the thunder-man Jambawul travels the skies on the huge thunderstorm clouds during the northern wet season. The raindrops are thought to carry spirit children from the clouds to the ground in search of a human mother. Melville Island Aborigines believe that the thunder-woman Bumerali produces lightning by striking the ground with her huge stone axe, which sends sparks flying around the sky.

Another Aboriginal thunder-deity is Mamaragan who lives in the wet season clouds and produces thunder by crashing the huge white mountains together and watches as the great sparks fly towards the earth.

Similar beliefs are associated with other societies such as the American Indians, Aztecs and Mongolians. Because of the direct influence of the weather on these societies and their lifestyles, the 'weatherman' was an important person, with great power over decision making. The first weathermen were usually high priests, witchdoctors or medicine men, and their duties were far more difficult than those of the modern-day meteorologist. Not only did these early weathermen have to predict the weather, but where necessary, they also had to modify it to suit the needs of their people. They did this by arranging and directing the various rites, ceremonies and sacrifices necessary to persuade the gods to act appropriately.

Probably the most famous 'weather modification' ceremony is the rain dance, common to several civilisations including various American Indian tribes and the Australian Aborigines.

The weather could also be used as a weapon in warfare, provided of course that gods were sympathetic to the cause in question. Perhaps the best known examples of this were the two occasions, in 1274 and 1281, when Kublai Khan's naval forces were smashed by typhoons while amassing to invade Japan. The Japanese people

According to Aboriginal legend the thunder-god Mamaragan lives in the wet season clouds.

believed that this was the result of their god sending a divine wind—or *Kami Kaze*—to rout the enemy and protect their country.

Folkloric Era

Gradually the belief in the 'divine' nature of the weather was supplanted by a form of folklore that consisted of a loose collection of observations regarding the behaviour of plants, animals and cloud formations. These observations applied to the local area of origin, and are just as interesting from a geographical viewpoint as from the meteorological one.

Probably the best known 'bridge' between the Divine and Folkloric eras was provided by the Greek poet Aratus. In his poem *Phaenomena* which was written about 275 BC and was regarded in both Greek and Roman antiquity as the definitive work on the weather, Aratus noted that although Zeus controlled the weather, he also gave valuable hints of things to come through cloud formations, the state of the moon and stars, as well as the behaviour of plants and animals.

Aratus wrote of Zeus:

> We are indeed his children; and he in kindness to men gives helpful signs and rouses people to work, reminding them of their livelihood, tells when the soil is best for oxen and mattocks, tells when the seasons are right for planting trees and sowing all their seeds. For Zeus himself has fixed the signs in the sky, demarking the constellations, and organised for the year stars to give the most reliable signs of the seasons to men, so that everything may grow without fail.

Aratus's lengthy poem also contains many observations that time has shown have no connection with the weather; however relevant information also was noted, for example, '...

when the Sun delays his appearance before dawn and reddish clouds are visible here and there, the fields do not go unwatered on that day,' and 'often when rain is coming, clouds before it appear looking very like fleeces.'

Aratus knew that weather forecasting was a tricky business and remarked:

> For often a man on a calm night secures his ship in fear of the sea at dawn. Sometimes trouble strikes on the third day or the fifth, sometimes it arrives unexpectedly; for we men as yet do not learn everything from Zeus, still much is hidden, whereof Zeus, if he wishes, will enlighten us anon.

Although it is now nearly twenty-three centuries since these words were written, 'still much is hidden' is indeed an accurate statement of our current knowledge of the weather.

As the centuries rolled past the days of Aratus, meteorology made surprisingly little progress. Other areas of human endeavour forged ahead impressively during the Middle Ages, with significant steps forward occurring in mathematics, chemistry and physics. Meteorology, however, was bogged down in a morass of trite sayings, doggerel and inane verse that was passed down and accepted from generation to generation. Many of these old sayings have lasted through the ages and are still known today. They fall into two broad categories, namely the behaviour of the plant and animal kingdoms, and the appearance of the sky.

Behaviour of the Plant and Animal Kingdoms

Some plants and animals are 'weather sensitive', that is, they react on occasion to meteorological conditions. Precisely what they are reacting to is not clear; it may be changing moisture content of the air (humidity), fluctuating temperature, light or barometric pressure. It may be some combination of all of these things.

Animal folklore attempts to correlate the present behaviour of various animals with the impending weather, for example, the old English proverb 'The lark soaring high heralds a blue sky'. The American saying 'When the cuckoo calls throughout the day, a cold year is on the way' attempts long-range forecasting. Donkeys provided the inspiration for the Spanish proverb 'When asses their ears do toss and sway, rain before the end of day.' And from Norway comes the advice: 'When a black cow scratches her flanks, she foretells bad weather.'

Cats also provided several rules of thumb, for example from Holland comes the saying 'When cats wash themselves, rain will come'; from Britain, 'When cats scratch the table legs, a change is coming'; from the United States, 'If a cat looks out the window, it is looking for rain'; and from Iran, 'When cats stand and lick their paws, it will soon be sunny out of doors'.

Much of the animal lore, however, is contradictory, for example, 'If toads call today, the Sun's on the way' from Japan but also, 'When toads loudly call, rain's sure to fall' from England. Apparently toads sometimes find themselves in the same dilemma as the modern-day meteorologist when making weather forecasts.

The behaviour of plants and crops also found its way into weather folklore in various sayings such as 'Mushrooms galore, much snow in store; no mushrooms at all, no snow will fall' (German origin) and 'When the leaves of wheat are narrow and short, there will be much snow' (Japanese origin).

Appearance of the Sky

This aspect of the Folkloric era contains some useful information and observations, which have solid roots in modern-day meteorology. Some examples from around the world are:

> 'When the sun is at home [encircled by a halo], it will soon rain' (Zuni Indians of New Mexico).

> 'A rainbow at night is a sailor's delight. A rainbow in the morning is a sailor's warning' (British origin).
> 'Red sky in the morning, shepherd's warning; red sky at night, shepherd's delight' (British origin).
> 'A rainbow in the eastern sky, the morrow will be fine and dry; a rainbow in the west that gleams, rain tomorrow falls in streams' (Chinese origin).

Sayings such as these were colourful but not accurate, and they did not further the study of meteorology. Real progress in meteorology, which is a combination of several of the scientific disciplines, including physics, chemistry and mathematics, could not take place until several key inventions and discoveries had slotted into place.

The invention of the thermometer by Galileo Galilei in 1607 and the invention of the barometer by Evangelista Torricelli in 1643 allowed the concepts of temperature and atmospheric pressure to be quantitatively measured and this was an important step in the history of meteorology. As Lord Kelvin, a nineteenth century Scottish physicist, was later to remark:

> When you can measure what you are speaking about and express it in numbers, you know something about it, and when you cannot measure it, when you cannot express it in numbers, your knowledge is of a meagre and unsatisfactory kind. It may be the beginning of knowledge but you have scarcely in your thought advanced to a stage of science.

Another giant stride forward came with the discovery of Boyle's Law in 1659. (This stated that at constant temperature, the volume of a given mass of gas is inversely proportional to its pressure.) This was followed in 1735 by George Hadley's explanation of the broad wind regimes of the earth including the effect of the planet's rotation. The pieces of the meteorological jigsaw puzzle were falling into place.

Atmospheric air as a 'cocktail' of various gases such as nitrogen, oxygen and carbon dioxide was described by Antoine Lavoisier in 1783 and important work on the physics and chemistry of water vapour condensation was performed by John Dalton in 1800. All these events laid the foundation for the birth of the Scientific era of meteorology. Only one factor now stood in the way and this was the lack of a method for fast communication over long distances.

As far back as the eighteenth century scientists had realised that weather travelled in organised masses of air and that in Europe and America the movement was roughly from west to east. In 1816, H. W. Brandes of the University of Breslau drew the first known isobaric weather chart using European observations taken some thirty years previously. This chart confirmed that weather sequences corresponded with giant atmospheric circulations of high and low pressures that moved around the earth.

This information meant that if only there was some fast and reliable method of communication between one township and another, advance warning of approaching bad weather could be given. Because of this general west-to-east movement of air, it was realised that if a fast method of trans-continental communication was available, a weather warning system could be operated; if, for example, people over the central parts of the United States learned that the west coast States were being battered by severe storms, they also could reason that bad weather was on the way. This information could, in turn, be passed on to the eastern seaboard. From ancient times, fast methods of communication had evolved in various civilisations. Many African tribes used drums or tom-toms to pass news around quickly and reliably. The American Indians used smoke signals and the Australian Aborigines also used signal fires to communicate with each other.

After European settlement in Australia, various

versions of eighteenth and nineteenth century communications were tried. Signalling by displaying different flags had long been a naval technique, and both Sydney and Melbourne had their flagstaff hills from which messages were displayed to the public; the Sydney suburb of Pennant Hills was so named because it was the site of one such signal station.

Another technique was the semaphore, which was usually a tower or pole on which were mounted moveable arms signifying certain predetermined messages. An early semaphore system used in Australia was between Port Arthur and Hobart Town in the early 1800s. If a convict escaped from the penal colony at Port Arthur, this news was rapidly signalled back to Hobart by a sequence of semaphores on the intervening hilltops. Systems involving flashing lights by night and mirrors by day were also practised by various groups and individuals.

None of these techniques, however, was sufficiently fast or reliable to transmit meteorological information in enough detail. The breakthrough came in 1844 when Samuel Morse demonstrated his electric telegraph by transmitting messages between Washington and Baltimore. This was the last piece of the jigsaw puzzle to fall into place, and heralded the Scientific era for meteorology. At last it was possible to tackle the problem of forecasting the weather in a constructive and serious way.

Scientific Era

As if to make up for centuries of lost time, meteorology now blossomed in several countries. In the United States Joseph Henry, the Secretary of the Smithsonian Institute, wrote to the Institutions Regents in 1847:

> It is proposed to organise a system of observations which shall extend as far as possible over the North American continent ... The citizens of the United States are now scattered over every part of the southern and western portions of North America, and the extended lines of the telegraph will furnish a ready means of warning the more northern and eastern observers to be on the watch for the first appearance of an advancing storm.

Similar systems of observation, which were linked by the electric telegraph, were developed around the world and an international network was soon linked up.

Another important step forward was made in 1892 when observations of wind and temperature at upper levels of the atmosphere were achieved on a systematic basis in France by Georges Besançon and Gustave Hermite using small free-floating balloons towing aloft tiny instrument packages to record the required information. This is the same system we use today.

With this background of rapid meteorological development following the birth of the Scientific era, we can now look at the development in Australia which followed a slightly different course to other parts of the world.

Meteorology in Australia

An interesting point about early meteorology in Australia is the fact that the Folkloric era was only brief and transient. The reasons for this are fairly obvious; European settlement in Australia was followed only fifty-six years later by the invention of the telegraph. This meant that only half a century was available to develop a weather folklore for Australia, and as a result there are few peculiarly Australian weather sayings. Instead many are transplants or adaptations of earlier English or European versions. This is seen as a lack of meteorological culture by some and as an advantage by others, because old ways did not have to be unlearned before a real understanding of the weather could begin.

Australia's formal entry into meteorology began with the arrival of the First Fleet. On board the HMS *Supply* was a man who is recognised as Australia's first non-Aboriginal 'weatherman', Lieutenant William Dawes. Dawes had been allocated some astronomical and meteorological instruments, including a barometer and thermometer, and he was ordered by Governor Phillip to set up an observatory as soon as possible after disembarkation.

Phillip wanted desperately to build up a picture of the climate of Sydney Cove in order to work out the feasibility of certain crop growths which would be vital to the survival of the settlement. In accordance with his wishes, Dawes set up his observatory on the adjacent promontory and kept records of the weather, including temperature, pressure and rainfall, for three years. This was the first, continuous formal documentation of Australia's weather ever conducted. The site of this first observatory, near the south-west pylon of today's Sydney Harbour Bridge, is known as Dawes Point, a fitting tribute to this efficient and industrious officer.

Lieutenant William Dawes, recognised as Australia's first non-Aboriginal 'weatherman'.

Australia's first observatory was set up on what is known today as Dawes Point.

Meteorology in Victoria was pioneered by a Bavarian ship's officer, Georg Balthesar von Neumayer, a most unusual man with extremely diverse interests. He obtained his doctorate in Munich in 1849, intending to become a teacher. Instead he went to sea, arrived in Melbourne in 1852 and spent some time, apparently with little success, on the Victorian goldfields.

A rather complex sequence of events then followed, during which von Neumayer returned home only to sail again to Melbourne, arriving in 1856. He had somehow persuaded King Maximilian of Bavaria to equip him with various meteorological instruments and he quickly set up an observatory on Melbourne's Flagstaff Hill. Soon he had established an observation network, consisting mainly of lighthouses, throughout Victoria. He continued to be funded by the benevolent King Maximilian. His exemplary work was recognised by the Government of Victoria in 1859 when he was appointed Government Astronomer. Before he returned to Europe in 1863 he had laid the foundation for Victoria's

Cumulonimbus is the tallest cloud in the atmosphere. The clouds shown here do not have the characteristic flattened top known as the anvil. (See Chapter 6.)

Broken altostratus, Flinders Ranges, SA. (See Chapter 6.)

Georg von Neumayer was appointed Victoria's Government Astronomer in 1859.

Sir Charles Todd, supervisor of the building of the Overland Telegraph Line from Port Augusta to Port Darwin.

weather service so establishing a perpetual bond of meteorological history between Australia and Germany.

The driving force behind the development of the infant science in South Australia was Sir Charles Todd, a man of vast energy and high organisational ability. He arrived from England in 1855 wearing the two hats of Superintendent of Telegraphs and Government Astronomer for South Australia. Undaunted by the vast distances and inhospitable countryside, he focused his attentions on the construction of a telegraph system, and soon had Adelaide connected with Melbourne and Sydney.

By 1872 he had completed what must rank as one of the great construction feats of all time with the building of the telegraph line between Adelaide and Darwin, through some of the hottest and most unforgiving country on earth. Having set up this extensive telegraph system, he then made the collection and transmission of weather observations a routine duty of all his telegraph operators.

Todd continued his distinguished career into old age, achieving numerous honours and distinctions along the way. He retired as Postmaster General at the age of eighty, dying a few years later in Adelaide in 1910. His immortality is assured, however, in the world of meteorology.

Much of the meteorological pioneering work in Queensland was performed by an eccentric and lively man called Clement Wragge (nicknamed 'Inclement' by his opponents) who was Queensland's Government Astronomer between 1887 and 1902. As with his counterparts in the other colonies, he was a man of boundless energy, who threw himself into his work with great enthusiasm. By 1893 he had established nearly one hundred meteorological stations in Queensland, together with four hundred rainfall stations, so laying the meteorological foundation for Queensland. He also began the tradition of naming tropical cyclones, initially with letters from the Greek alphabet, then with characters from Greek and Roman mythology. He also began to name the cyclones after the politicians of the day, on the grounds that both were national disasters. This did not endear him to people in high places, and probably counted heavily against him in later years.

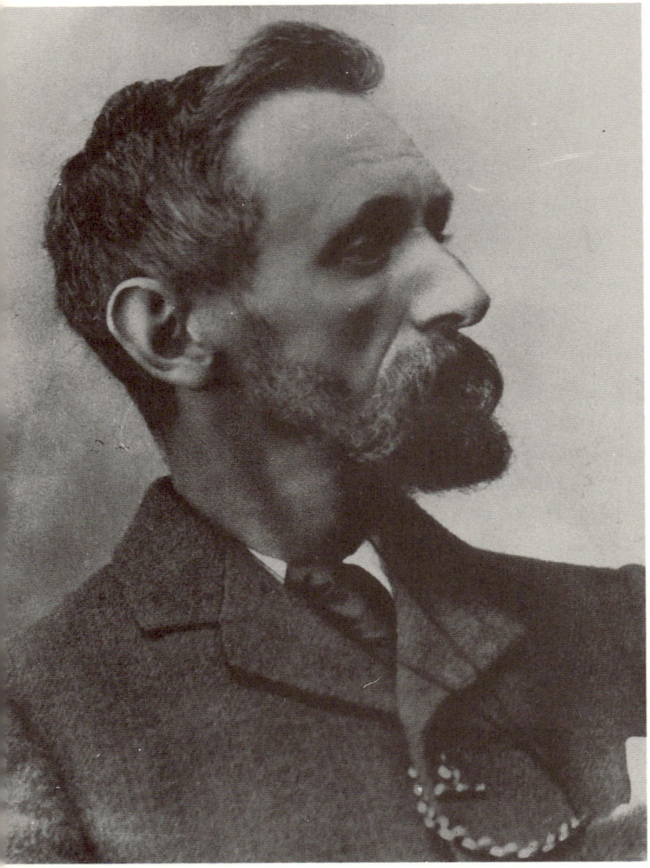

Pioneering meteorologist Clement Wragge was nicknamed 'Inclement' by his opponents.

Assisted by a young man called Inigo Jones, Wragge also began to issue long-range forecasts for Queensland using a European technique, which had been suitably modified. This was the beginning of the tradition of 'alternative forecasting' techniques, carried on today by Jones's pupil, Lennox Walker, with the issuing of forecasts for particular locations several months ahead.

Embracing this facet of meteorology further eroded Wragge's position with his peer group, but the real parting of the ways occurred in a rather bizarre way. In 1902 a drought afflicted a great deal of eastern Australia, including much of Queensland. Wragge had been impressed with the European idea of creating rain by firing large vertical cannon into the atmosphere and amid much publicity he installed Steiger Vortex Guns in a ring around Charleville. These funnel-shaped cannon, which produced large explosions and rapidly rising smoke rings, were discharged at various intervals while much of Australia watched with interest. Modern calculations show that any energy produced by such an experiment would be negligible as far as the atmosphere is concerned, and would be comparable to trying to stop a tidal wave by tossing a brick into the sea. Predictably the experiment was a failure and Wragge had to endure the ridicule and public displeasure familiar to the modern-day meteorologist after a forecast failure. He left Queensland soon after.

It is easy to label Wragge as a crank but his contribution to the fledgling science of meteorology in Australia is undeniable. In addition to the work already mentioned, he established the first weather observatories on Mt Wellington, near Hobart, and on Australia's highest mountain, Mt Kosciusko. He also represented Australia at an International Meteorological Organisation (IMO) meeting in Europe, helping to cement Australia's place at the forefront of meteorology.

Another surprising contribution to the Australian weather scene was made by G. W. Goyder, who was in fact the Surveyor General of South Australia during the mid-1860s. He was a small man, not much more than 1.5 m in height, with red hair and pallid complexion. This unimpressive physique, however, housed a human dynamo who performed his duties honestly, meticulously and with great accuracy. 'Little Energy', as he was nicknamed, was the perfect choice for the job of Surveyor General. During the early 1860s, much of the good farming land in South Australia had already been taken, and the government was under great pressure to open up the vast tracts of land further north towards the Flinders Ranges. Goyder was ordered to report on the feasibility of this idea and following a detailed survey in 1865, he drew a loop on the map outside of which, he claimed, farming would not be feasible. This loop, which became known as 'Goyder's Line', ran up the eastern side of Spencers Gulf, along the southern flank of the Flinders Ranges and then south-east passing near Peterborough, Jamestown, Burra and Swan Reach. Goyder's observation on the vegetation in the area had led him to believe that outside this line, farming would not be sustainable because of insufficient rainfall.

This was a bold prediction, as no detailed rainfall records were then available on which to base his belief. It was also not what the politicians of the day wanted to hear as it put added pressure on them to make the unpopular decision of keeping the backblocks closed to agriculture.

Predictably enough, Goyder's Line created a turmoil of tirade and filibuster, including parliamentary debate, during which it was urged that the line be pushed further north, preferably out of South Australia altogether. It was even suggested that Goyder was on the payroll of the pastoralists who wanted to protect their land from agricultural farming. This was a great injustice to Goyder who was a man of unimpeachable integrity. Caving into this pressure, the government went against Goyder's advice and allowed farming allotments to be sold well north of his line and hundreds of people began wheat farms in the backblocks of South Australia. 'Lady Luck' seemed to smile on these farmers and for the next few years good rains came and bumper wheat crops were produced from the 'Golden North'.

The farmers said that Goyder had forgotten the truth of the old saying 'rain follows the plough', a relic from the European Folkloric era. By breaking up the soil, so the theory went, more moisture was released into the air and became available for rainfall. Protracted drought during the early 1880s forced many farmers into ruin and the rest to their knees. Eventually most walked off their land and returned to Adelaide, disillusioned and embittered. Derelict homesteads and abandoned farm machinery still dot the area as monuments to the fact that weather cannot be ignored and must be legislated for in our day-to-day activities.

Goyder had made one of the early comments on the climatology of the continent, namely that most areas of South Australia have insufficient rain to support general agriculture. It is not known exactly how he reached this conclusion but more than a hundred years of subsequent rainfall data show that Goyder's Line was a very accurate comment on the rainfall of the area.

Milestones of Australian Meteorology

With such remarkable men focusing their talents on the new science, development was rapid. Greater organisation between the colonies was arranged in 1879 when a meteorological conference, attended by the Government Astronomers from New South Wales, Victoria

Central office staff of the Commonwealth Bureau of Meteorology in 1910.

and South Australia, was convened in Sydney. Further conferences were held in 1881 and 1889, during which time the network of observational stations was enhanced and the standardisation of instruments, weather codes and means of telegraph reporting of observations was begun.

A system evolved that dictated that although there should be free and frequent exchange of meteorological information between the various capital cities, each colony would be responsible for weather services within its own boundaries. Today the Commonwealth Government maintains regional offices in each capital city.

In the meantime a very significant event occurred on 5 February 1877, when Australia's first weather map was published in the *Sydney Morning Herald*. It was prepared by the then New South Wales Government Astronomer, Henry Chamberlain Russell, who was Australia's first native-born Government Astronomer. The map showed reports from a number of New South Wales, Victorian and Queensland stations on the telegraphic network and showed a low-pressure cell centred somewhere over north-eastern New South Wales. This was a forerunner of the daily weather chart that is now an essential part of our newspaper and television news services.

It was soon realised that rather than have a piecemeal organisation run by individual State governments, it was best to monitor the weather on a national scale. The Bureau of Meteorology was established in 1908 and its head was the first Commonwealth meteorologist H. A. Hunt. He began operations with a total staff of forty-nine to provide a national weather service for the population of Australia, which was then around four million.

Hunt and his staff inherited a solid base of

Henry Chamberlain Russell, Australia's first native-born Government Astronomer.

observational sites and telegraph systems pioneered by the nineteenth century Government Astronomers, together with extensive meteorological records extending back to the early times of European settlement. This was an invaluable inheritance and it enabled the embryonic Bureau to provide effective services from the beginning. The development of the system was also a tremendous achievement because of the vast distances involved and the generally inhospitable nature of the countryside on which observational sites had to be located and connected by telegraph.

The Bureau of Meteorology grew steadily over the years, increasing its range of services to cover both capital city and State forecasts and, with the advent of airline passenger traffic, flight forecasts for aeroplanes. The size of the organisation increased further during World War II when the Bureau was incorporated into the RAAF for the duration of the war.

Many of the Bureau staff were posted to the South Pacific theatre during World War II to provide aerodrome forecasts for operational squadrons in action against the Japanese. Many also saw action in north Australia. Post-war expansion in the Bureau was on a modest scale, but a greater public interest in the weather grew after 1956, when television presentations on 'tomorrow's forecast' were begun. There has also been a renewal of interest in the great outdoors over the last thirty years or so, with people engaging in 'weather sensitive' activities in increasing numbers. These include such pastimes

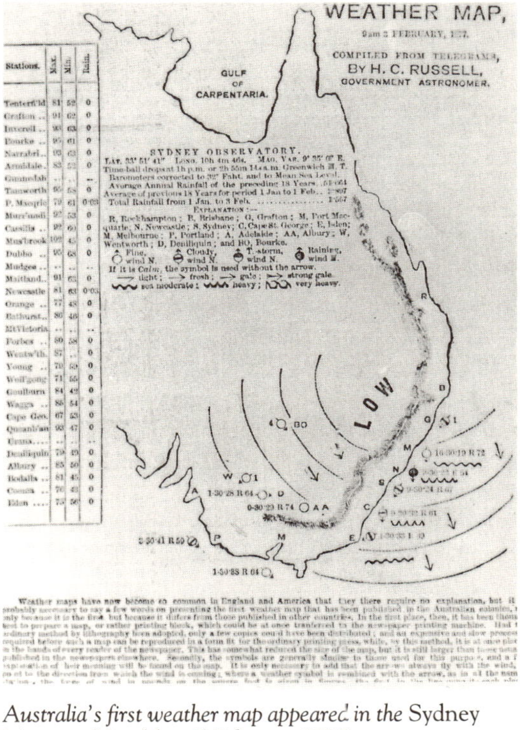

Australia's first weather map appeared in the Sydney Morning Herald *on 5 February 1877.*

A balloon flight in wartime New Guinea. These instruments are still used to monitor the atmosphere.

as recreational boating, surfing, hang-gliding, bushwalking, camping, windsurfing, parachuting, ballooning, four-wheel driving, and fun-running.

In addition to these added demands for forecasting the weather, there has also been an increase in requests for weather statistics for planning purposes. Some examples of this include information on solar and wind power, rainfall rates for drainage and dam design, generalised data for farm and crop planning and wave statistics for oil rig operations.

The Bureau of Meteorology now issues more than one million forecasts and warnings annually, together with a similar number of aviation briefings. Ten million calls are made to the telephone weather service and around half a million queries and documentations are requested per annum.

The Australian weather service now ranks with the best in the world. It has been recognised by the World Meteorological Organisation, which nominated three World Meteorological Centres—Washington, Moscow and, as its Southern Hemisphere city, Melbourne.

2. The Climate of Australia

If the climate of Australia had to be summarised in one word, that word would surely be 'diverse'. Because of its size and location, Australia's climate covers a spectrum of climatic classifications ranging from pure tropical over the northern quarter to alpine over the highlands of southern New South Wales, Victoria and Tasmania.

Rainfall

Australia is a dry continent; more than half its land area is desert and less than 30 per cent receives sufficient rainfall to support general agriculture. Figure 2.1 shows that a large proportion of the landmass receives, on average, less than 300 mm of rain annually.

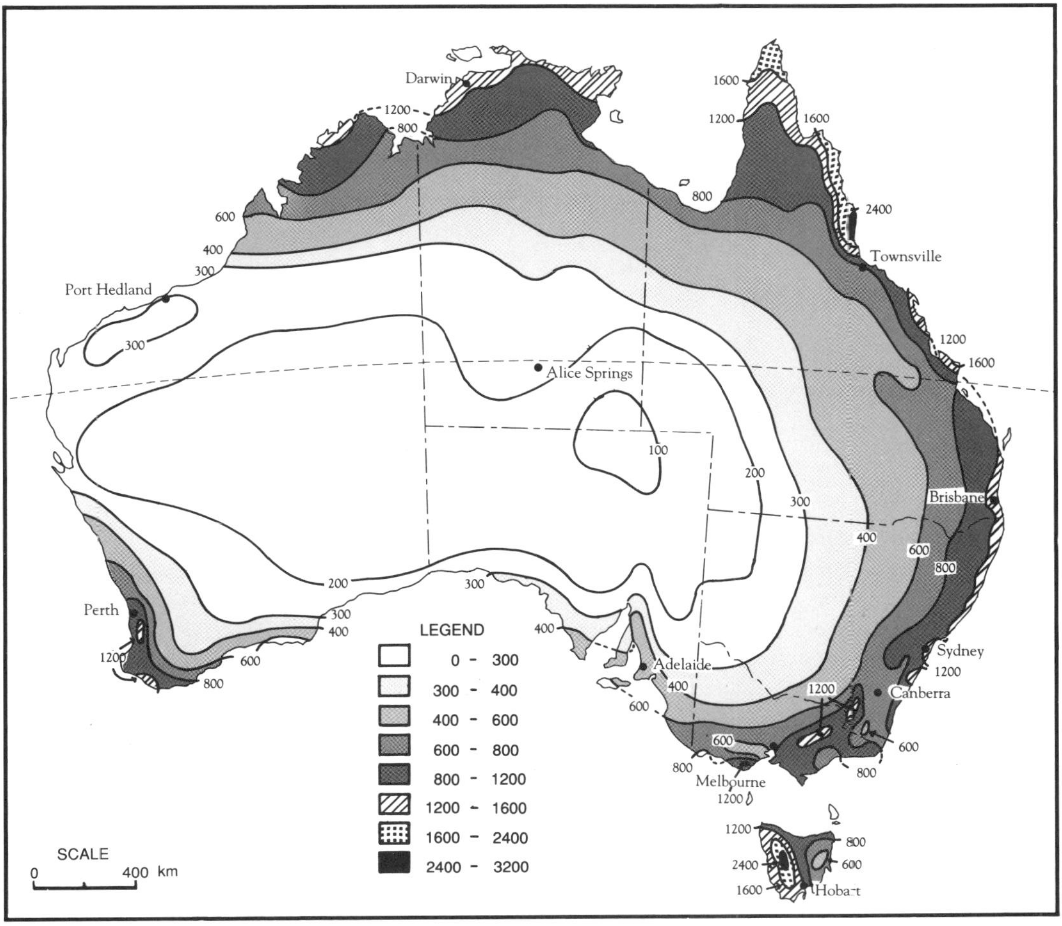

Figure 2.1—Annual rainfall in millimetres.

Overleaf: Figure 2.3—Climatic zones of Australia, according to rainfall.

Bountiful, reliable falls occur only in a coastal strip, extending from western Victoria through Tasmania, New South Wales, Queensland, the Northern Territory and into north-western parts of Western Australia. A small chunk also clings to the south-west corner, near Perth. Broadly speaking, the rains south of about 35°S are winter rains, and those north of 25°S are summer rains. The area in between is a mixture of both.

A good illustration of this is provided by considering the rainfall patterns of Hobart, Sydney and Darwin, as shown in Figure 2.2. Hobart has a winter rainfall maximum, Darwin a summer one, and Sydney has a double peak, that is, one in summer and one in winter.

Figure 2.2—Rainfall in millimetres, Darwin, Hobart and Sydney.

	Darwin	Hobart	Sydney
Month	Mean monthly	Mean monthly	Mean monthly
No. of years of record	86	100	123
January	391	48	102
February	330	41	115
March	260	47	133
April	103	54	123
May	14	49	122
June	3	58	133
July	1	53	102
August	2	52	78
September	13	52	68
October	50	63	77
November	126	56	79
December	243	56	78
Yearly Totals	1536	629	1215

Figure 2.3 shows the climatic zones of Australia, which are broken up according to rainfall. To underline the great variation in rainfall across the continent, it is interesting to note that the

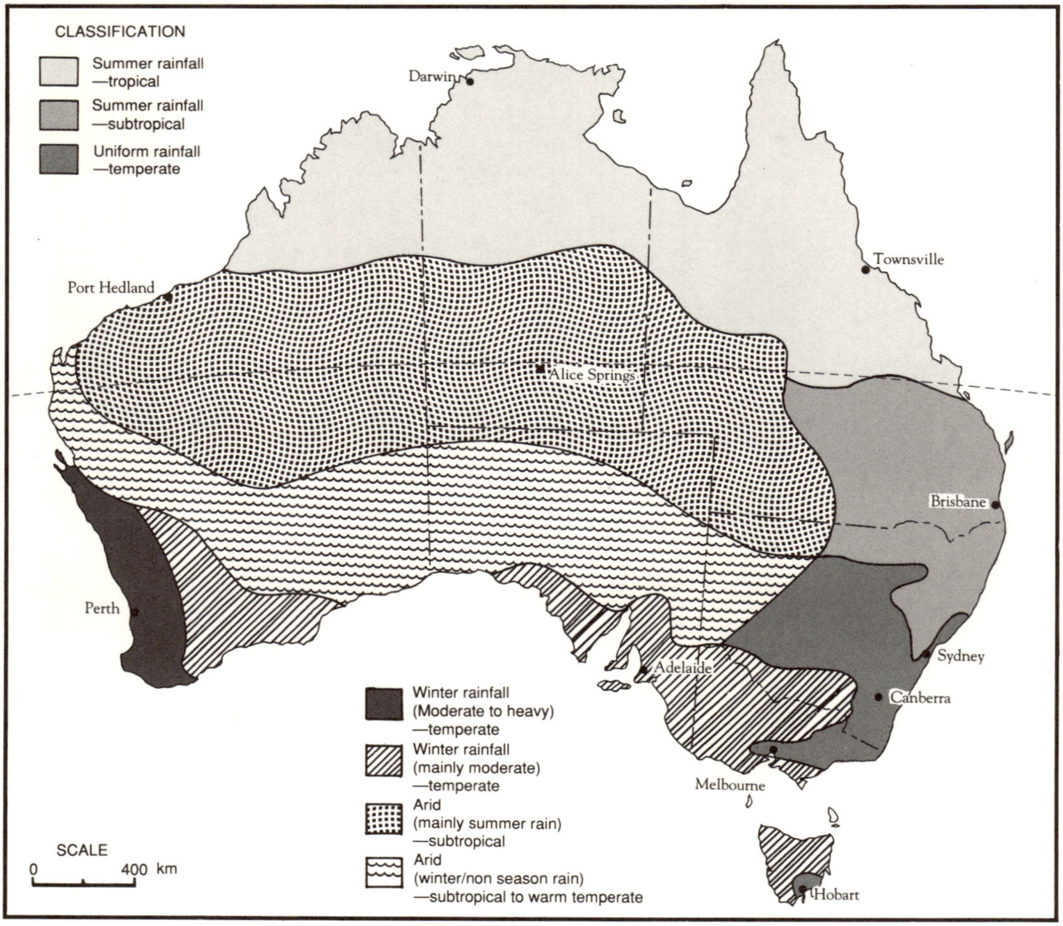

Figure 2.4—Rainfall in millimetres, capital cities.

	Adelaide		Brisbane		Canberra		Darwin		Hobart		Melbourne		Perth		Sydney	
Month	Mean monthly	Mean no. of days of rain	Mean monthly	Mean no. of days of rain	Mean monthly	Mean no. of days of rain	Mean monthly	Mean no. of days of rain	Mean monthly	Mean no. of days of rain	Mean monthly	Mean no. of days of rain	Mean monthly	Mean no. of days of rain	Mean monthly	Mean no. of days of rain
No. of years of record	140	140	130	122	43	43	86	79	100	100	126	126	106	102	123	123
January	20	4	165	13	61	8	391	20	48	11	48	8	8	3	102	13
February	21	4	164	14	61	7	330	20	41	10	49	7	12	3	115	13
March	24	5	145	15	53	7	260	19	47	11	53	9	20	4	133	14
April	44	9	86	11	48	7	103	8	54	13	58	11	45	8	123	13
May	68	13	71	9	49	9	14	1	49	14	58	14	124	14	122	13
June	72	15	68	8	39	9	3	Nil	58	15	50	14	183	17	133	12
July	66	16	56	7	38	10	1	Nil	53	15	48	15	174	18	102	11
August	61	15	46	7	45	12	2	Nil	52	16	51	15	137	17	78	11
September	51	13	47	8	52	10	13	2	52	15	58	14	80	14	68	11
October	44	11	75	9	69	12	50	6	63	17	68	14	55	11	77	12
November	31	8	99	10	62	10	126	11	56	14	60	12	21	6	79	12
December	26	6	130	12	52	8	243	17	56	13	58	10	14	4	78	12
Yearly Totals	528	119	1153	123	629	108	1536	104	629	164	659	143	873	119	1215	148

driest place in Australia is Mulka (South Australia) with an average annual rain-fall of 103 mm, while Bellenden Ker (Queensland) is the wettest place with an average of 8352 mm of rain per year.

Figure 2.4 shows some rainfall data from around the continent. Darwin has the highest average yearly rainfall (1536 mm) with Sydney the second highest (1215 mm); Adelaide is the driest capital; Sydney has nearly twice the annual rainfall of Melbourne; Darwin's rainfall is nearly three times that of Adelaide; and Brisbane holds the capital city record for the maximum 24-hour fall, which was 465 mm on 21 January 1897.

Temperature

As with rainfall, there is a great diversity of temperature ranges across Australia. The below 0°C blizzard conditions of the Australian Alps in the winter contrast with occasional 50°C plus temperatures over the inland during summer. The lowest temperature ever recorded in Australia was –22.2°C at Charlotte Pass, New South Wales, on 14 July 1945 and 22 August 1947 while the highest shade temperature was 53.1°C, recorded at Cloncurry (Queensland) on 16 January 1889. Figures 2.5 and 2.6 show the distribution of average daily maximum and minimum temperatures for January and July based on long-term records collected by the Bureau of Meteorology.

Figure 2.7 is a table showing temperature data for the capital cities. Some interesting points from the table are that Darwin is the hottest capital with Brisbane coming second; the hottest month on average in both Sydney and Melbourne is January with Melbourne being slightly hotter than Sydney; July is the coldest month in all capitals; Canberra is the coldest capital; and the average maximum temperature of Darwin in July is warmer than the maximum for all other capitals for their hottest months. Figures 2.8 and 2.9 show tables of extreme maximum and minimum temperatures for each State.

With a prolonged period of high temperatures a heatwave is often experienced. Parts of inland Australia frequently record more than three successive days of 40°C plus temperatures, and some parts of the northern inland often experience twenty consecutive days of 40°C plus. Marble Bar, in the north-west of Western Australia, lays claim to being one of the hottest places on earth, with a record of 161 consecutive days in excess of 37.8°C, which occurred between 30 October 1923 and 7 April 1924.

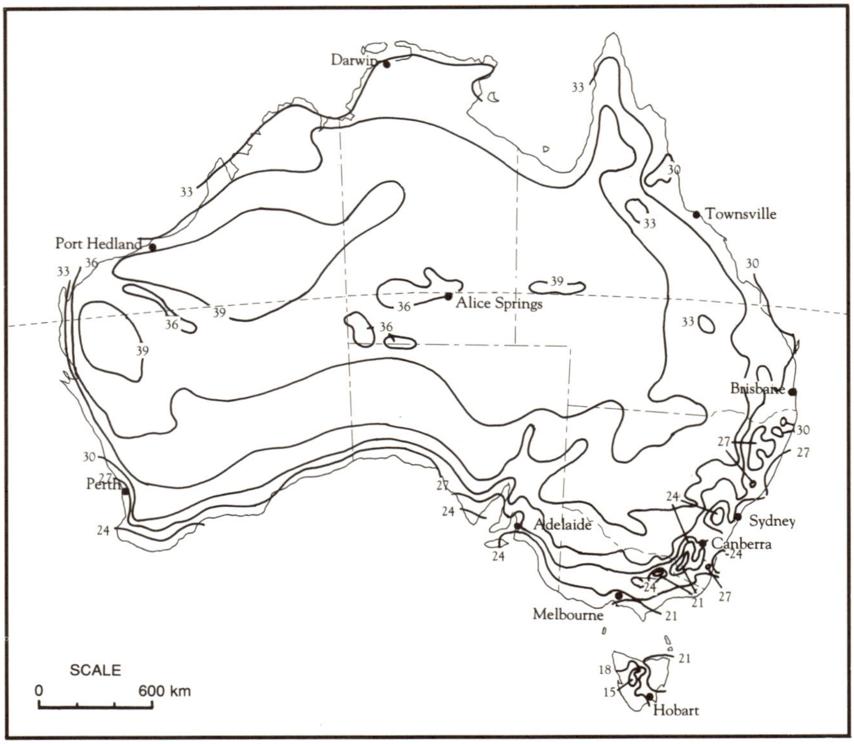

Figure 2.5—Average daily maximum temperatures for January.

Figure 2.6—Average daily minimum temperatures for July.

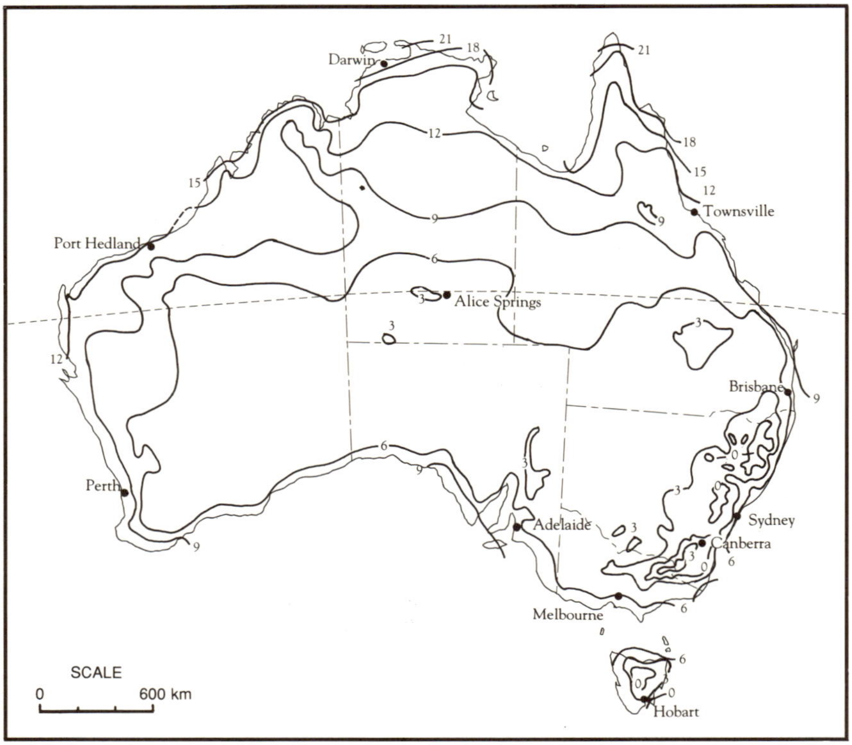

Figure 2.7—Air temperature (daily readings in °Celsius), capital cities.

	Adelaide		Brisbane		Canberra		Darwin		Hobart		Melbourne		Perth		Sydney	
Month	Mean max.	Mean min.	Mean max.	Mean min.	Mean max.	Mean min.	Mean max.	Mean min.	Mean max.	Mean min.	Mean max.	Mean min.	Mean max.	Mean min.	Mean max.	Mean min.
No. of years of record	122	122	95		43	43	95	95	98	98	126	126	85	85	123	123
January	29.5	16.4	29.4	20.7	27.6	13.1	31.7	24.7	21.4	11.6	25.8	14.0	29.6	17.7	25.5	18.4
February	29.3	16.6	29.0	20.6	26.8	12.8	31.4	24.5	21.5	11.8	25.7	14.3	29.9	17.9	24.6	18.5
March	26.8	15.1	27.9	19.4	24.4	10.6	31.8	24.3	20.0	10.6	23.7	12.9	27.8	16.6	24.5	17.4
April	22.7	12.6	26.1	16.6	19.7	6.4	32.6	23.8	17.1	8.8	20.1	10.6	24.5	14.1	22.2	14.5
May	18.7	10.3	23.2	13.3	15.0	2.9	31.8	21.8	14.2	6.7	16.5	8.4	20.7	11.6	19.4	11.3
June	15.8	8.3	20.8	10.9	12.1	0.9	30.4	19.8	11.8	5.1	13.9	6.7	18.2	9.9	16.7	9.1
July	15.0	7.3	20.4	9.5	11.1	-0.3	30.3	19.2	11.5	4.4	13.3	5.7	17.3	9.0	15.9	7.9
August	16.4	7.8	21.8	10.3	12.7	0.8	31.2	20.5	12.8	5.1	14.8	6.4	17.9	9.1	17.5	8.8
September	18.9	9.0	24.0	12.9	15.9	2.9	32.4	23.0	14.9	6.2	17.1	7.7	19.4	10.1	19.7	10.9
October	22.0	10.9	26.1	15.8	19.1	5.9	33.0	24.9	16.8	7.6	19.5	9.3	21.2	11.5	21.9	13.4
November	25.1	12.9	27.8	18.2	22.4	8.4	33.1	25.2	18.5	9.0	21.8	10.9	24.6	14.0	23.5	15.4
December	27.7	15.0	29.1	19.9	26.2	11.1	32.5	25.1	20.2	10.6	24.1	12.6	27.3	16.2	25.0	17.3
Yearly Averages	22.3	11.9	25.5	15.7	19.4	6.3	31.8	23.1	16.7	8.1	19.7	9.9	23.2	13.1	21.4	13.6

Figure 2.8—Extreme maximum temperatures, all years to July 1994.

Station	°Celsius	Date
New South Wales		
Bourke	52.8	17.1.1877
Walgett	50.1	2.1.1903
Wilcannia	50.0	11.1.1939
Victoria		
Mildura	50.8	6.1.1906
Swan Hill	49.4	18.1.1906
Queensland		
Cloncurry	53.1	16.1.1889
Winton	50.7	14.12.1888
Birdsville	50.0	24.12.1972
South Australia		
Ooodnadatta	50.7	2.1.1960
Kyancutta	49.3	9.1.1939
Western Australia		
Eucla	50.7	22.1.1906
Mundrabilla	49.8	3.1.1979
Forrest	49.8	13.1.1979
Madura	49.4	7.1.1971
Tasmania		
Bushby Park	40.8	26.12.1945
Hobart	40.8	4.1.1976
Northern Territory		
Finke	48.3	2.1.1960
Jervois	47.5	3.1.1978
Australian Capital Territory		
Canberra (Acton)	42.8	11.1.1939

Figure 2.9—Extreme minimum temperatures, all years to July 1994.

Station	°Celsius	Date
New South Wales		
Charlotte Pass	–23.0	29.6.1994
		22.8.1947
Kiandra	-20.6	2.8.1929
Kosciusko Hotel	-14.4	3.7.1929
		6.7.1939
Cooma	-11.2	13.7.1898
Victoria		
Mount Hotham	-12.8	13.8.1947
Omeo	-11.7	15.6.1965
Bairnsdale	-7.2	16.8.1896
Queensland		
Stanthorpe	-11.0	4.7.1895
Mitchell	-9.4	15.8.1979
Nanango	-9.3	16.7.1918
South Australia		
Yongalla	-8.2	20.7.1976
Kyancutta	-7.0	9.7.1960
Western Australia		
Booylgoo	-6.7	12.7.1969
Wandering	-5.6	1.6.1964
Tasmania		
Oatlands	-12.8	20.5.1902
Bothwell	-12.5	24.6.1972
Northern Territory		
Alice Springs	-7.5	12.7.1976
Tempe Downs	-6.9	24.7.1971
Australian Capital Territory		
Canberra	-10.0	19.7.1924
		11.7.1971

Snow

By world standards Australia is a warm climate. Snow is a very rare or unknown phenomenon in most areas and there is no permanent snowfield as occurs in parts of Europe and North America. Isolated pockets of snow do persist throughout the summer months around Mt Kosciusko but are usually not suitable for skiing.

Major cold outbreaks moving over south-eastern Australia from the south during the winter months account for most snow in Australia. In extreme cases snowfalls will penetrate along the Great Dividing Range as far north as Brisbane and a case of snow on the ranges as far north as Mackay has been recorded. Snowfalls over the capital cities are mainly confined to Canberra and Hobart, although Melbourne sometimes experiences light falls and Mt Lofty, near Adelaide also sees snow on occasions. Snow on the ground occurred once in Sydney's central business district in 1836. Snow falls in the national capital, Canberra, about once every two years although a higher frequency occurs over the Australian Capital Territory as a whole.

Some of the more notable snowfalls from around Australia can be found in the Bureau of Meteorology's records.

1836	27–28 June	Snow on ground in Sydney
	3 and 5 July	Snow on ground in Sydney
1882	20 June	8 cm of snow in Hobart
	13 July	Heavy snowfalls in Hobart
	26 July	Snow on ground lasted all day in Hobart
1900	5 July	Unprecedented snowfalls in New South Wales central districts Nearly a metre of snow fell at Bathurst, and Forbes reported its first known snowstorm since European settlement
1951	19 July	Extensive snow over Melbourne covered most suburbs; snow persisted in some areas for 24 hours
1969	12–13 September	Heavy snow in Hobart, down to sea level in some areas; significant dislocation of vehicular traffic
1974	July	Frequent falls throughout the month over Tasmania; highways cut and skiers stranded
1976	4–5 August	Extensive snowfalls over Tasmania; severe stock losses; several Hobart suburbs snowbound and residents skied to work
1981	21–23 June	Snowfalls in South Australia as far north as Wilpena, and in most districts of Victoria; first snow in some areas for at least twenty-five years

Frost

At the other end of the temperature spectrum is the phenomenon of frost. Frost is formed when the temperature at ground level drops below 0°C and the water vapour in the atmosphere condenses and freezes into ice crystals. Most frosts in Australia are caused through heat loss from the soil by the radiation of heat away from the ground. Clear, still, winter nights are needed for this process, as cloud tends to form a blanket in the atmosphere that holds the remnants of daytime heat in, and therefore prevents the necessary cooling.

Black surfaces lose heat faster at night than light coloured ones, so in an area that has a mixture of light and dark coloured soils, the darker areas would be more prone to frost. Because cold air is denser and heavier than warm air, it tends to fall to the lowest levels, and in mountainous terrain on still, clear nights the coldest areas are the valleys, while the warmest areas are the peaks. Valleys are therefore more prone to frost over the winter season.

Figure 2.1C—Average first month of occurrence of a minimum temperature of 2.2°C.

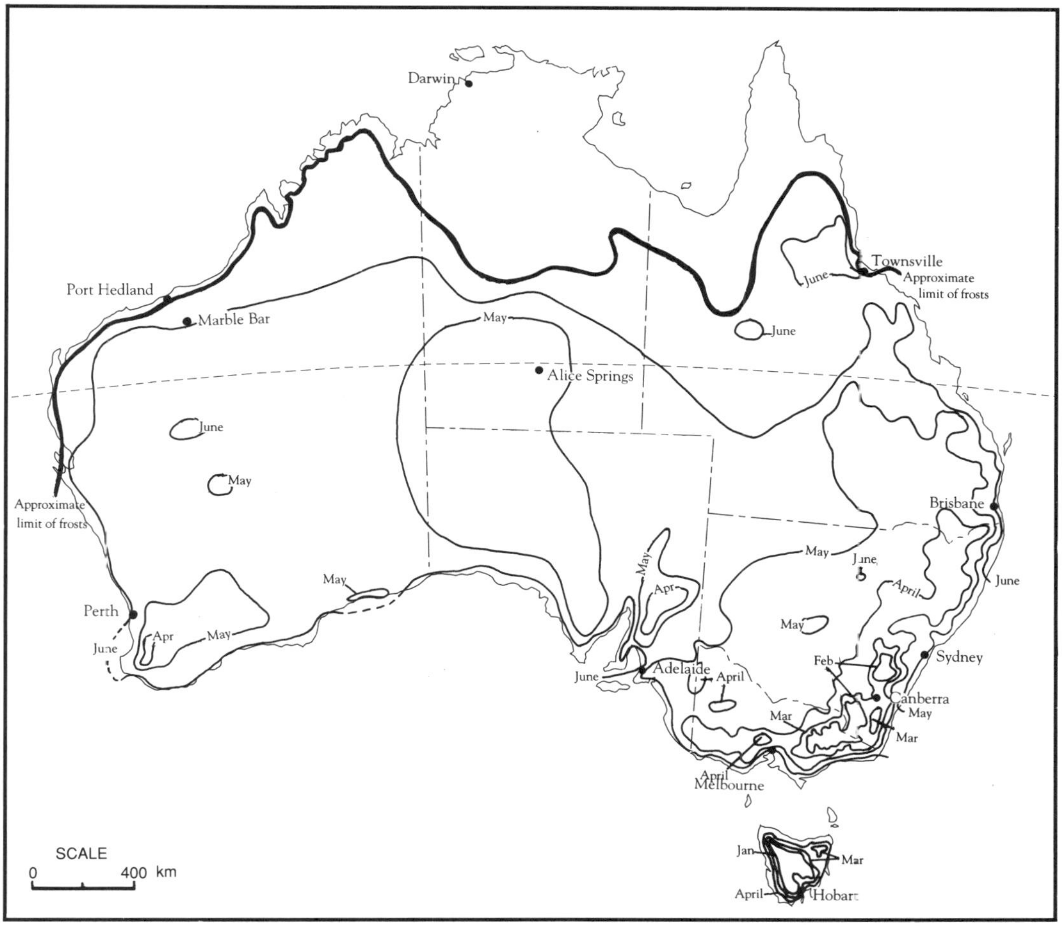

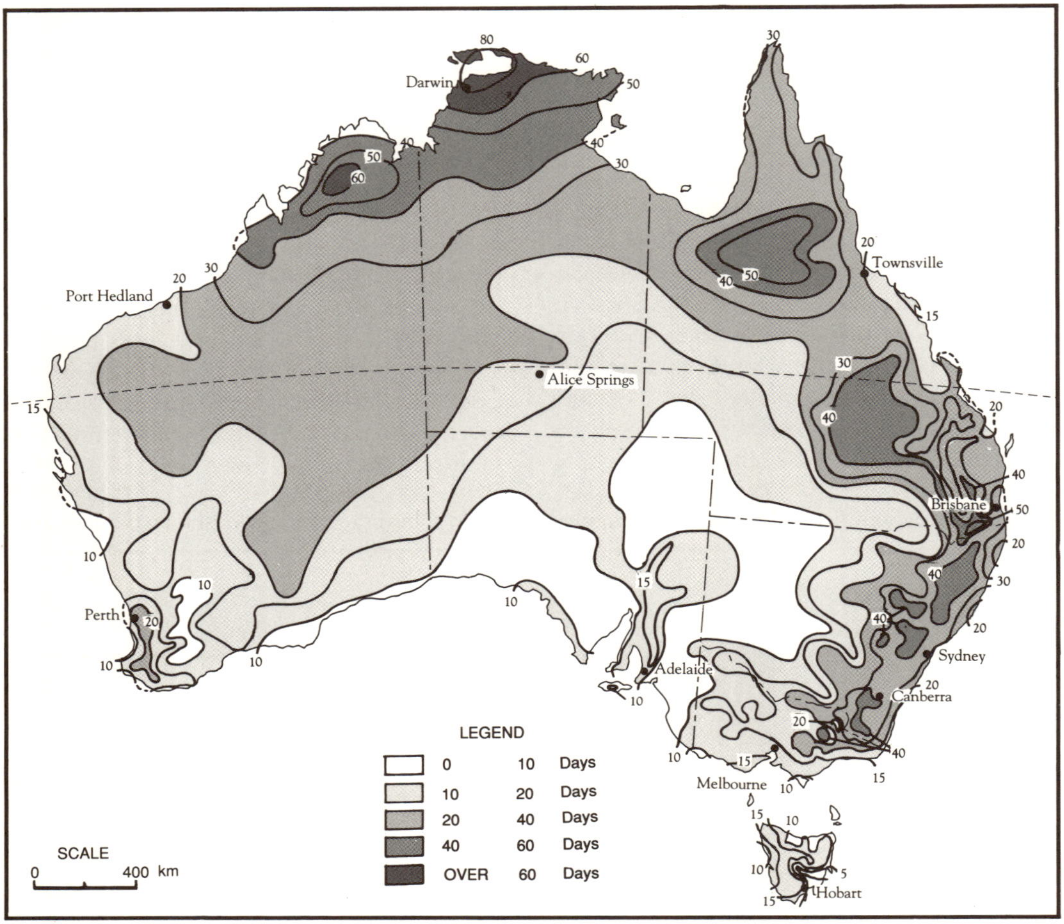

Figure 2.11—Average number of days on which thunderstorms are observed over a particular locality.

In Australia frosts generally occur in anticyclonic conditions when clear nights and light winds can be expected. This effect is enhanced markedly if during the previous 24–48 hours an outbreak of cold polar air has occurred that has chilled the ground, enabling the subsequent overnight cooling to begin at a much lower temperature.

Figure 2.10 shows the average first month of occurrence of a minimum temperature of 2.2°C. (This temperature, measured in a Stevenson Screen—see Chapter 7 for more details—about a metre off the ground, corresponds approximately to a ground temperature of 0°C.) An interesting feature of the map is the line denoting the approximate limit of frosts for the mainland. Contrary to popular belief, the line is well into the north of the continent, although it reaches about 27°S along the Western Australian coast.

It is important to note that there are frost free pockets in many areas that are not taken into account with the drawing of this line. This is particularly true in coastal areas, where the proximity of the ocean can keep the temperature above frost level. An illustration of this is found in Sydney where the official city records are taken at Observatory Hill, a location virtually on the shores of Sydney Harbour. There has never been a frost recorded at Observatory Hill, although some of the inland suburbs frequently experience below 0°C temperatures during the winter months.

Thunderstorms and Hail

Figure 2.11 shows the average number of days on which thunderstorms are observed over a particular locality. Lines joining places of equal annual frequency are called iso-bronts and they conveniently delineate areas of maximum and minimum thunderstorm activity. Not surprisingly, the tropical north of Australia experiences the highest number of thunderstorms with some areas exceeding fifty thunderstorm days per year.

A similar situation exists over south-east Queensland, where a combination of summer tropical air and the proximity of the Great Dividing Range create ideal conditions for the breeding of thunderstorms.

Hail, the occasional product of severe thunderstorms, can occur during any season but most small hailstorms over southern Australia are produced by cold frontal activity during winter and spring. Summer thunderstorms are commonplace along the Great Dividing Range and adjacent coastline and occasional episodes have been noted when hail in excess of golf ball size has fallen. A celebrated example was the New Year's Day thunderstorm of 1947 in Sydney, when orange-sized hail fell over the southern and eastern suburbs, causing widespread damage and personal injury.

Figure 2.12 —Average hours of bright sunshine over the year.

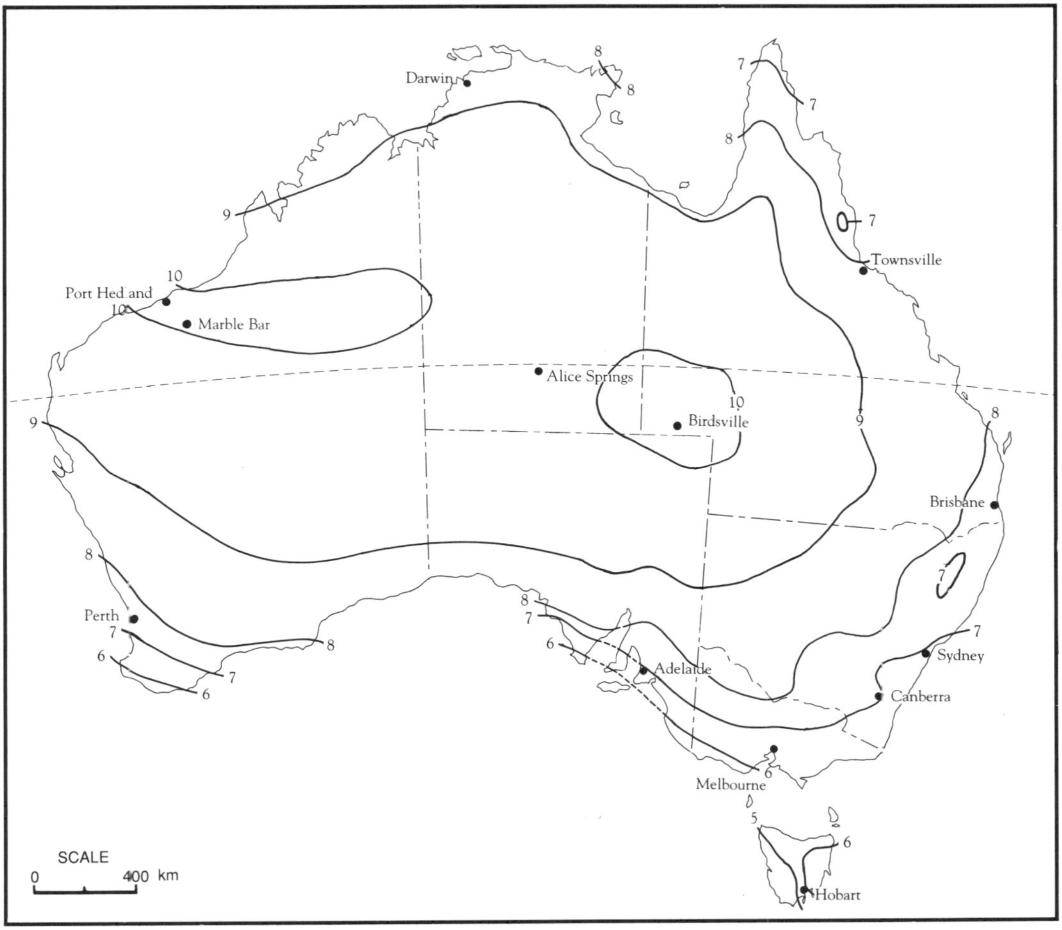

Hours of Sunshine and Cloud Cover

By world standards, Australia receives large amounts of bright, unimpeded sunshine. This is of course reflected in the low rainfall–high temperature pattern that affects most of the continent. This pattern makes Australia eminently suitable for solar-powered devices and many households today use solar-powered hot water services as a cheap energy alternative. Solar-powered pumps are also available as an alternative to electric generators or windmills.

Figure 2.12 shows the average hours of bright sunshine over the year calculated using all available records up to 1974. Two extensive areas of greater than 10 hours per day exist. One near the Queensland–South Australian border and the other over Western Australia. The hours tend to decrease towards the coast and also decrease with increasing latitude. Closely related to the hours of sunlight is the cloud cover and Figures 2.13, 2.14, 2.15 and 2.16 show the average cloud cover at 9 a.m. and 3 p.m. in both January and July.

Cloud cover is estimated in oktas, that is, an observer estimates how many eighths of the sky are covered by cloud. If the sky is completely overcast, this means there are 8 eighths of cloud, or 8 oktas. If only half the sky is covered, there are

Figure 2.13—Average cloud cover, January at 9 a.m.

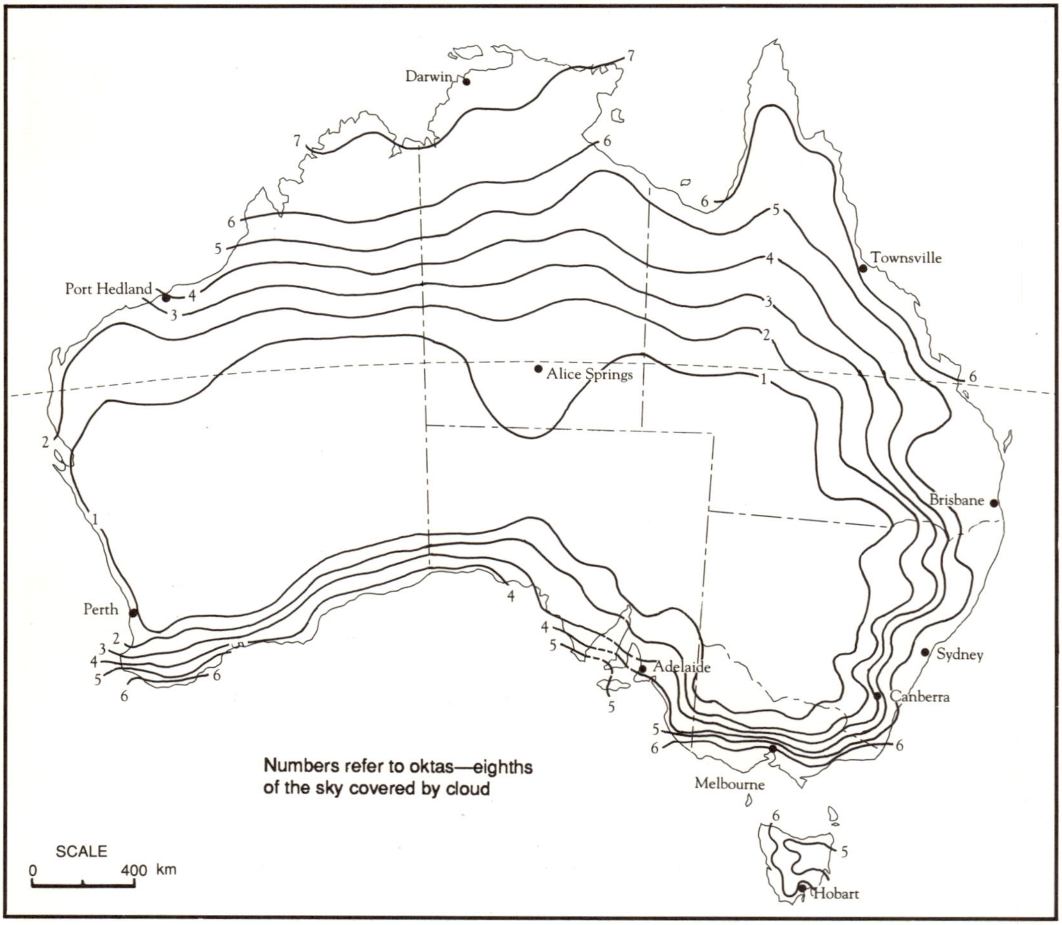

Top: Frozen dew, Mt Donna Buang, Vic. (See Chapter 2.)

Above: Winter wonderland of snow, Kosciusko National Park, NSW. (See Chapter 2.)

Severe frost, Falls Creek, Vic. (See Chapter 2.)

Extensive valley fog, Leura, Blue Mountains, NSW. (See Chapter 2.)

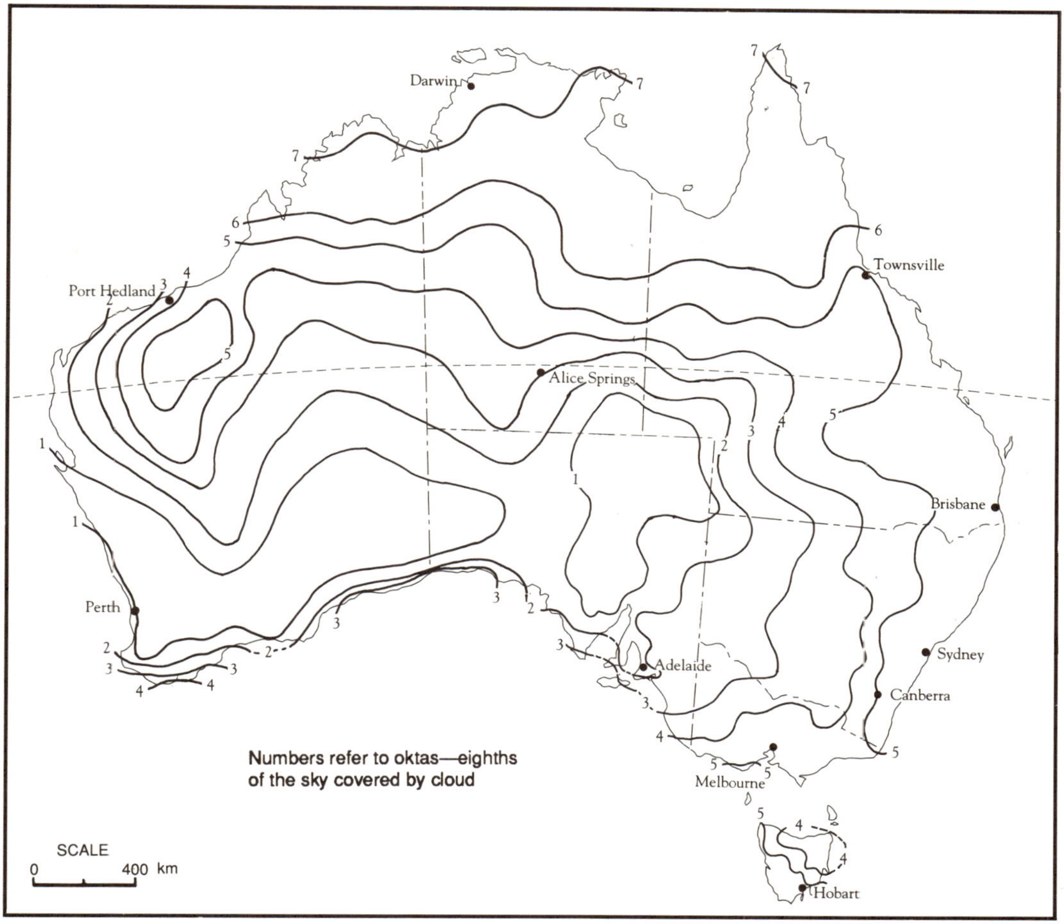

Figure 2.14—Average cloud cover, January at 3 p.m.

4 oktas; 0 oktas means that the sky is clear.

These figures are interesting because they illustrate both the daily and seasonal variation in cloud cover. In January there is generally more cloud in coastal areas and over the tropical north. At 9 a.m. there are 5 or more oktas of cloud along the south coast of Western Australia, South Australia and Victoria, as well as the New South Wales and Queensland coasts. At 3 p.m. this cloud has decreased but cloud over the inland has increased. This is because of the growth of the afternoon cumulus cloud over the hot land. Of particular interest is the area to the south-east of Port Hedland, Western Australia. Cloud in this area has increased markedly between 9 a.m. and 3 p.m. because of the development of afternoon convective cloud. As a result of the very high afternoon temperatures a 'heat low' is frequently a feature of the synoptic chart over this part of Western Australia during the summer months. The picture for July is very different, with far less cloud over the tropics because they are experiencing their dry season during the winter months. More cloud is evident over the southern extremities of the continent and this is a reflection of cold frontal activity that passes over the southern areas during the winter season. There is also less difference between the 9 a.m. and 3 p.m. cloud cover than there is during the summer because the land is not as hot and the tendency to form afternoon convective cloud is less.

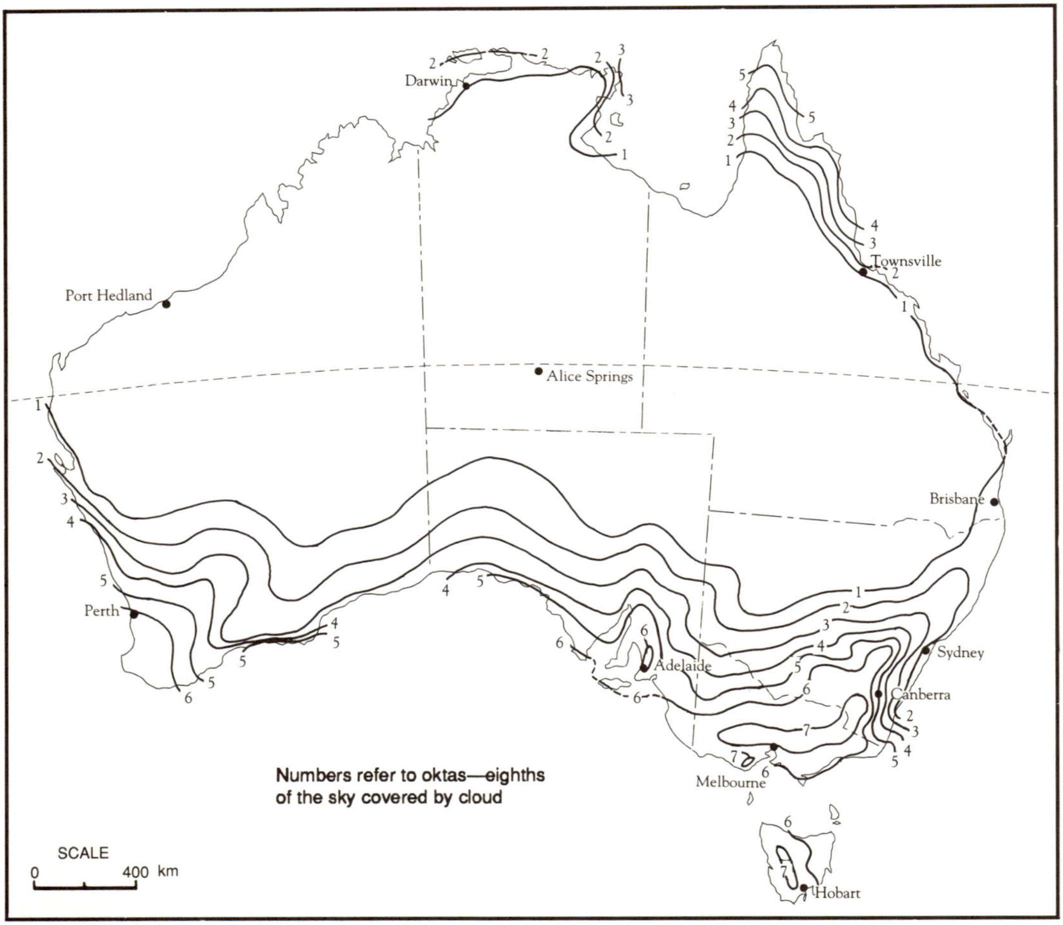

Figure 2.15—Average cloud cover, July at 9 a.m.

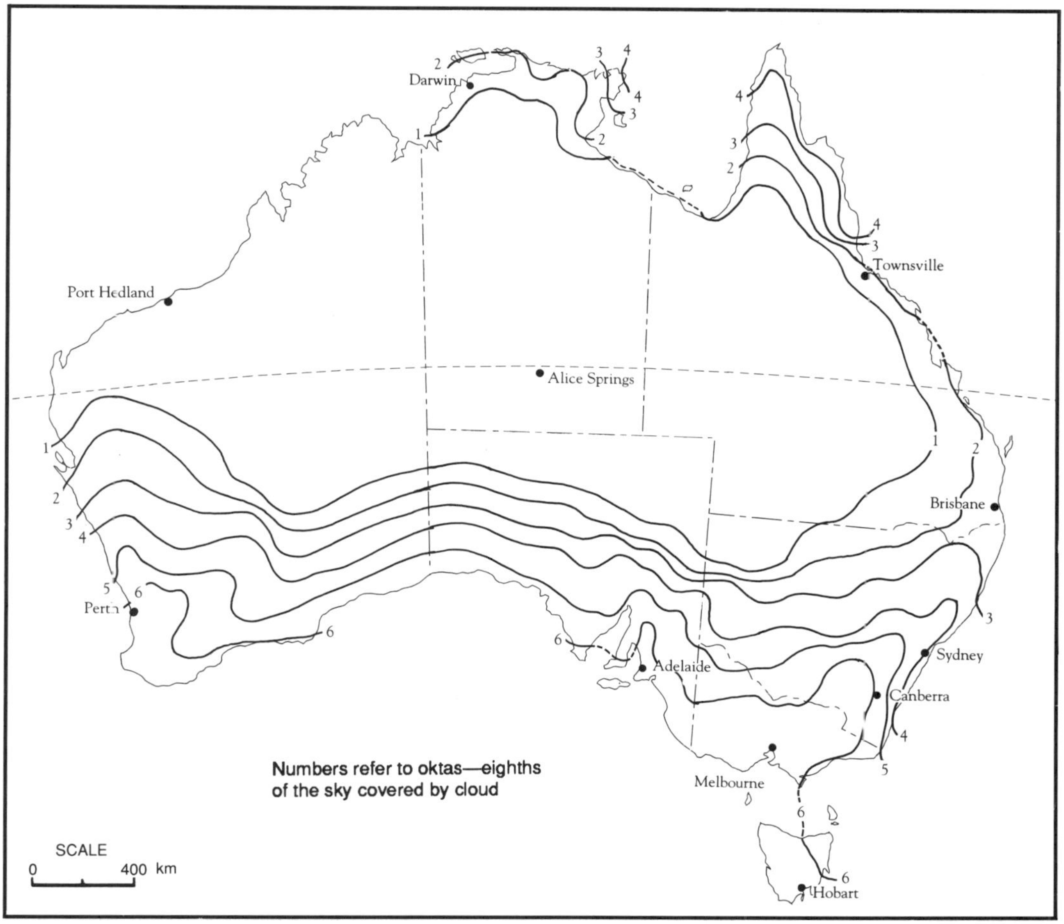

Figure 2.16—Average cloud cover, July at 3 p.m.

Evaporation

Evaporation can be thought of as the opposite of rainfall. With rainfall water vapour is condensed in the air into liquid form but with evaporation surface water is changed from liquid form back into gaseous water vapour and re-enters the atmosphere. For most areas of Australia evaporation is greatly in excess of rainfall, as can be seen by comparing the average annual evaporation map (Figure 2.17) with the average annual (median) rain map (Figure 2.1).

In the centre of Australia, evaporation is some eighteen times greater than annual rainfall because of the generally high temperatures, low humidities and high numbers of hours of sunshine. There are some areas, however, where the rainfall is on a par with evaporation. Such zones are usually heavily vegetated because they are always very moist and humid. In Australia these localities include the highlands of the west coast of

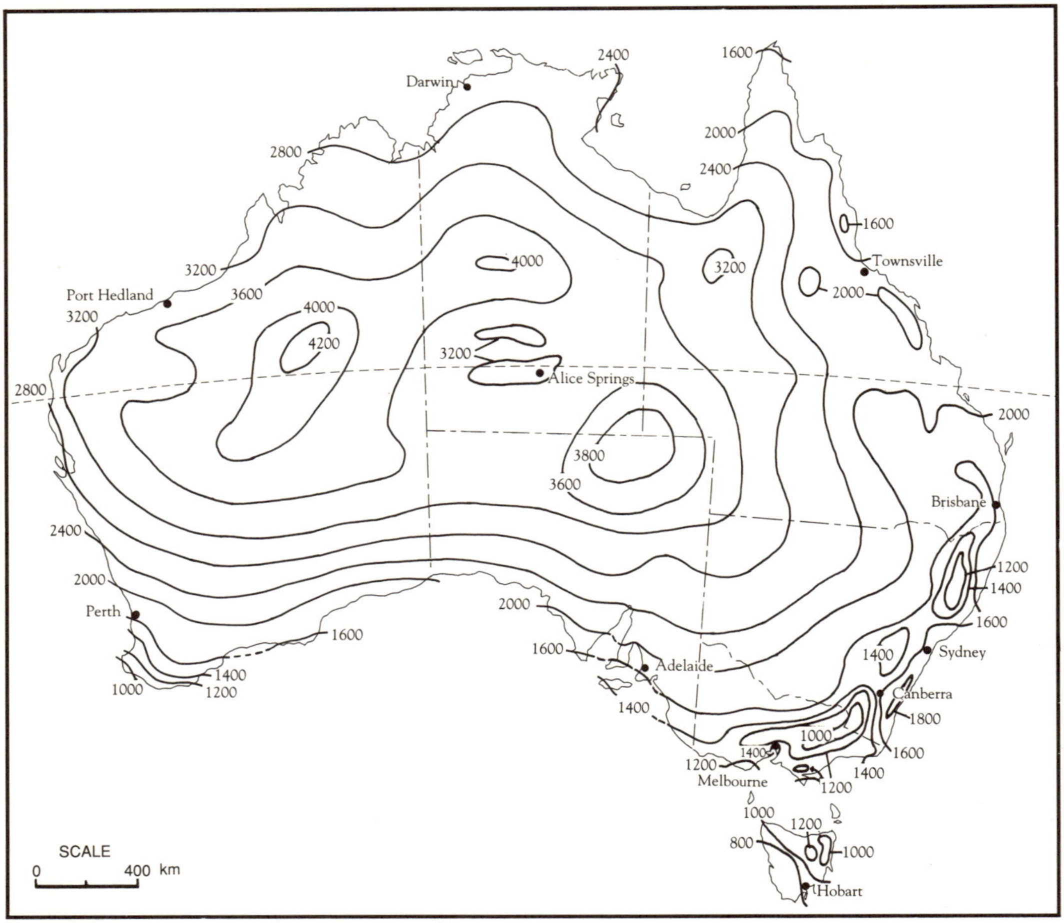

Figure 2.17—Average annual evaporation in millimetres.

Tasmania, the Queensland coast in the vicinity of Innisfail and parts of the east coast of Victoria. (For details on the measurement of evaporation, see Chapter 7.)

Drought and Flood

Dorothea Mackellar poetically summarised much of Australia's climate in her work *My Country* when she wrote:

> I love a sunburnt country,
> A land of sweeping plains,
> Of ragged mountain ranges,
> Of droughts and flooding rains;

Flood and drought are indeed part of the Australian weather scene, even though we only have a limited overview of these phenomena because of the comparatively short time over which records have been taken. In general, the term 'drought' means acute water shortage. Obviously lack of rainfall is the main factor behind this but evaporation and soil moisture are also important contributors.

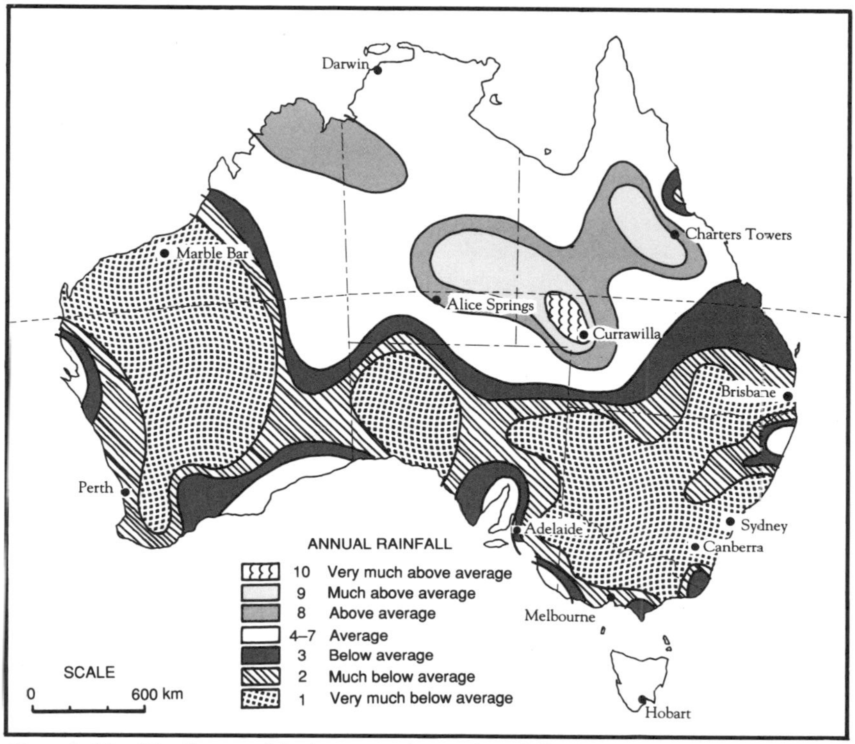

Figure 2.18—Distribution of decile ranges of annual rainfall, 1944.

Figure 2.19—Distribution of decile ranges of annual rainfall, 1950.

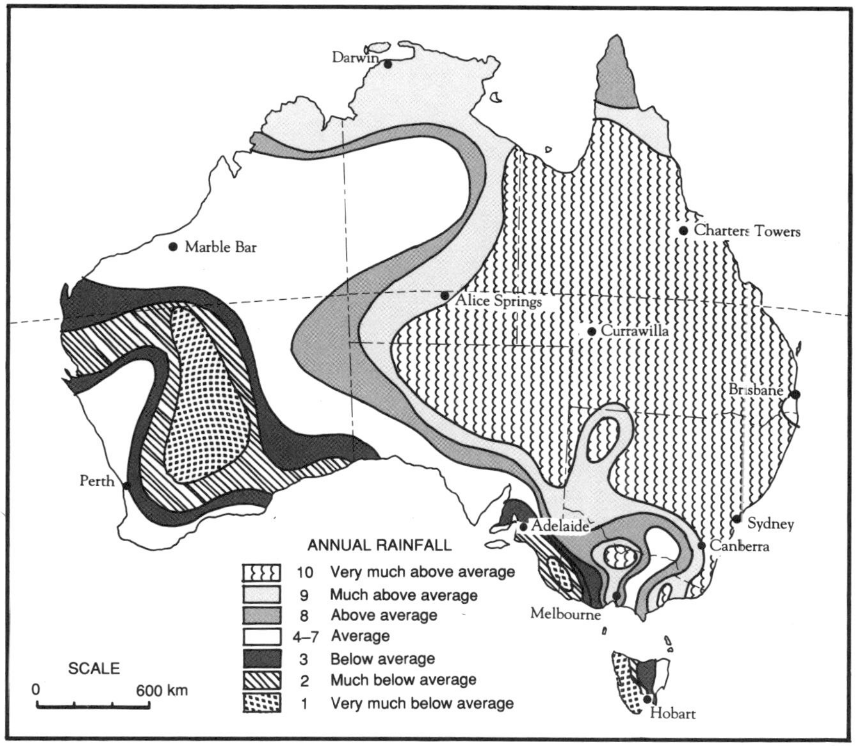

Definitions of drought vary but a convenient one was used by Gibbs and Maher in *Rainfall Deciles as Drought Indicators*, Bureau of Meteorology, 1967. They described a drought year for a particular location as one in which rain fell within the first decile range (the first decile range is the lowest 10 per cent of all recorded rains, decile 5 is the midpoint (median) of all recorded rains, and decile 10 is the highest 10 per cent). When a yearly rainfall map of Australia is reviewed, there is nearly always some area that has experienced a drought during that year. It is only occasionally, however, that very widespread droughts have occurred, and since European settlement, we have experienced eleven major droughts, several of which have extended over a number of years. All of these were notable and widespread droughts for various parts of Australia. It is interesting to note, however, that even in these freakish years of below average rainfall, other parts of the continent experienced above average rains. This illustrates the highly localised nature of rainfall and the difficulties associated with long-range forecasting. Consider, for

Figure 2.20—Distribution of the 'index of drought'.

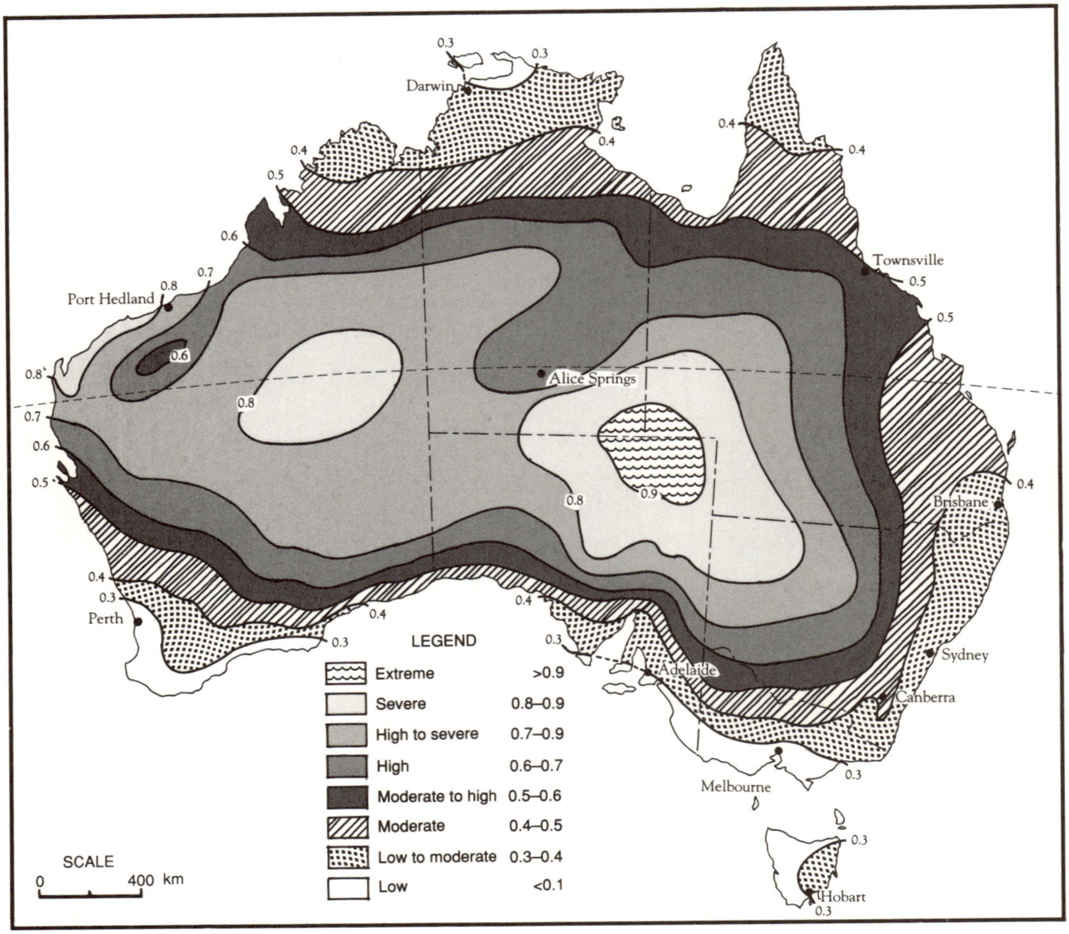

example, the year 1944 (Figure 2.18). As a long-range forecaster in 1943 you may have predicted widespread drought over eastern Australia. Certainly the residents of New South Wales would have been impressed with your forecast but those over much of Queensland would not have been. In fact the Currawilla area over south-western Queensland experienced decile 10 rainfall for 1944, which represents flooding from time to time during the year.

The year 1950 provides another example of this phenomenon (Figure 2.19), with decile 1–2 rainfall over significant parts of Western Australia along with some of the highest rainfall on record over eastern Australia. While it is always possible to make statements such as 'there will be severe drought over parts of Australia next year', a perusal of the records will reveal that this is nearly always so. The real test is to delineate which areas will experience drought and which areas will suffer from floods. Until recently modern science had not succeeded in producing a recognised method of doing this.

A method of calculating drought incidence in Australia was developed by Desmond Gaffney (1975) which analysed the distribution of annual rainfalls less than the median. What was called an 'index of drought incidence' was defined as $I = \frac{50-10}{30}$ percentile. The range between the 50 and 10 percentile gives a measure of the variation of annual rainfalls less than the median (50 percentile). This is then divided by the 30 percentile to give the drought deficiency index.

Figure 2.20 shows the distribution of this 'index of drought' across Australia, based on observation points with thirty or more years of record to the year 1979. Note the high values over north-western New South Wales, south-western Queensland and northern South Australia. This makes all these areas, at best, unsuitable for general agriculture. The comparatively low area near Wittenoom Gorge in Western Australia is also reflected in the cloud cover map (Figure 2.14) showing the average cloud cover for January at 3 p.m., which is caused by the formation of a summer 'heat low' over the area.

Flooding is caused when rainfall occurs at a rate or in an amount greater than the soil in the area can absorb. Run-off then begins and is greatly worsened if any watercourses nearby overflow. Floods can occur in any part of Australia, even over the desert areas from time to time, but it is more frequent in the higher rainfall areas of the tropical north and along the east coast.

The potential for flooding was realised from the earliest days of European settlement when during 1789 Governor Phillip and a party of sailors explored the river that emptied into Pittwater. They sailed and rowed some 145 km upstream, during which time Phillip remarked on the extensive masses of debris hanging high in the treetops, which is always indicative of intermittent major flooding. The early settlers were soon to confirm this when the Hawkesbury (as Phillip named it) flooded prodigiously in 1799, devastating the infant settlement of Green Hills (now Windsor).

It is interesting to note that apparently the Aborigines warned these settlers of an impending flood well before the event took place but their advice was largely ignored. The Aboriginal name for this river was *Deerubbin* and the local tribes were apparently well aware of the periodic floods that took place and the sort of weather likely to produce them. It was to be sometime before the white settlers were able to share this knowledge.

Flooding in Australia has a significant economic impact, and is believed to cost, on average, about $30 million annually. The most financially damaging floods are those involving the river systems of the eastern and south-western parts of the continent, where a great deal of agriculture and industry is concentrated. One of the most widespread and intensive floods of this nature occurred in 1955 (see Figure 2.21) when vast tracts of inland New South Wales were flooded for extended periods. As well as heavy property and stock losses, large areas of land were

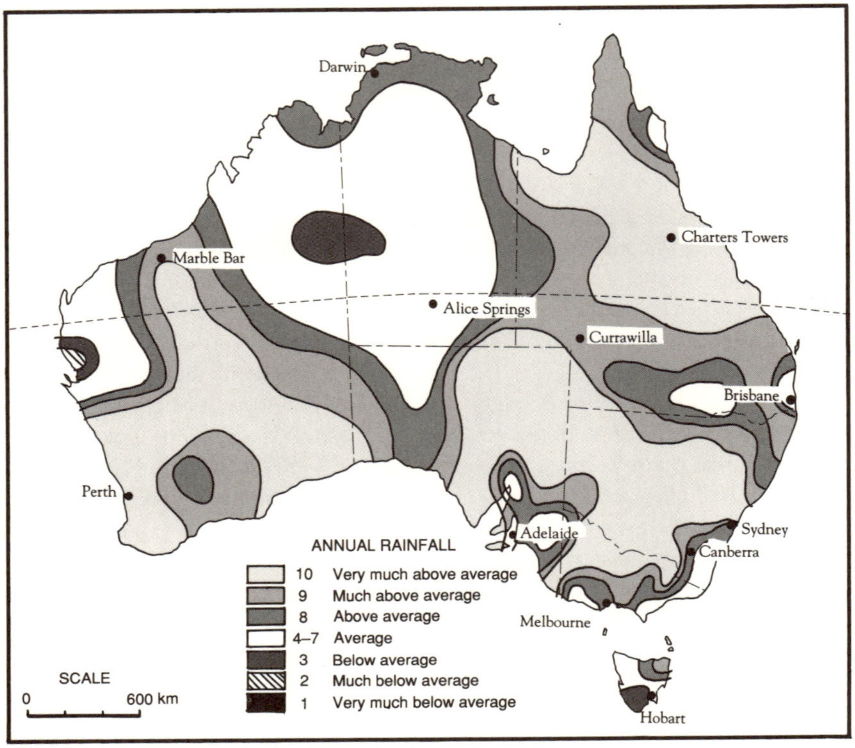

Figure 2.21—Distribution of decile ranges of rainfall, 1955.

Figure 2.22—Distribution of decile ranges of rainfall, 1939.

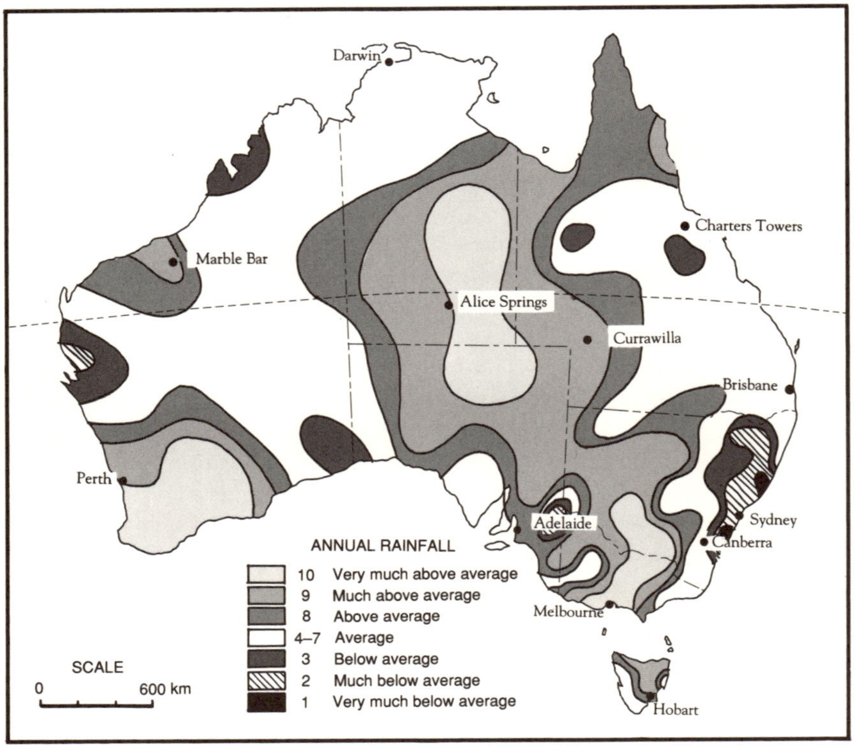

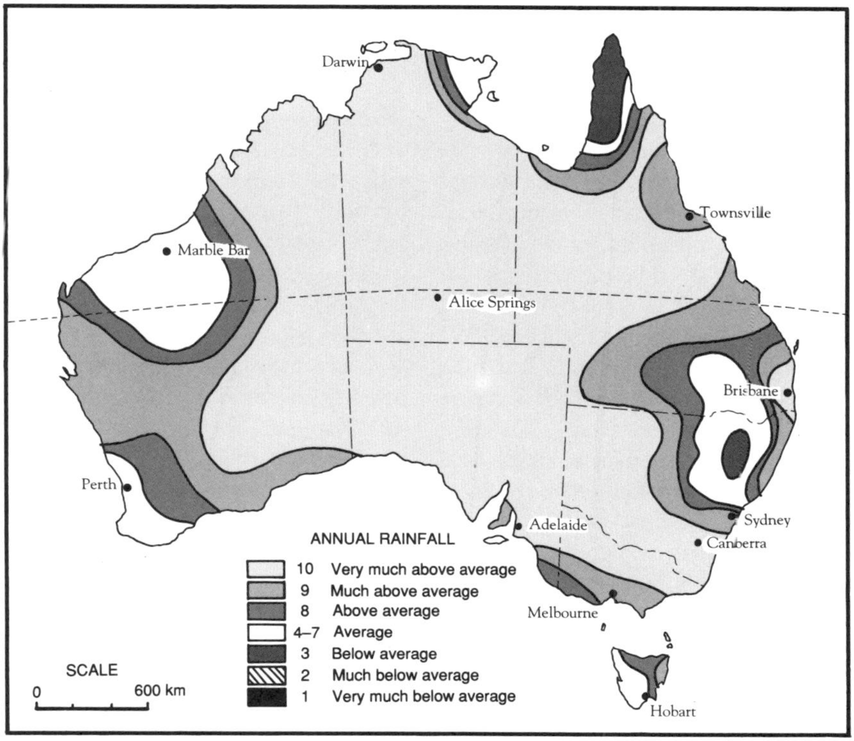

Figure 2.23—Distribution of decile range numbers of rainfall based on district averages, 1974.

Figure 2.24—Typical paths of tropical cyclones over Australia.

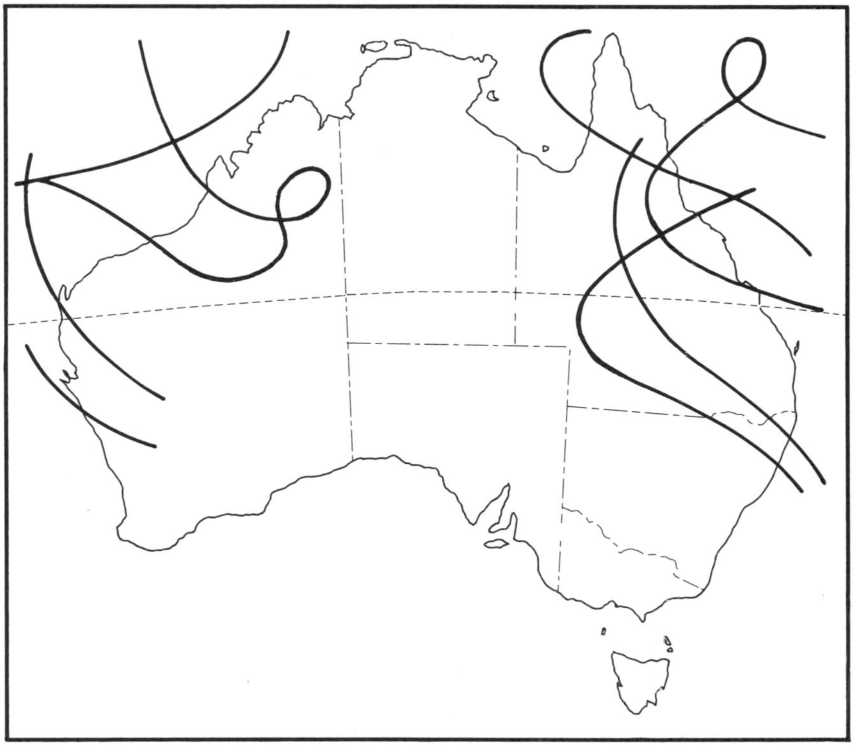

rendered unproductive for agriculture because of heavy deposits of sand carried by the flood.

Figures 2.22 and 2.23 show some other years when extensive flooding occurred over parts of Australia. (The simple definition of decile 10 rainfall to indicate a flood has been used here.) It is clear that even in a flood year, there are also adjacent areas experiencing drier than normal conditions. A good example is the year 1950 (Figure 2.19) when most of eastern Australia experienced flooding rains but western Victoria suffered a drought. In south-eastern Australia, flooding occurs mostly between April and November because of the development of slow-moving low-pressure systems in the western Tasman Sea. In 1934 much of Victoria, including a large section of the Melbourne metropolitan area was inundated causing loss of life and millions of dollars worth of stock and property damage.

Over northern Australia, extensive flooding often occurs because of the activity of tropical cyclones, but flooding is also part of the average wet season that extends usually from November to March. The economic impact of these floods is normally less severe than those over south-eastern Australia because of the less dense population in the area. Nevertheless frequent disruption to roads, local services and stock movements accompanies these events. Some of these floods have been of spectacular proportions such as the 1940 Roper River flood when the river reached a width of 11 km in places and a depth of nearly 20 m. A similar huge body of water was produced in 1966 when tropical cyclone Joy flooded the Ord River, which reached a depth of 25 m and flowed at a rate of about 30 000 m^3/sec.

On occasion, flooding of the rivers of northern Australia will be of sufficient magnitude for water to drain southwards and reach Lake Eyre. Normally, a flow of this nature is largely lost because of the long gauntlet of seepage and evaporation it has to run; sometimes, however, so much is produced that Lake Eyre becomes an extensive, shallow, lake—perhaps the fabled inland sea of the early explorer's imagination.

As its name suggests, flash flooding is a rapidly developing, short-term event when rain falls at a rate faster than the run-off can clear it from the surrounding area. In this case there is a dramatic build-up of water that often surges over the ground in a huge wave and can uplift cars, destroy buildings and carry away livestock. Urban areas are more prone to this sort of event than rural areas because a greater percentage of water falling in a city runs off rather than percolating into the soil. This is an obvious consequence of covering large areas with impervious substances such as concrete, bitumen and tile.

While the normal drainage system will cope with rainfall rates usually encountered, when extreme rates occur, flash flooding will sometimes result. A famous example of this is the Melbourne flood of February 1972 when a slow-moving thunderstorm deposited 83 mm of rain over the city in less than one hour. Another case occurred in Sydney on 6 August 1986, when 328 mm of rain fell in 24 hours causing urban havoc, property damage and widespread disruption of services.

Such events differ from the 'normal' flood in that they are usually short lived and clear quickly as soon as the rain itself begins to ease. Flash floods can happen also along any watercourse over which rainfall occurs at a rate faster than the water can flow away. The main cause of this phenomenon is the slow-moving thunderstorm that remains in the same area for an extended period of time (for example, one to two hours) causing continuous heavy rain throughout the period.

Over the years increasingly sophisticated flood forecasting techniques have evolved, linking automatic recording stations with the Bureau of Meteorology, which liaises closely with local State emergency organisations. If warning can be given of imminent flooding, the impact of the flood when it does occur should be less because of the preventative measures that can be taken. Evidence so far shows that such a warning service is highly economical as the savings that result are well in excess of the cost of running the service. A further improvement is likely over the next decade as increasing instrumentation, greater computing power and superior mathematical models become available.

Tropical Cyclones

Tropical revolving storms, known variously as hurricanes, typhoons or tropical cyclones, are one of nature's most destructive phenomena. A tropical cyclone is a cyclonic, low-pressure system of tropical origin, which in the Southern Hemisphere rotates in a clockwise fashion.

The central pressure of a tropical cyclone will in some cases be below 960 mb and surface winds of over 200 km/hr have been recorded. Tropical cyclones generally occur between latitudes 10°S and 25°S in the Southern Hemisphere, but sometimes reach as far as 30°S, which is roughly Geraldton on the west coast and Coffs Harbour in the east. This means that about two-thirds of the Australian coastline is susceptible to tropical cyclone crossings, and is the reason so much time

Figure 2.25—Satellite photograph showing tropical cyclone activity.

and effort is expended on locating and identifying this type of storm.

The cyclone season is November to April, for during this time cloud masses tend to form near the equator, break up, re-form and sometimes develop into a fully fledged tropical cyclone. The subsequent movement is very erratic (see Figure 2.24) although it is generally away from the equator. If the cyclone crosses the coast it tends to rapidly weaken and become a rain depression, bringing the menace of flood to replace that of strong wind.

Some cyclones cross the coast, weaken and then move out to sea again, strengthening as they go. Others will move to the far south and become intense mid-latitude low-pressure systems; there have been numerous occasions when tropical cyclones have passed across into the Tasman Sea to lash New Zealand as a strong, extra-tropical low-pressure cell.

Fortunately for Australia, most of the capital cities are beyond the reach of cyclones and much of the coastline where crossings are likely is uninhabited. Perhaps the best known cyclone of modern times is Cyclone Tracy which devastated Darwin on Christmas Eve/Day 1974, virtually flattening the city and killing sixty-five people in the process.

Cyclone Tracy was by no means Australia's most destructive cyclone. In 1899, the era before a comprehensive cyclone warning system was instituted, three hundred people drowned when a cyclone struck northern Queensland. While errors still occur in the prediction of cyclone movement, the old days of fishing fleets, for example, putting to sea into the path of cyclone should not occur any more. With the modern system, people should be well informed that a cyclone is in the area, even if the subsequent movement is uncertain.

As well as cyclones being readily identifiable from satellite photography (see Figure 2.25), they can also be accurately tracked by radar when within range of the instrument (up to 250 km away). The radar image of a tropical cyclone will show the clear area forming the 'eye', surrounded by spiral bands of cloud converging inwards.

Tropical cyclones begin as a cluster of cumulus and cumulonimbus cloud, which usually persists for 2–3 days before further development takes place. The Coriolis force gradually exerts its influence and the cluster begins to rotate in a clockwise fashion and the system takes on its characteristic spiral configuration. An eye develops, which is an area of relative calm a few kilometres across at the centre of the cyclone. This eye is surrounded by a wall of cumulonimbus cloud that can reach up to 10–20 km. (The strongest surface winds are usually close to the eye, but outside the clear area.)

Winds

Any discussion about wind is a difficult matter because wind varies a great deal in both direction and speed. Look at a weathervane for a few minutes to see the irregular but frequent changes in direction. Changes in wind speed are referred to as 'gusts', and these occur continuously over very short time intervals. Wind is recorded on an anemograph, which marks wind speed and direction on a chart attached to a clockwork recording drum (see Chapter 7).

From this we can see how frequently and rapidly wind changes direction and speed and how the top of the gust speed is significantly greater than the mean wind speed. The convention for measuring the wind is to view the anemograph trace for a period of ten minutes and then to average the speed and direction over this period of time. This variable nature of the surface wind is largely produced by the turbulence of the wind blowing over the ground with all its roughness and irregularity. In addition wind varies greatly from place to place because of topography; occasionally it also varies with the seasons. Coastal winds are very complex because of the sea-breeze effect, which reaches a maximum during the

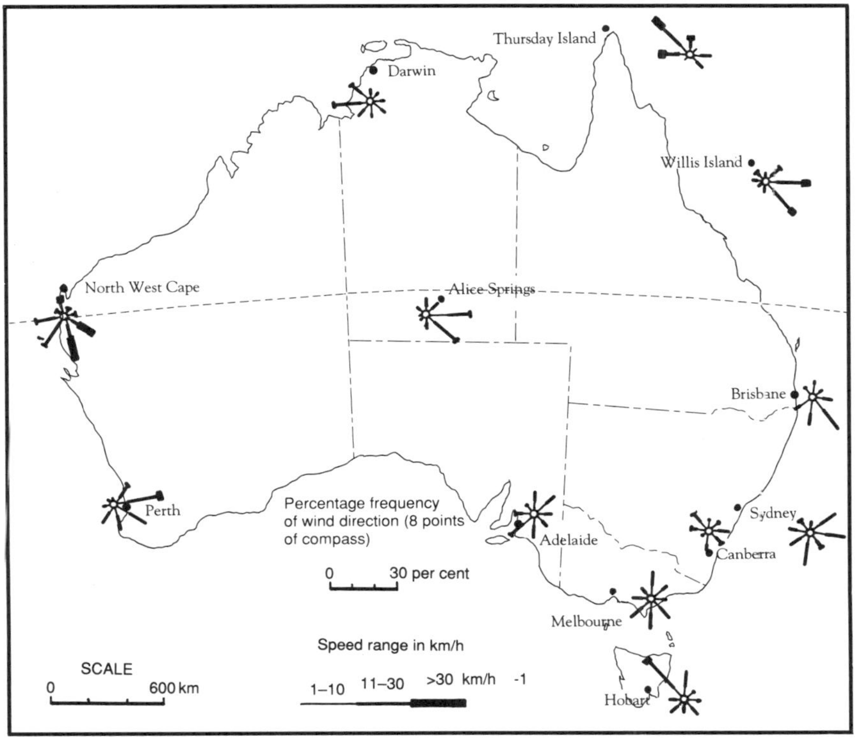

Figure 2.26—Wind 'roses', January at 9 a.m.
Figure 2.27—Wind 'roses', January at 3 p.m.

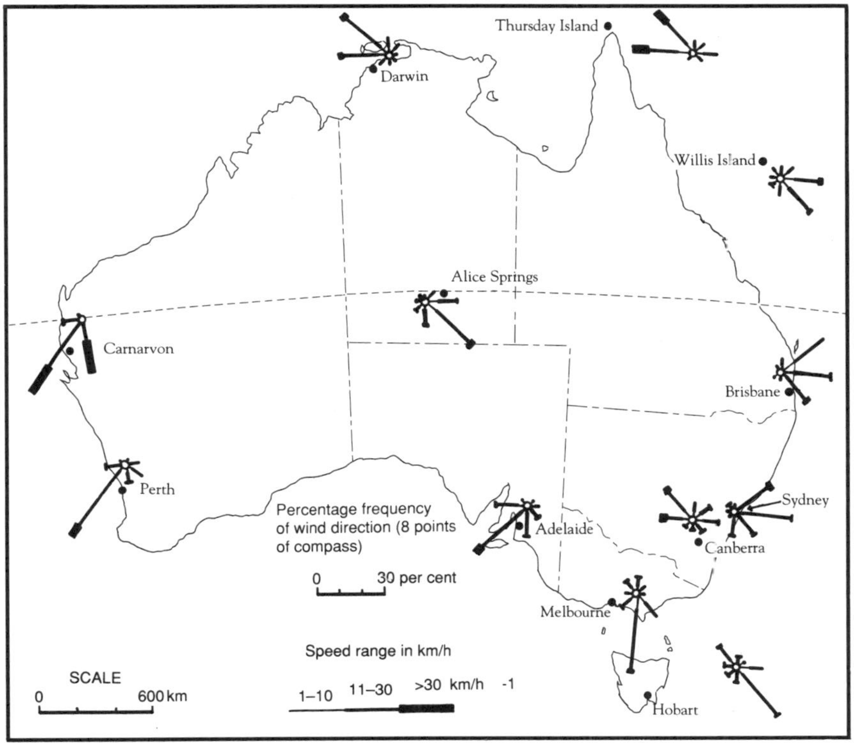

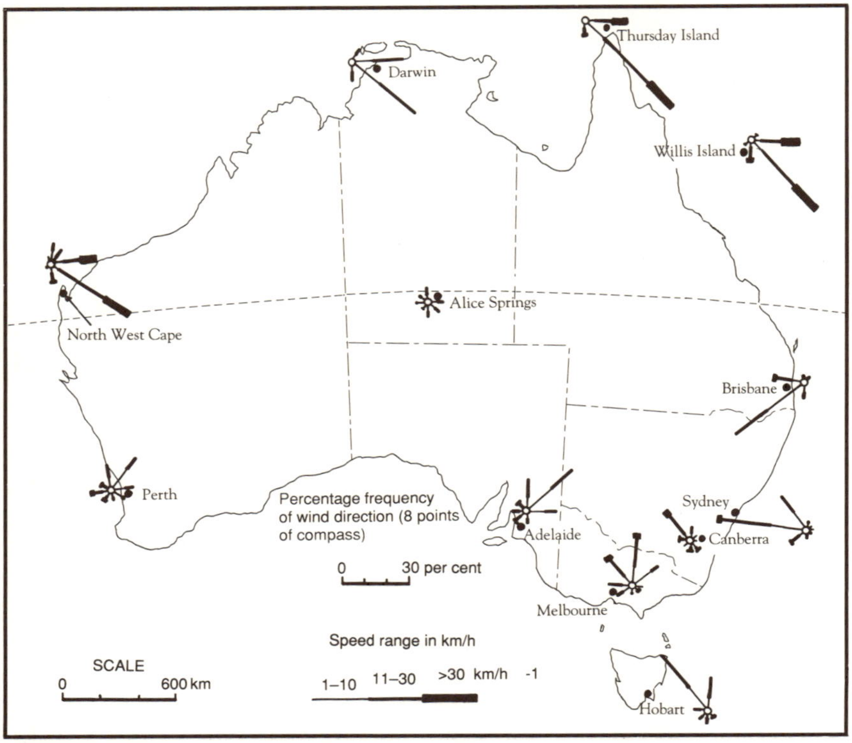

Figure 2.28—Wind 'roses', July at 9 a.m.

Figure 2.29—Wind 'roses', July at 3 p.m.

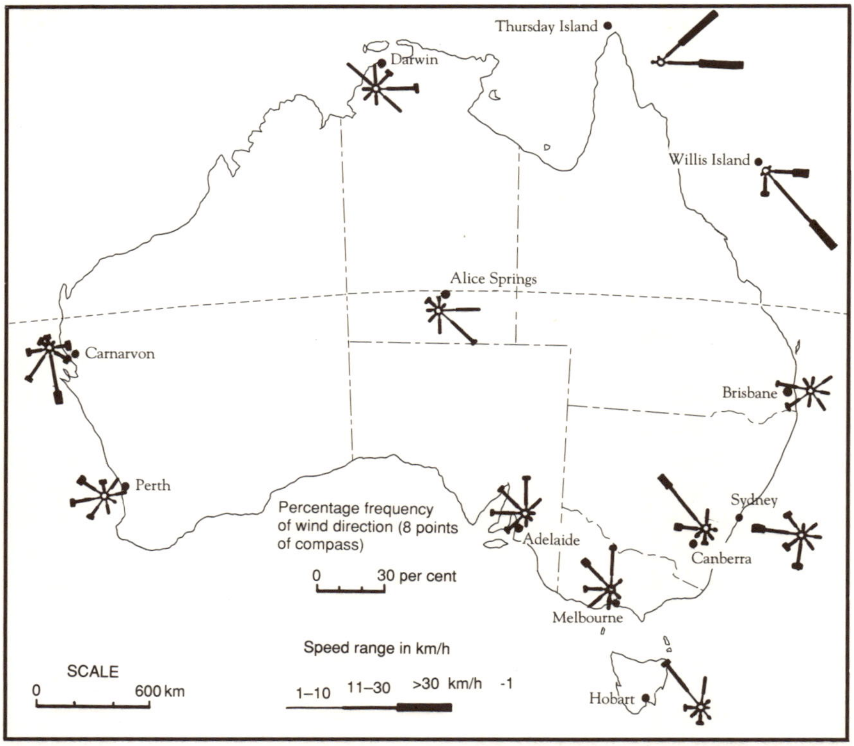

day and degenerates during the night.

Sea-breezes are deflected to the left in the Southern Hemisphere by the Coriolis force, which is a deflecting force produced by the rotation of the earth. (See Chapter 4 for more details.)

Broadly speaking, the sea-breeze along the east coast will be from the north-east, along the south coast from the south-east, along the west coast from the south-west, and along the north coast from the north-west. Local variation is produced by topography and coastline orientation but the broad sea-breeze regime is as indicated. A good example of local variation occurs at Hobart where an east-north-east sea-breeze would be expected but where in fact a south-east occurs in practice. This is because of a deviation in the wind flow caused by the orientation of the Derwent River.

Sea-breezes are a welcome feature of Australia's climate during the summer months. They can reduce the temperature along the coastline by as much as 10°C, and they are probably a key reason for the vast majority of Australia's population clinging to the coastline. So welcome is the beginning of the sea-breeze in summertime Perth that it has been known for many years as the 'Fremantle Doctor'. It brings relief from the often savage heat of high summer. Winds over the inland are much less complicated and closely reflect the position of the synoptic systems dominant at the time.

Figures 2.26, 2.27, 2.28, and 2.29 show wind 'roses' around Australia for the months of January and July, both at 9 a.m. and 3 p.m. These maps are based on long-term averages from all the locations in question and show both speed and direction. (The longer the 'telescope', the greater the frequency of the wind from the direction indicated; the broader the 'telescope' the greater the wind speed.) January at 9 a.m. shows generally light winds in most areas with a fairly uniform distribution of direction. At 3 p.m. the sea-breeze effect can be seen to take hold along the coast, while the inland stations remain generally light and variable. The picture for July is quite different, with the first observation to note being that there is not a great change between 9 a.m. and 3 p.m. This is because the sea-breeze effect is much weaker during the winter months. Also there is much greater preference for specified direction during July. The south-east trade winds are very prominent along the north Queensland coast, while south of about 30°S, winds from the western quadrant predominate. This is consistent with the average position of the synoptic systems for winter, which is a high centred over southern Queensland and westerly flow over the southern portion of the continent. The wind regimes at other times of the year can be thought of as transition periods between January and July.

Humidity

This meteorological element is a measure of the amount of water vapour in the existing air-mass. There is always a certain amount of water vapour 'dissolved' in the air around us; sometimes there is only a very small amount present and we say that the air is dry. Usually this involves air that has blown across the land for extended periods, such as north-westerly winds for Melbourne and Sydney, and easterly winds at Perth. Physically we can interpret these conditions by feeling dry and experiencing chapped lips or by noticing that hair crackles with static electricity when brushed or combed. Air that has come off the ocean, on the other hand (such as a sea-breeze), carries far more water vapour with it and we feel this as humid. Some physical manifestations of this include a higher tendency for the human body to sweat, and also for wet items (such as towels) hung up indoors to remain damp for extended periods.

Humidity is closely linked to human discomfort because of its effect on perspiration. If the body becomes hot the pores open and release sweat in order to cool the skin. It is not the fluid itself that produces the cooling, because the temperature of the perspiration is the same as that of the body.

Rather it is the evaporation of the sweat that produces the desired cooling because the process of evaporation absorbs heat—that is, it cools.

If the air-mass surrounding the body already contains a lot of water vapour it does not readily absorb more, and the process of evaporation is slowed. This means if a human body becomes hot in a humid air-mass (after physical exertion, for example), cooling by the process of perspiration will be inhibited. If this process is prolonged, heat exhaustion may occur, and this phenomenon is sometimes experienced by athletes when distance running events are held in humid conditions.

Vapour pressure is one way in which humidity is measured. This is defined as the pressure exerted by the water vapour in the air, and as such is a measurement of the actual amount of water vapour present. Unfortunately, common usage has settled on another, more complex measurement that is known as relative humidity. This is a percentage ratio of the actual vapour pressure to the saturated vapour pressure at that temperature. Because the relative humidity

Figure 2.30—Average percentages for relative humidity, January at 9 a.m.

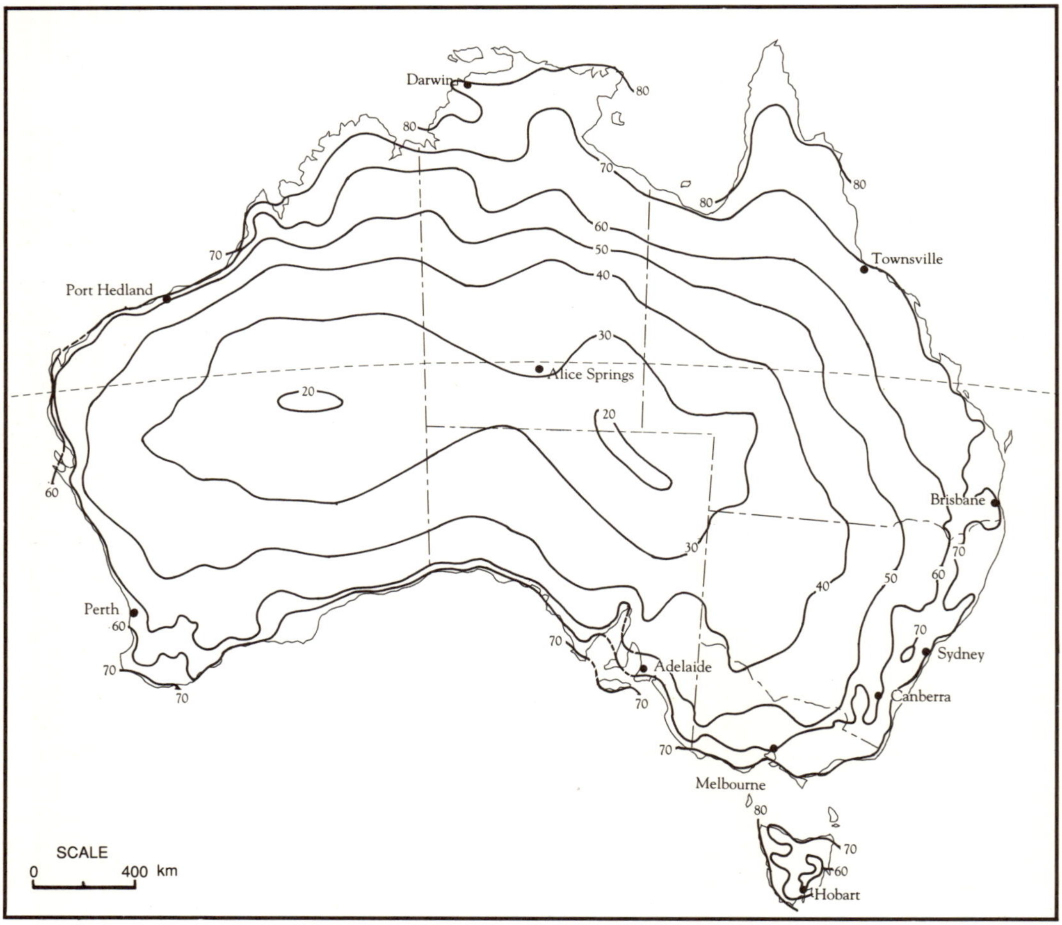

Top: Stratocumulus deck over Broken Hill, NSW. (See Chapter 6.)

Above: Developing cumulonimbus, Mt Buffalo National Park, Vic. (See Chapter 6.)

Rainbow over the Lake Mungo area, NSW. (See Chapter 2.)

depends on temperature, it varies markedly throughout the day even if the actual water vapour content stays fairly constant. Relative humidity tends to be greatest during the early morning when the temperature is at a minimum; and at its lowest around early afternoon.

Figures 2.30, 2.31, 2.32 and 2.33 give long-term averages for humidity for January and July, both at 9 a.m. and 3 p.m. As we would expect, humidity tends to be higher near the coast, and the effect of the afternoon sea-breezes is apparent on the January at 3 p.m. map.

The predominance of south-east winds along the north Queensland coast during the winter months is also visible as a belt of high relative humidity during July at 3 p.m. Over the interior there is a marked dryness that is centred to the north-west during the winter months and more over central Australia during the summer. Over northern Australia, the higher values occur during January, which is close to the middle of the wet season. For the southern half of the continent, however, the highest values occur during July, which corresponds to the winter rainy season.

Figure 2.31—Average percentages for relative humidity, January at 3 p.m.

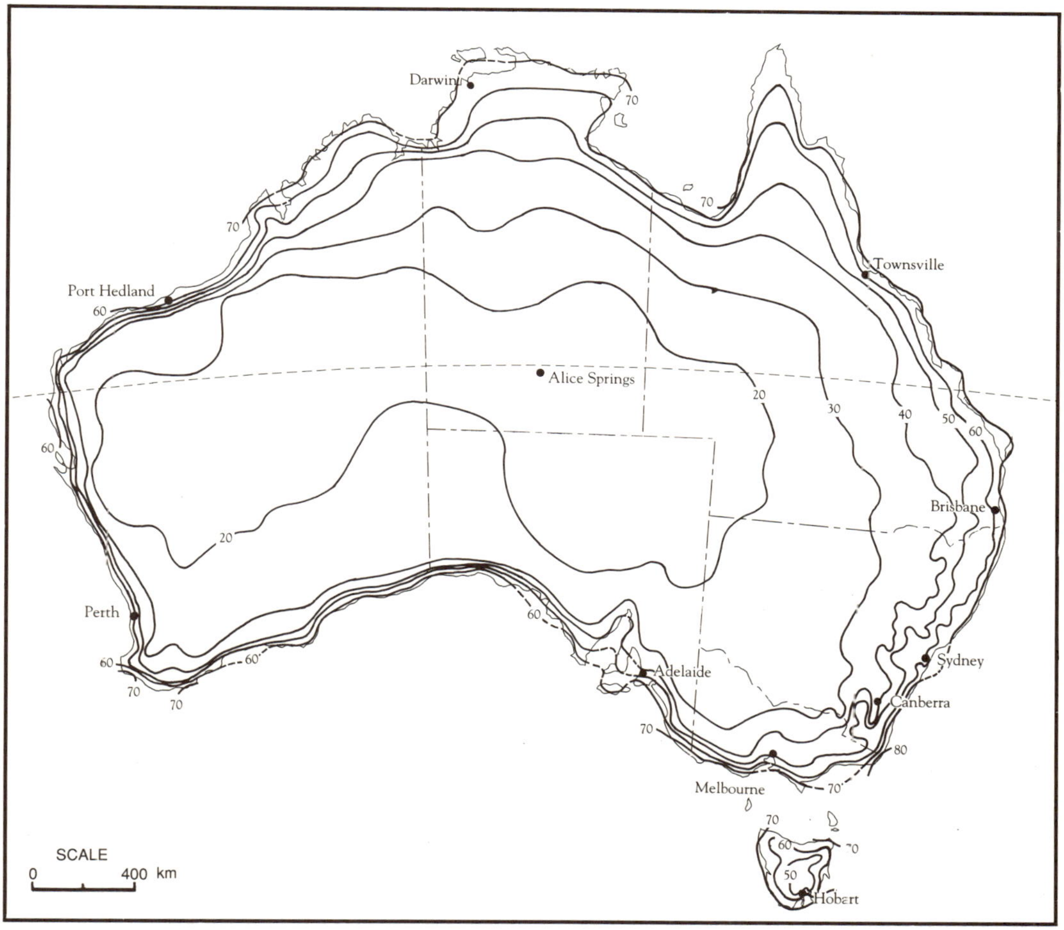

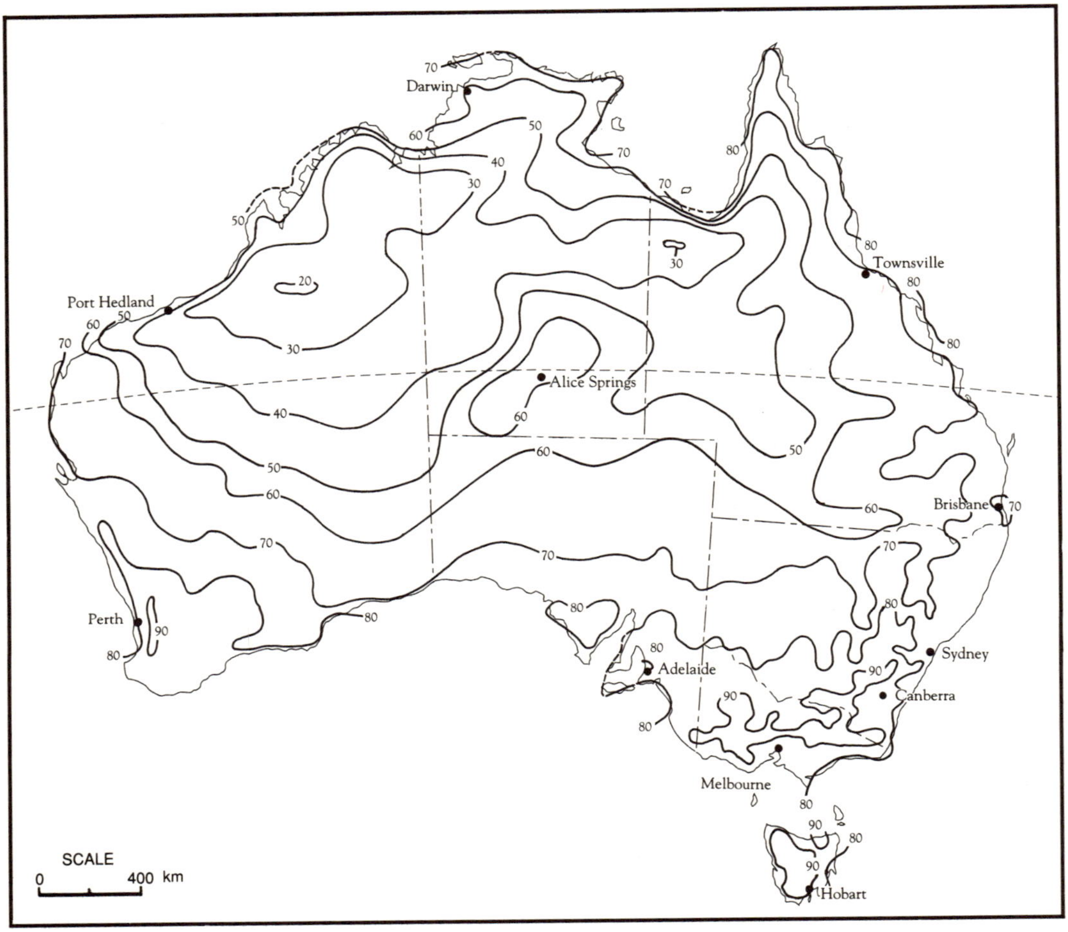

Figure 2.32—Average percentages for relative humidity, July at 9 a.m.

Climatic Discomfort

Climatic discomfort is a highly personal matter. Because of the great variation in metabolisms, some people are comfortable in meteorological conditions that cause discomfort in others. For example, some people are able to walk around in shirt-sleeves in temperatures that cause others to wrap up in a coat or jumper.

Some standardisation of climatic discomfort has been achieved, however, due mainly to the work done by the American Society of Heating, Refrigerating and Air Conditioning Engineers. Some work was also performed by the American military forces during the Korean War (1950–53) when large numbers of troops were exposed to below 0°C temperatures for extended periods. The established measurements of climatic discomfort that have evolved are called effective temperature and relative strain index.

Effective temperature is a combination of temperature, humidity and wind speed and is based on the fact that differing humidities and wind speeds can cause the temperature

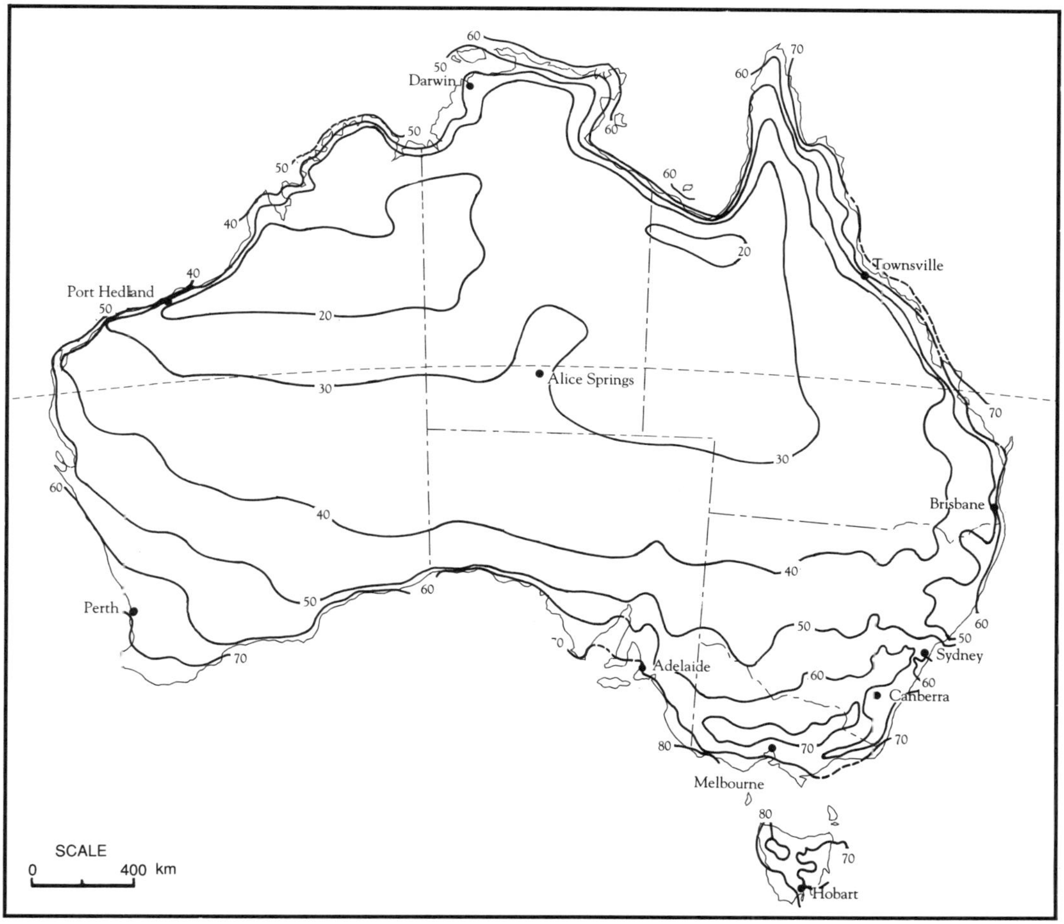

Figure 2.33—Average percentages for relative humidity, July at 3 p.m.

experienced by the body to 'feel' different from that indicated by the thermometer. Technically it is defined as the temperature of still, saturated air in which a normally clothed sedentary worker would feel the same level of comfort or discomfort. Decreasing humidity cools the effective temperature, as does increasing the wind flow. Conversely, increasing the humidity and decreasing the wind flow increases the effective temperature.

It has been found that the normally clothed sedentary worker is comfortable when the effective temperature lies between 15°C and 27°C. Above 27°C effective temperature usually produces heat discomfort and below 15°C produces cold discomfort. Effective temperature is a limited concept because it only refers to indoor conditions and normal clothing.

Relative strain index takes into account not only temperature, humidity and wind but also solar radiation for outdoor purposes, metabolic heat rate and insulation of clothing. It is normally applied as a measure of heat discomfort and as Australian weather produces heat discomfort on a far greater frequency than cold discomfort, it is a useful climatic labelling device.

Figure 2.34 is a heat discomfort map which

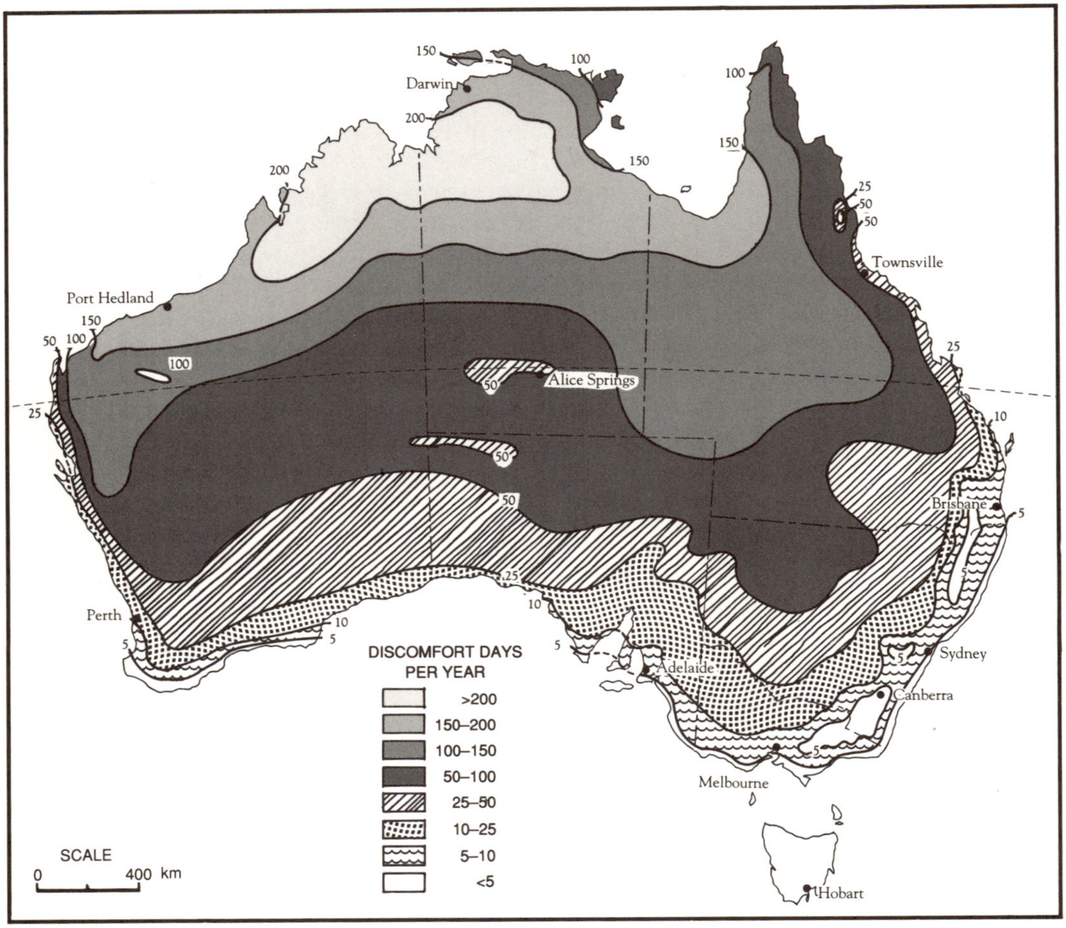

Figure 2.34—Heat discomfort.

shows the average number of days per year when the relative strain index at 3 p.m. exceeds the critical discomfort level (which has been set at 0.03) assuming standard conditions (indoors, manual activities, light clothing and air movement of 1 m/sec.). The area of greatest discomfort is the north-west of Western Australia which averages in excess of two hundred heat discomfort days per year over a considerable area. This illustrates the effect of wind in reducing heat discomfort as the north Queensland area of similar latitude has only between fifty and one hundred such days a year. This is because the Queensland coast has prevailing onshore winds for much of the year.

The moderating effect of altitude is also obvious, even where the Atherton Tablelands form an 'island' of comparative comfort in the surrounding hot and humid tropical sea.

One of Australia's greatest assets is its climate. By world standards, the capital cities experience generally mild weather which means that the people require a comparatively low expenditure on heating and cooling.

3. General Circulation of the Atmosphere

A knowledge of the general wind circulation of the atmosphere is necessary for any understanding of the causes of weather and climate. The atmosphere is a fluid which behaves according to physical laws which are known to a fair degree of precision but the complexity of the circulation makes it difficult to predict its details with accuracy.

This chapter deals with the broad-scale features of the general circulation and describes the main physical laws which determine its structure.

Chemical Composition of the Atmosphere

The atmosphere consists of a thin layer of gases above the surface of the earth which are held there by the earth's gravitational attraction. If the earth is visualised as a balloon, the thickness of the atmosphere would be represented by the thickness of the rubber of the balloon.

The gases of the atmosphere continually take part in a set of complex chemical reactions that result in a constant transfer of chemicals between the atmosphere and the surface of the earth and the biosphere. In spite of such an active chemical environment, the proportion of each of the chemical constituents that makes up the atmosphere remains almost constant.

The main component of the atmosphere is nitrogen. It makes up about 78 per cent of the volume of the atmosphere. The second most abundant gas is oxygen, which comprises about 21 per cent. The remainder of the volume of the atmosphere is made up of various gases, shown here.

Gas	Percentage by volume
Nitrogen	78.084
Oxygen	20.946
Argon	0.934
Carbon dioxide	0.033
Neon	0.00182
Helium	0.00052
Others	0.00066

The gases are generally well mixed and their proportions, with the exception of carbon dioxide, ozone and water vapour, are almost constant up to an altitude of about 80 km. However, water vapour is almost entirely restricted to the troposphere and its concentration is very variable. There had been little change in the composition of the atmosphere for a long period of time but since AD 1800 carbon dioxide at low levels has increased from 275 parts per million by volume to 348 parts per million today. Increases in ozone have also occurred in the lower levels of the atmosphere at some locations through the chemical reactions that occur in photochemical smog. In the stratosphere there have recently been dramatic decreases in the amount of ozone, especially over the Antarctic region.

The small amounts of ozone, carbon dioxide and water vapour in the atmosphere belie their importance for the welfare of life on earth. Stratospheric ozone protects surface life from the harmful effects of ultraviolet radiation. Carbon dioxide has an important role in maintaining the temperature of the earth at an acceptable level. Without water vapour many of the familiar weather occurrences would not exist. It has a capacity to absorb large amounts of energy that can be released under appropriate conditions to drive such weather phenomena as tropical cyclones.

Vertical Structure of the Atmosphere

There is no definite top to the atmosphere. It is most dense near the surface of the earth and becomes less dense with increasing distance from the earth's surface until it merges into the very thin interplanetary space.

Figure 3.1 shows the wide variation of temperature throughout the atmosphere. The atmosphere's temperature distribution is the result of the delicate relationship between the wavelength of the incident radiation, the atmospheric density and the amount of radiation absorbed.

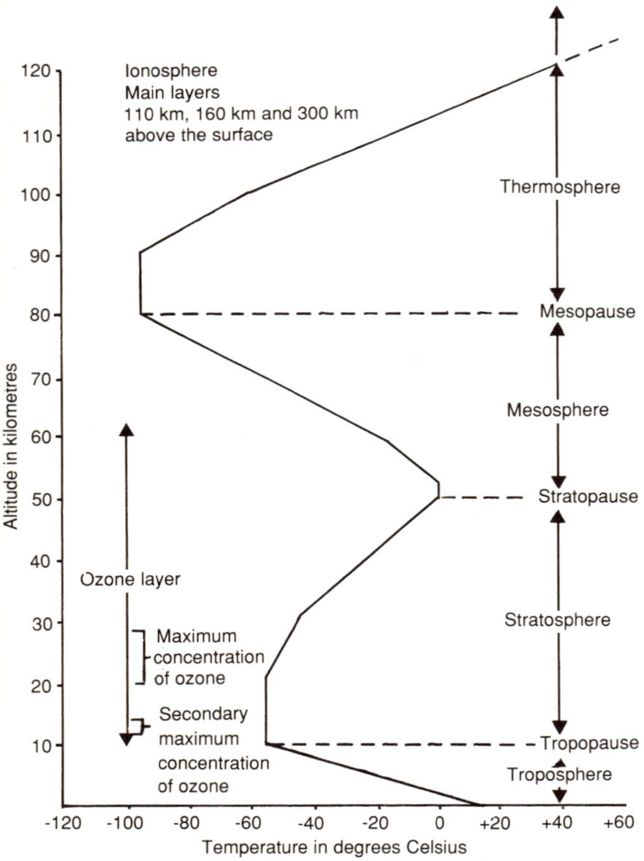

Figure 3.1—Vertical temperature structure of the atmosphere.

The visible light we see is only a small proportion of the radiation the sun emits. Figure 3.2 shows the distribution of wavelengths emitted which varies from very short invisible X-rays to long infra-red radiation (also invisible).

Some of the sun's radiation is absorbed by the atmosphere. At very high altitudes X-rays and other very short wavelength radiation are absorbed by the sparsely distributed molecules of the upper atmosphere. This absorption of high-energy radiation causes the very high temperatures of the thermosphere. The radiation is so powerful it knocks electrons off the molecules and atoms forming electrically charged ions. This area of the atmosphere is called the ionosphere. Its electrical properties reflect and refract radio waves and make long distance radio reception possible by bounding radio waves back to earth. The longer wavelength solar radiation is not absorbed by the low-density gases of the thermosphere and passes through virtually unimpeded to the higher density lower altitudes.

The absorption of radiation in the upper reaches of the atmosphere filters out the short wavelength radiation and less is available for heating the lower atmosphere so that the temperature falls in the thermosphere with decreasing altitude. But closer to the earth, in the region called the mesosphere, the atmospheric density increases to such a value that the oxygen molecules absorb ultraviolet radiation. This imparts energy to the atmosphere and increases the temperature as the altitude decreases. Maximum absorption and heating occurs at the stratopause at an altitude of about 50 km. When ultraviolet is absorbed by the oxygen molecules they split into two oxygen atoms, which then react with oxygen molecules to form ozone. The ozone sinks under the influence of gravity to form

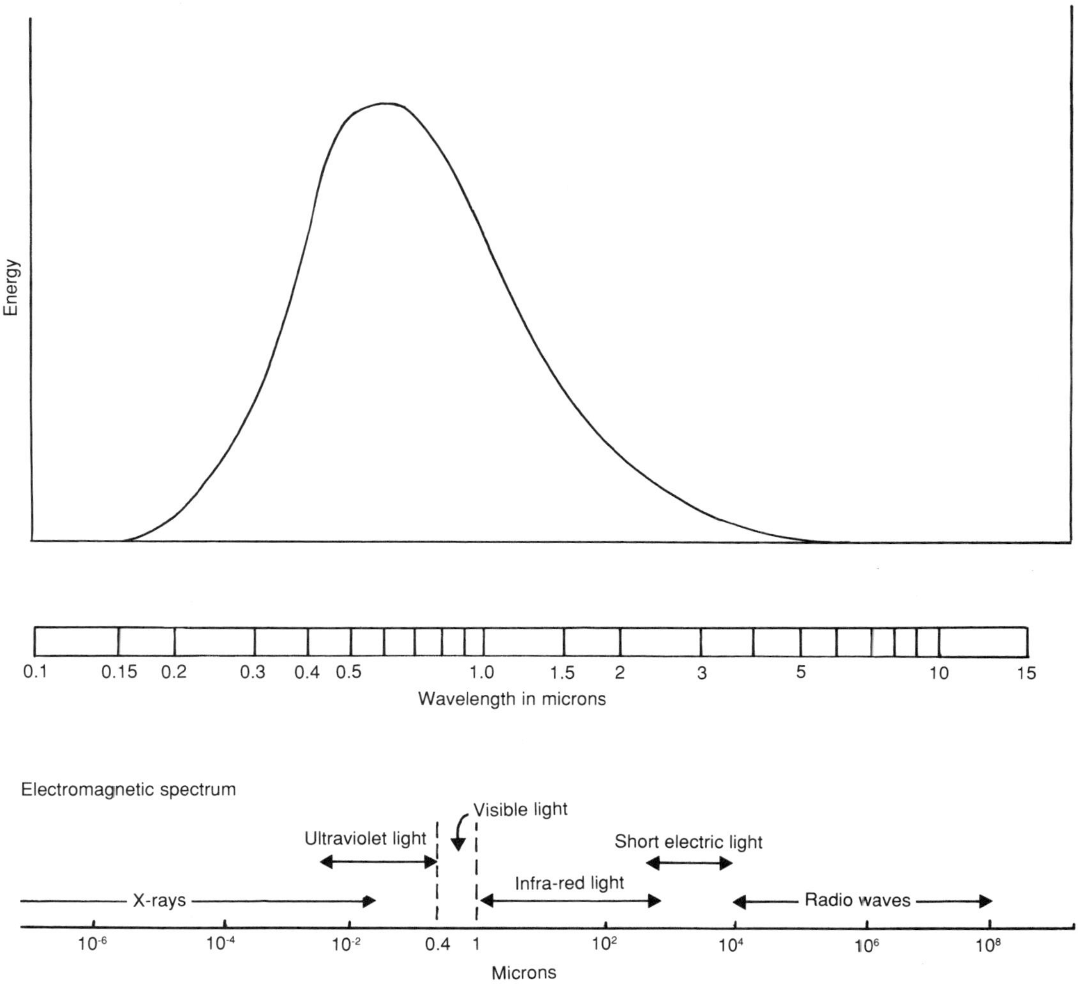

Figure 3.2—Spectral distribution of radiation from the sun.

a layer of maximum concentration at an altitude of about 20–28 km and a secondary layer at 16 km. These compose the so-called ozone layer. Most of the ultraviolet radiation is absorbed as it descends to lower altitudes, less is available for heating and the temperature decreases. This region, between the stratopause and the tropopause (see Figure 3.1), is called the stratosphere.

Eventually the radiation strikes the ground and heats the surface, which in turn heats the adjacent air. Warm air becomes less dense than its surroundings and rises and cools. This process mixes and heats the gases of the atmosphere close to the earth's surface in the zone known as the troposphere, the upper limit of which is the tropopause.

Wind Circulation of the Real Atmosphere

Meteorology is concerned with the circulation of air within the atmosphere and its associated weather. Energy in the form of latent heat is stored in water vapour that, when it condenses to form droplets, usually in the form of cloud or fog, releases sensible heat. This important source of energy drives many familiar weather phenomena. As very little water vapour exists above the tropopause, the weather is largely restricted to the troposphere.

Atmospheric Scales

The atmosphere is characterised by phenomena that vary greatly in both size and length of life cycle. In size they range from the molecular scale of heat conduction to planetary waves with an extent of 10 000 km. Similarly the length of the life cycle of atmospheric phenomena varies from the very short, such as the vibration of sound waves of less than a second, to ice ages, which may last ten million years.

None of these phenomena is discreet; together they form part of a continuum that is the atmospheric system. Many classification schemes of atmospheric phenomena have been proposed in an attempt to subdivide them into manageable classes for study. There is now a reasonable consensus that uses a horizontal distance scale based on a classification proposed by Smagorinsky (1974). There is a considerable amount of overlap of scales and in summary they are as follows.

Microscale	10^{-2} to 10^{3} metres
Local Scale	10^{2} to 5×10^{4} metres
Mesoscale	10^{4} to 2×10^{5} metres
Macroscale	10^{5} to 10^{8} metres

Mean Winds

Figure 3.3 is a schematic representation of the tropospheric wind circulation averaged over a long period. The actual winds that occur at any particular time may vary considerably from the average. There are six main features of the mean surface flow.

Polar highs These occur at both poles and are the result of very cold sinking air. At the surface the air spreads out resulting in easterly winds around the highs.

Temperate latitude low-pressure systems These are regions of variable winds converging into low-pressure areas that are located about 60°S and 60°N and are often the 'anchor points' of fronts.

Westerlies These are regions of belts of predominantly westerly winds approximately between latitudes 40°S and 60°S and 40°N and 60°N. Often fronts are embedded in the westerlies.

Subtropical anticyclones These are regions of high pressure approximately between latitudes 30°S and 40°S and 30°N and 40°N. Surface winds are light and variable.

Trade winds These occur in the region between the equatorial trough (also called the intertropic convergence zone) and latitudes 30°S and 30°N. They are south-easterlies in the Southern Hemisphere and north-easterlies in the Northern Hemisphere.

Intertropical convergence zone This is a shallow belt of low pressure on or near the equator. Winds are usually light and variable.

The vertical motion of air within a hemisphere can be divided into three main cells.

The Hadley cell Rising air over the intertropic convergence zone forms the equatorward side of the Hadley cell. Sinking air over the subtropical high-pressure belt forms the poleward side of the cell. As the air approaches the ground some moves towards the pole and some towards the equator. The equatorward moving air forms the surface return flow back to the equatorial trough.

The Ferrel cell The poleward moving air referred to above forms the surface section of the Ferrel cell; the equatorward side is formed by the descending air over the subtropical ridge. Air

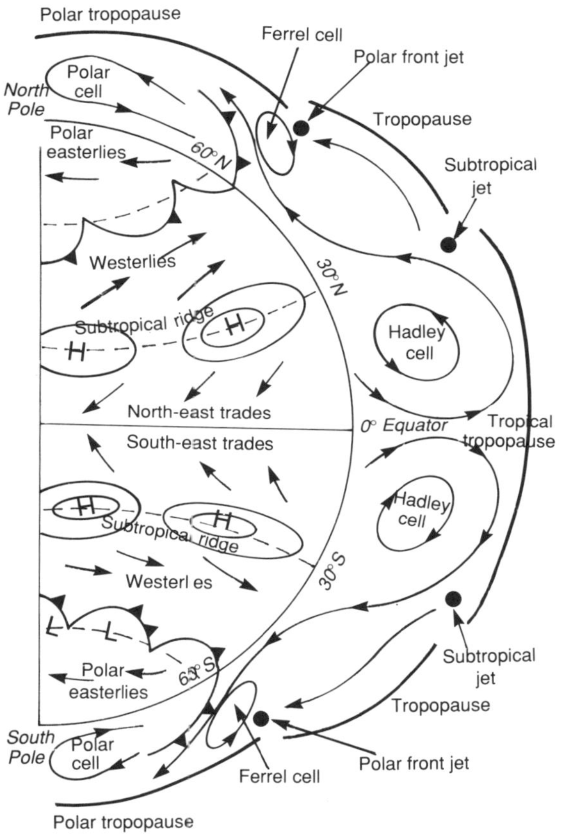

Figure 3.3—Winds in the troposphere.

rising over the cold dome of polar air forms the poleward arm. The Ferrel cell is a weak indirect circulation.

The cell over the polar region The tropopause acts as a lid on the rising air. As the warm air rises over the cold dome, some is deflected equatorwards to form the top arm of the Ferrel cell and some is deflected polewards forming the upper-level arm of the polar cell. The poleward arm of the cell is formed by the cold air sinking over the poles. On reaching the surface the air spreads out towards the equator forming the surface arm of the polar cell.

The boundary between the sinking dome of cold air and the warmer lower latitude air is the polar front.

Two other features of the mean circulation are the very strong westerly winds that occur just below the tropopause. The polar front jet occurs above the polar front at an altitude of about 10 km and is associated with a gap in the tropopause on its poleward side. The subtropical jet occurs over the subtropical ridge and is also associated with a gap in the tropopause on its poleward side. It usually occurs at an altitude of about 12 km and wind speeds are often greater than 280 km/h: wind speeds of 540 km/h have been recorded.

Instantaneous Global Wind Circulations

The daily weather chart illustrated in Figure 3.4 shows the wind circulation at a particular time. On such charts it may be difficult to identify many of the features of the mean circulation patterns that, because they are averages, emphasise those aspects of the wind circulation that persist for a considerable period of time. The daily circulation patterns can for convenience be divided into three regions: the polar region, the middle- and high-latitude region and the tropical region.

Wind Circulation in the Polar Region

The cold air over the poles subsides. Subsidence and intense cold causes the air to be extremely dry with only very weak horizontal thermal gradients. The energy, stored in strong thermal gradients and the latent heat of vaporisation of water vapour, which drives the major atmospheric disturbances is absent in polar regions. In the Northern Hemisphere there is a fairly well defined

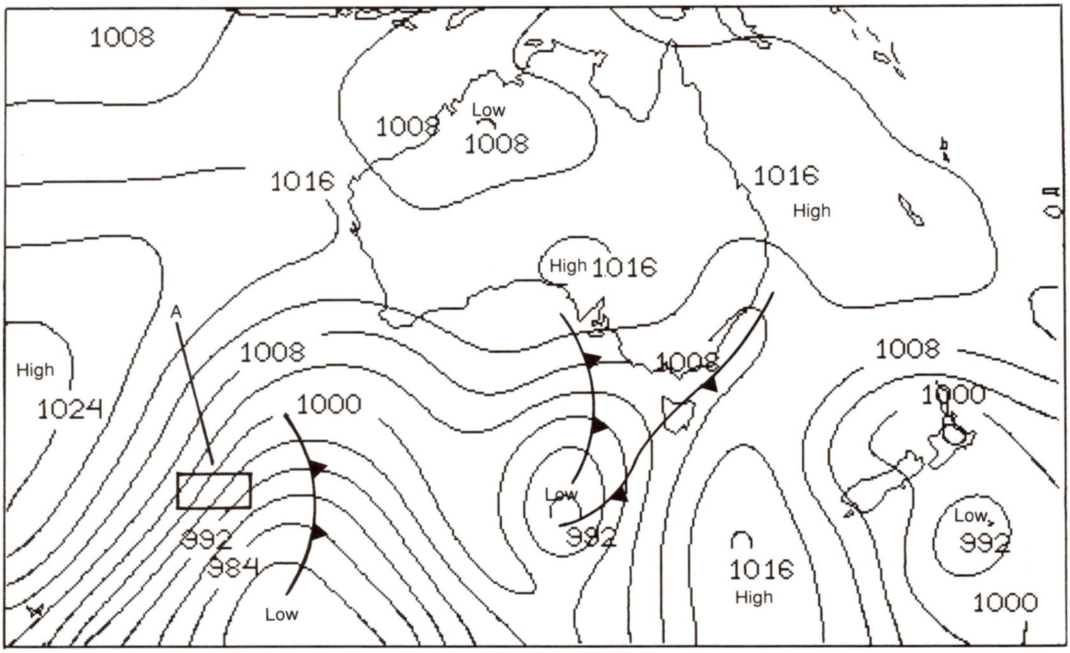

Figure 3.4—Mean sea level pressure analysis.

low-energy circulation north of about 70°N, which is north of the main westerlies, but the boundary of this weak circulation and the high-latitude westerlies is not as clearly defined in the Antarctic region where very strong winds do occur at times. These are usually katabatic winds caused by the cold air sliding down the Antarctic continent towards the Southern Ocean.

Wind Circulation in the Middle- and High-Latitude Region

The day to day variability of the circulation is perhaps greatest between latitudes 40°S to 70°S and 40°N to 70°N. The daily weather map (see Figure 3.4) indicates there is a progression of highs and lows across the earth's surface.

As the polar air moves towards the equator it picks up moisture and heat. Where it encounters the warmer air moving from the equator, strong horizontal thermal gradients occur. The thermal gradients, the moisture and the heat provide an enormous energy source to drive the often violent weather of these latitudes. The general westerly flow in this area is extremely unstable and breaks down into a stream of large eddies; the familiar highs and lows, which generally move eastwards across the surface. These huge eddies move more slowly than the westerly flow at higher altitudes and have a maximum complexity at the surface. This is illustrated by three simultaneous charts showing the mean sea level pressure pattern (Figure 3.4); the 500 hPa contour pattern, which is in the middle of the troposphere at an altitude of about 5500 m (Figure 3.5); and the 250 hPa contour pattern; near the top of the troposphere at an altitude of about 9000 m (Figure 3.6). The large eddies of the surface chart are more complex than the patterns in the middle and upper troposphere. They are typically 1000 to 3000 km across. Such closed circulations occur

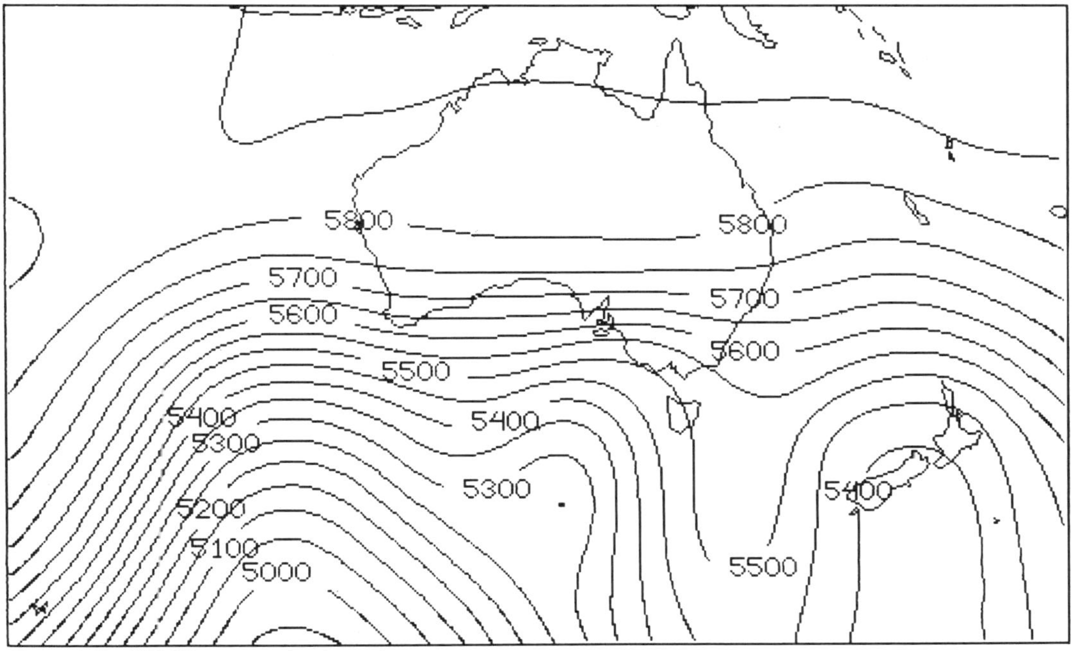

Figure 3.5—500 hPa contour height analysis.

Figure 3.6—250 hPa contour height analysis.

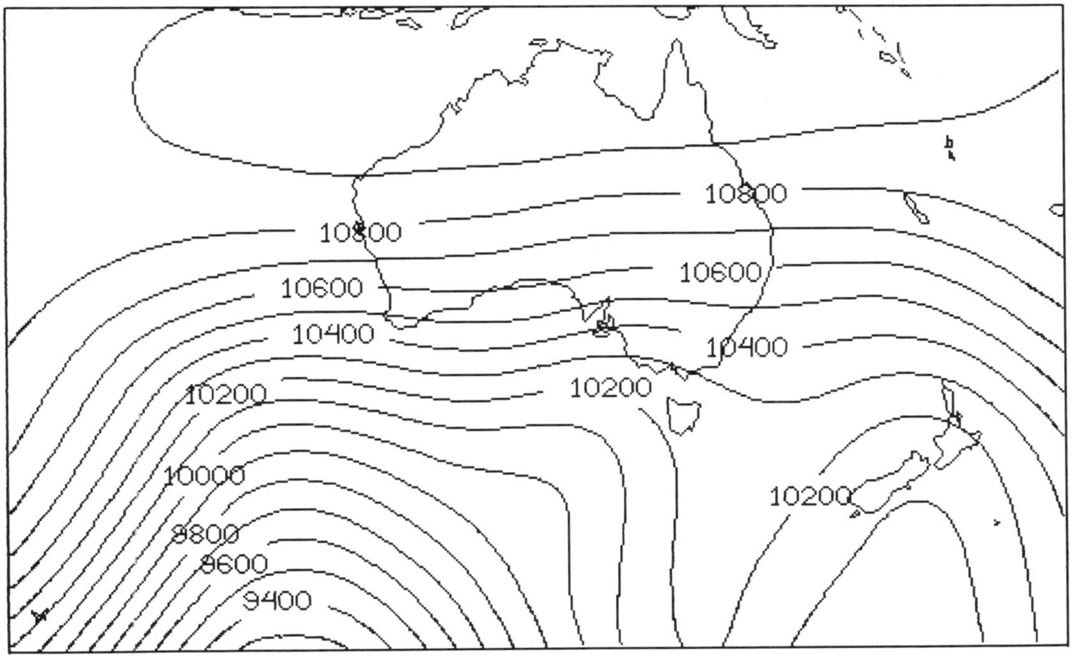

much less commonly at 500 hPa where they are generally replaced by a wave pattern of large meanders usually of dimensions considerably larger than the surface eddies. At 250 hPa there are typically four or five such large meanders or waves around the globe that are known as long waves or Rossby waves after C. G. Rossby who first investigated their properties.

On a day-to-day basis the troughs and ridges not only migrate around the earth but there is also great variation in their intensity and spatial arrangement, which is described by the zonal index cycle. This index is essentially the difference between the mean surface pressures at two latitude circles, usually 35° and 55°. The atmosphere may take a month or more to exhibit the whole range of values of the index. Typical patterns of troughs and ridges in the middle troposphere with zonal indices ranging from high to low are illustrated in Figure 3.7.

Figure 3.7a illustrates a high zonal index pattern where the upper wind flow has a gentle meandering pattern. The wind is mainly westerly with very little north or south component. The surface eddies move quickly from west to east with little equatorward or poleward movement and there may be large areas of surface zonal (westerly) flow. As the flow becomes more disturbed, the amplitude of the upper waves becomes greater and the wavelength shorter as

Below, right and following page: Figure 3.7—The zonal index cycle illustrated by wind flow in the middle troposphere in the Southern Hemisphere. Arrows indicate windflow.

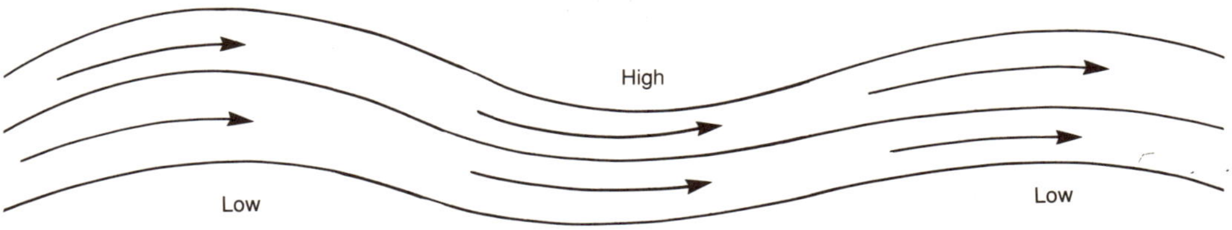

3.7a High zonal index

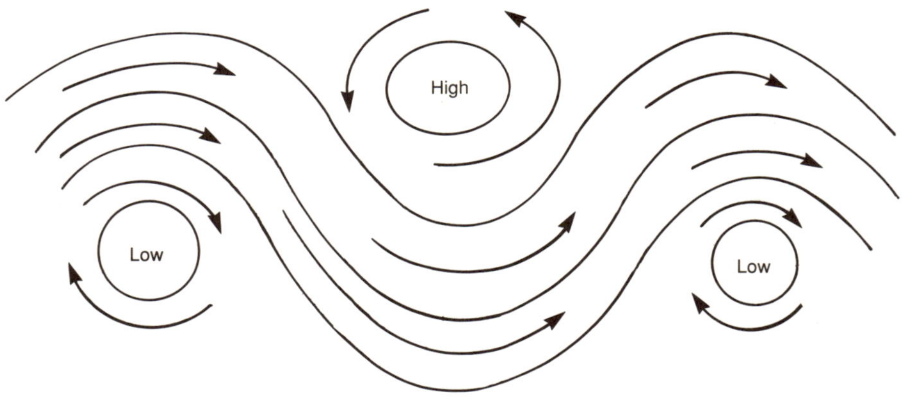

3.7b Medium to high zonal index

illustrated in Figure 3.7b. The surface eddies move more slowly and have larger meridional movement, greatly reducing the area of surface westerlies, which sometimes completely disappear. As the zonal index decreases further the flow becomes even more disturbed and the surface pattern consists entirely of closed circulations around highs and lows. The upper pattern also becomes more involuted as illustrated in Figure 3.7c. When the zonal index reaches its lowest value in the cycle the upper flow pattern illustrated in Figure 3.7d occurs. There is very little westerly flow, as the main components are poleward and equatorward. At the surface a large, very slow-moving high is associated with the upper ridge and a slow-moving low moves equatorwards and is associated with the trough. This results in the surface low being located equatorward of the high. It is known as a blocking pattern because the normal westerly flow around the globe is blocked. Frontal systems approaching from the west are steered to the poleward side of the block. Northern Hemisphere blocking patterns persist for up to about sixteen days but in the Southern Hemisphere they are more short lived and persist only up to a week.

Wind Circulation in the Tropical Region

The tropical region is that part of the globe, generally between latitudes 30°S and 30°N, which lies between the subtropical ridges. The winds in this region usually have an equatorward component, flowing into the equatorial trough.

The trade winds One of the most persistent and well-known features of the tropical wind circulation is the trades. The word 'trade' comes from Old English meaning 'path', and the winds are so named because of their regular course. Many cultures have a special word reserved for these persistent winds, for example in Arnhem Land the most common Aboriginal name is *Dir'mala*, while in Saharan Africa they are known as the *Harmattan*.

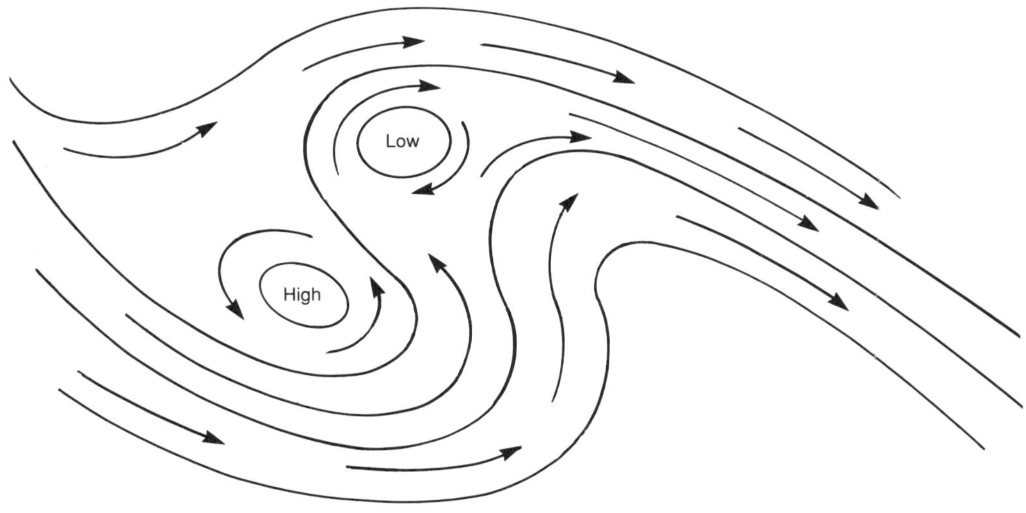

3.7c Low to medium zonal index

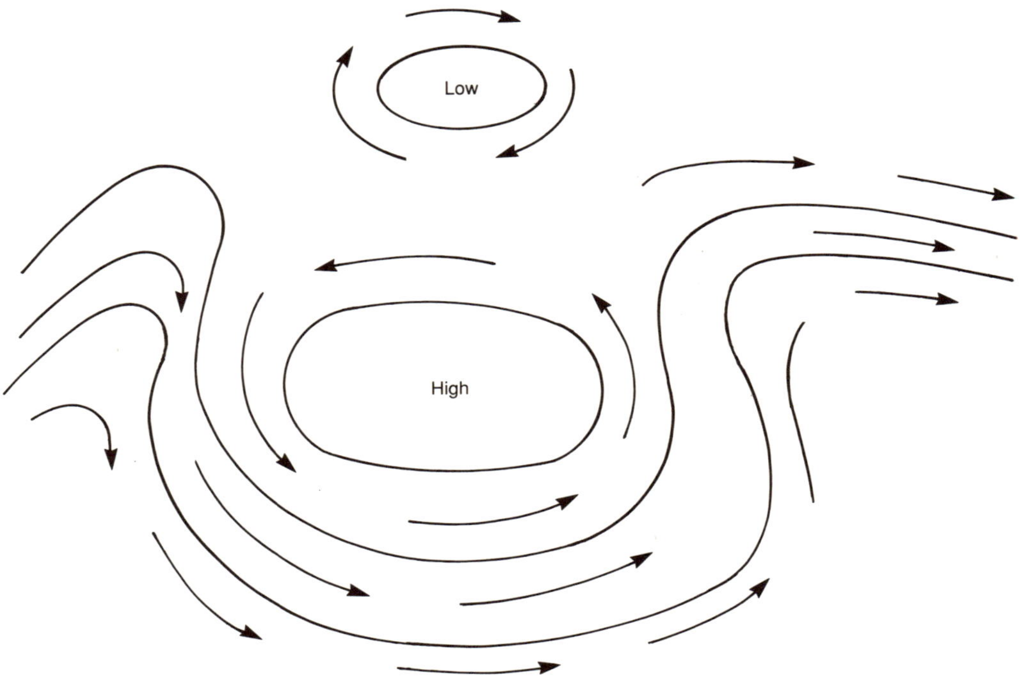

3.7d Low zonal index

In the Southern Hemisphere the winds blowing out of the subtropical highs are called the south-east trades; in the Northern Hemisphere they are called the north-east trades. If the equatorial trough is in the Northern Hemisphere the south-east trades turn to the south-west as they cross the equator. Similarly if the equatorial trough is in the Southern Hemisphere, the north-east trades become north-westerlies as they cross the equator. The trade winds are remarkably steady and occur over most ocean areas except the northern Indian Ocean. The persistence of the trades is a reflection of the permanence of the subtropical ridge, with the greatest variability occurring close to the subtropical ridge which consists of migrating highs. On the eastern side of the highs the trades have a strong southerly component in the Southern Hemisphere and a strong northerly component in the Northern Hemisphere, but to the west of the highs the flow is almost pure easterly. By the time the air has reached about 15°S or 20°N its direction becomes constant and this leads to very monotonous weather.

The vertical structure of the trades is determined by their source in the subtropical ridge. At and close to the surface, cool air (having been advected from the cooler poleward side of the high) circulates around a high and picks up moisture over the oceans by evaporation. Higher-level subsiding air in the ridge spreads out in all directions as it approaches the surface. But it is forced to the north and south of the ridge because other highs to the east and west prevent the air from moving eastwards or westwards at the latitude of the ridge. The strongest subsidence occurs on the eastern side of highs where the air warms as it subsides because of the increasing pressure. This causes a corresponding decrease in the relative humidity. Where the warmed air meets the cooler surface air circulating around the high, a temperature inversion forms at the level where the two streams meet. The height of the inversion varies from near the surface over the cold water oceans along the western desert sides of the continents to great altitudes over equatorial regions. Cloud tops are restricted to the bottom of the inversion, preventing moisture from being distributed throughout the depth of the atmosphere. It has been suggested that the latent heat contained in the water vapour of the surface trades results in a net transfer of heat to the equatorial region. If this is true the trades could be regarded as self generating and the cause of the intertropical convergence zone. However, further research is required on this aspect of the trades.

The equatorial trough The equatorial trough is a shallow area of low pressure where the trades from both hemispheres meet. It is fairly close to the equator, especially over the oceans. Figure 3.8 shows the mean positions of the equatorial trough for January and July. In January its position varies between latitudes 17°S and 8°N but in July it varies between 2°N and 27°N.

The equatorial trough is the belt across which there is no appreciable transport of heat. However, because there is a large excess of radiative energy, and therefore heat, in the summer hemisphere, the equatorial trough follows the summer sun to compensate for the energy imbalance of the Southern and Northern hemispheres. The ocean has a large capacity for storing heat and is able to compensate for the large hemispheric energy excess or deficit so that the equatorial trough migrates only slightly from season to season over the oceans. On the other hand the land areas have a very small heat storage capacity and the equatorial trough has to make large migrations polewards to permit an appreciable flow of heat across the equator to compensate for the hemispheric energy imbalance. In the central Atlantic and the eastern Pacific the equatorial trough moves as little as 5° of latitude between the seasons. Between longitudes 15°E and 120°E

Figure 3.8—Mean positions of the equatorial trough, January and July.

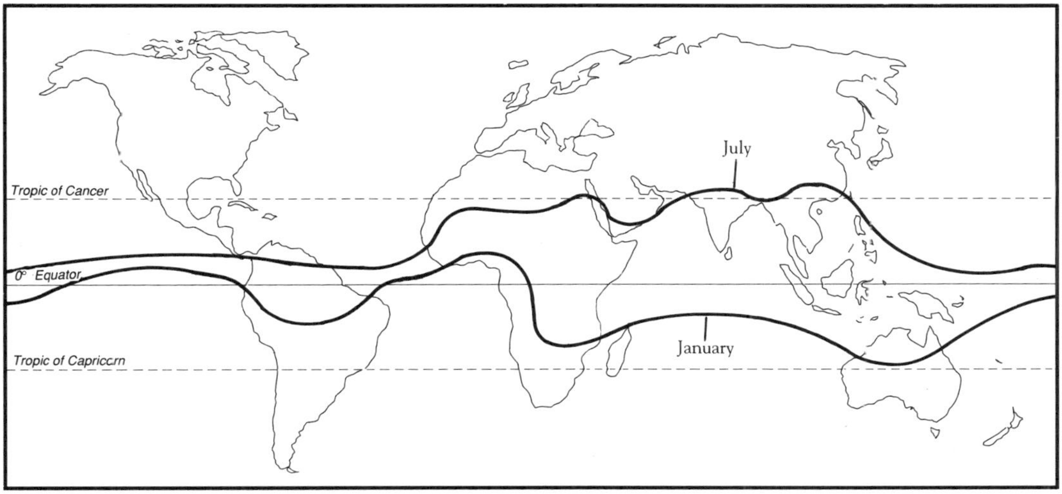

it moves about 40° of latitude during the seasons. This movement is related to the occurrence of the monsoon circulations that occur over the whole of southern Asia and northern Africa in the northern summer, and over Australia and southern Africa in the southern summer. The monsoon is discussed in more detail later in this chapter.

The equatorial trough is at times somewhat more complex than a single simple low-pressure trough stretching around the globe. Sometimes the equatorial trough is distinguished from the intertropical convergence zone. The equatorial trough is defined as the low-pressure trough lying between the trades of the two hemispheres where they meet at a small angle with no convergence. The intertropical convergence zone is also defined as the low-pressure trough where the trades of the two hemispheres meet, but at a large angle with marked convergence. Both terms are often used synonymously.

A wide range of weather conditions can be associated with the equatorial trough. If the trades are weak and there is no convergence there may be virtually no cloud or weather activity associated with it. On the other hand if the trades intensify, large masses of cumulonimbus may develop and result in heavy rainfall. At times there may be two separate convergence zones with clear weather in between.

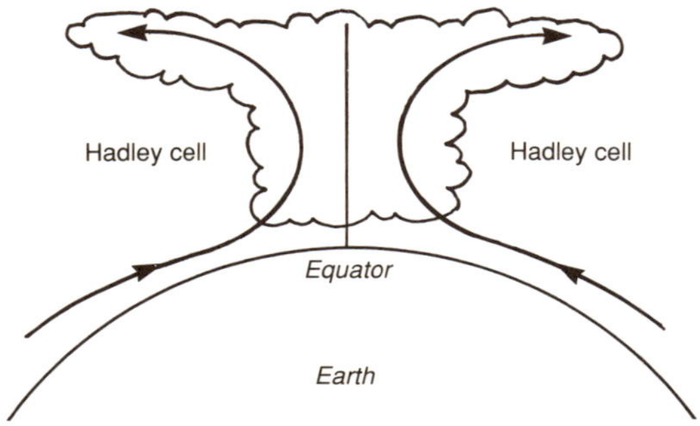

Figure 3.9—Simple model of the equatorial trough.

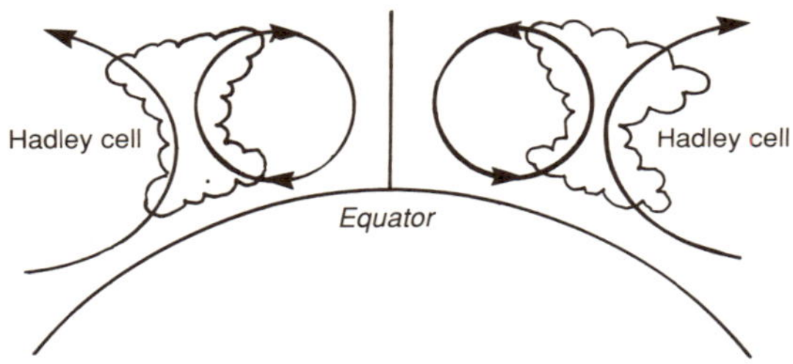

Figure 3.10—Simple model of the equatorial trough with double vertical circulation cells.

The classical model of the equatorial trough is that it is the common vertical arm of the Hadley cells of the Northern and Southern hemispheres, as illustrated in Figure 3.9. It has been suggested that this model is an over simplification. Cloud and rain produced by the above model allow for radiative cooling at the cloud tops and evaporative cooling in the lower layers. In these circumstances, if the cooling becomes sufficiently large the equatorial region becomes cooler than its surroundings and air starts to subside. Then a double vertical circulation forms between the Hadley cells, as illustrated in Figure 3.10. Two new convergence zones are formed, separated by a stable almost cloudless region. This double cell model, however, appears to be restricted to ocean regions. A third model has been suggested by Asnani (1968), which is illustrated in Figure 3.11. A single cell separates the two Hadley cells and the position of the intertropical convergence zone is determined by the rotation direction of the separating cell.

The equatorial trough could be thought of as the meteorological 'equator' separating the Northern and Southern hemisphere circulation systems. Like other meteorological phenomena, it is extremely complex with a structure which varies over time. There is evidence to suggest

Streaks of cirrocumulus, Wilmington, SA. (See Chapter 6.)

A pelican contemplates a bank of stratocumulus, Lake Illawarra, NSW. (See Chapter 6.)

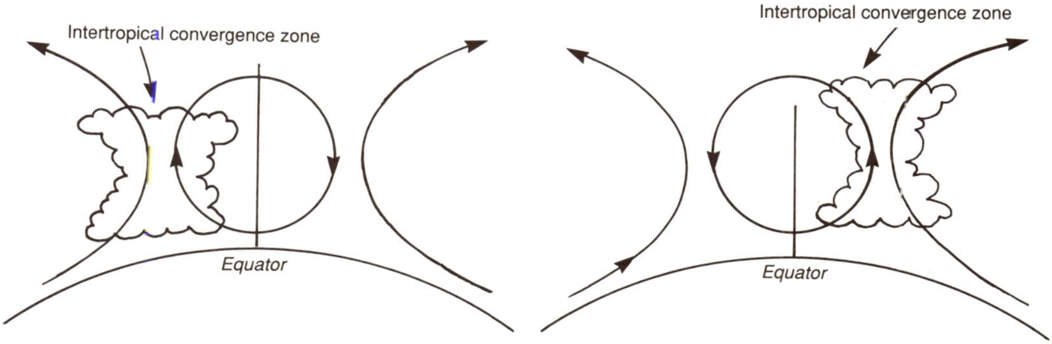

Figure 3.11—Simple model of an equatorial trough following Asnani (1968).

that all three models described above are valid but exist under different circumstances.

The Walker circulation In considering the tropical circulation, so far only the meridional (north–south) circulations have been described, but there is clear evidence that large vertical east–west circulations also occur in the tropical regions. In 1897, very early in the history of modern meteorology, H. H. Hildebrandsson discovered an inverse relationship between pressure anomalies at Buenos Aires and Sydney; that is, if the pressure is above average at Sydney it will be below average at Buenos Aires. These pressure anomalies were eventually recognised as evidence of a vertical latitudinal circulation in the tropics, which is of enormous significance to Australia's climate. The circulation became known as the Walker circulation, after Sir Gilbert Walker who did much pioneering work investigating such relationships between pressure, temperature and rainfall at various places around the world. Walker called this relationship the Southern oscillation to distinguish it from two other similar relationships in the pressure field, namely the North Atlantic oscillation and the North Pacific oscillation. The use of the term oscillation does not imply any regular periodic change in the pressure relationship between different parts of the globe, but merely indicates that there is an inverse relationship.

Figure 3.12 illustrates the vertical east–west circulation near the equator. The Walker circulation is a cell with rising air in the Indonesian–Australian region and sinking air near the west coast of South America. These are thermally driven circulations and the reason for their existence is the differing sea-surface temperatures of vast areas of the oceans.

Usually a very cold ocean current flows equatorwards along the South American coast and spreads out into the eastern Pacific in equatorial regions. However, in the Indonesian and northern Australian region water temperatures are above the average for that latitude. It was suggested by Bjerknes (1969) that the relatively low water temperature in the eastern Pacific causes the lower-level air above the sea to be too cold to take part in the ascending motion in the equatorial region between the two Hadley cells, as illustrated in Figure 3.9. Instead it flows westwards, absorbing heat as it travels over the warmer water of the western Pacific, until it reaches the Indonesian region where it rises to form vast clusters of thunderstorms producing heavy rain; it is this rising air that forms the western arm of the Walker circulation. The Walker circulation is the most marked of all the equatorial east–west vertical circulations.

It has been found that the Southern oscillation is very persistent, with the pressure anomalies

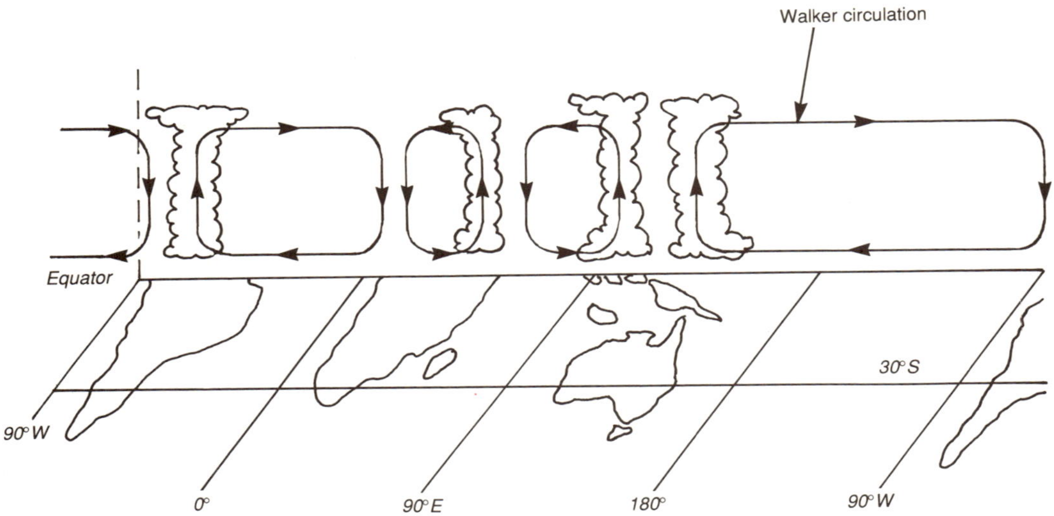

Figure 3.12—The Walker circulation.

lasting for several months. There is a tendency for them to reach a maximum from October to November and to break down from March to April. Rainfall over Australia is strongly correlated to the sign (positive or negative) and strength of these anomalies, providing a reasonably reliable method for forecasting seasonal rainfall. The strength of the Southern oscillation is measured by means of the Southern oscillation Index. In theory, this index measures the difference in mean sea level atmospheric pressure between sites in the South Pacific subtropical high-pressure region and the Australian–Indonesian low-pressure region. In practice, the index is calculated by subtracting the mean monthly pressure anomaly at Tahiti from the mean monthly pressure anomaly at Darwin.

Closely related to the Southern oscillation is the phenomenon of El Niño. Originally El Niño referred to a warm current that flows southwards along the coasts of Equador and northern Peru each year during summer when the south-east trades are at their weakest. It sets in just after Christmas in most years, hence the name El Niño (meaning, 'the child'). Usually this very shallow current of warm water penetrates to about 6°S, but in years when the south-east trades are exceptionally strong the warm waters may extend as far south as 12°S. Today common usage reserves the term El Niño for the exceptional event when the warm current extends south of 6°S and includes the influx, beneath the shallow surface current, of warmer water from the west and north-west.

There is a strong relationship between the strength of the south-east trades and the intensity of the El Niño event. This relationship is illustrated in Figure 3.13. The thermal structure of the top layer of the Pacific Ocean during the normal south-east trade season is illustrated in Figure 3.13a. The thermocline, the boundary separating the deep cold water from the warmer shallow surface layer, is deeper on the western side of the Pacific. It is caused by the solar heating of the surface water as it is pushed westwards by the south-east trades and piled up on the western side of the ocean. Sea level is about 0.4 metre higher in the northern Australian region than at the same latitude in the South American region. Figure 3.13b illustrates the situation during a

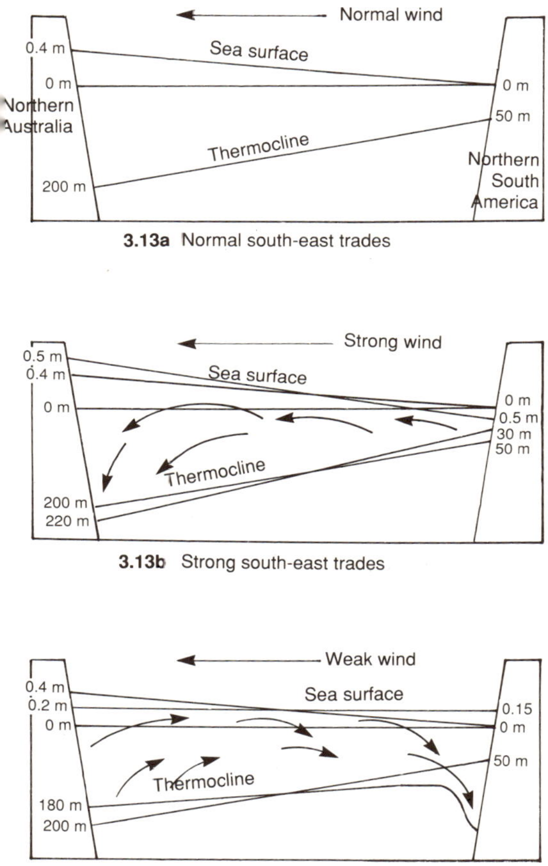

Figure 3.13—Relationship between sea temperatures and the strength of south-east trades.

period of very strong south-east trades. The stronger winds force the water to pile up even higher on the western side of the ocean and the slope of the thermocline across the Pacific increases so that on the eastern side the warm surface water is shallower and on the western side it is deeper and sea level is higher. Figure 3.13c illustrates the change in the thermal structure of the upper layer of the ocean when the south-east trades relax (weaken). The weak winds are unable to support the high sea level on the western side and the water sloshes back towards South America causing the sea level to rise and the thickness of the warm water layer to increase in the eastern Pacific.

The severe drought of 1982–83 in Australia, South-East Asia and the African Sahel corresponded to a very marked El Niño event.

Monsoons Monsoons are well-known features of the tropics. They are thermally driven winds that blow in response to the seasonal changes to the difference in pressure between land and sea, which is caused by their different temperatures. Originally the term was used to describe a persistent cool dry wind in winter blowing southwards across India from the Tibetan Plateau; in summer it described a warm and humid wind blowing northwards across India from the Indian Ocean, which often produced torrential rain. The term monsoon has now been extended to similar phenomena in other parts of the world.

Where large continents border the sea the differences in temperature are often great and result in vigorous winds. In 1686 Halley was the first to propose an explanation of the mechanism of the monsoon. In summer, air over the land is hotter and therefore less dense than air over the sea. This causes a low-pressure area to form over the land. In low-latitude areas, the Coriolis force, which deflects the wind to travel parallel to the isobars in higher latitudes, is very weak so that air flows across the isobars from the high-pressure area over the sea to the low-pressure area over the land, as illustrated in Figure 3.14a. The air from maritime regions is very moist and when it reaches the warm low-pressure area it rises and in doing so cools, forming widespread cloud and thunderstorms with heavy rain. In winter, the wind flow is reversed as shown in Figure 3.14b. The land cools more than the sea, which causes the air in contact with the land to become denser than the air over the sea. This results in higher pressure over the land than the sea. The cool dry wind that results is called the winter monsoon.

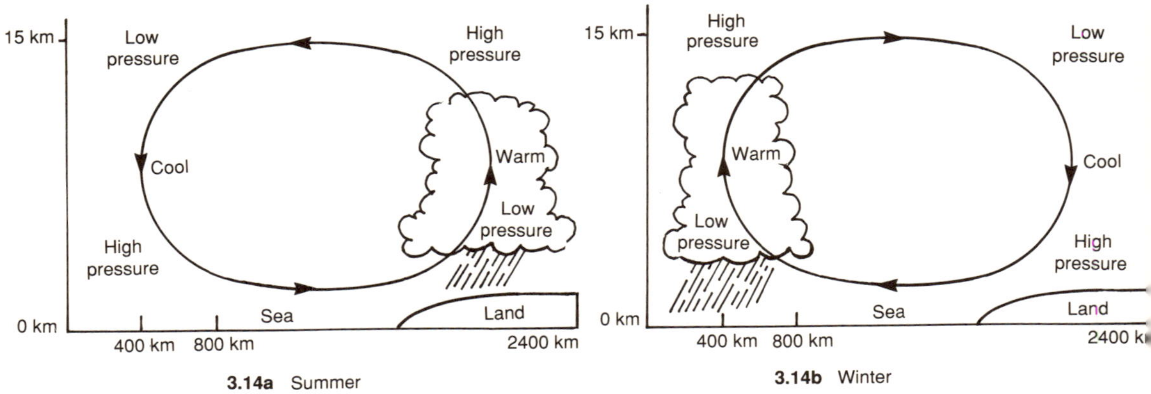

Figure 3.14—The monsoon circulation.

Any cloud and rain activity, if it occurs at all, will be over the sea.

A great deal has been learned about the monsoon circulations since the time of Halley. They are somewhat more complex than his general explanation suggests. Monsoon circulations occur in equatorial regions in Africa, Asia and northern Australia, although in Australia the monsoonal climate is much less marked. The areas affected are shown in Figure 3.15. There is a considerable variation in monsoonal circulations caused by the relative positions of the landmasses and the oceans and by the presence of the massive Himalayan Mountains and Tibetan Plateau.

The Asian monsoon is strongly influenced by the presence of the Himalayan Mountains and Tibetan Plateau, the topographical features of which are tall enough to deflect the subtropical

Figure 3.15—Areas affected by monsoonal climate.

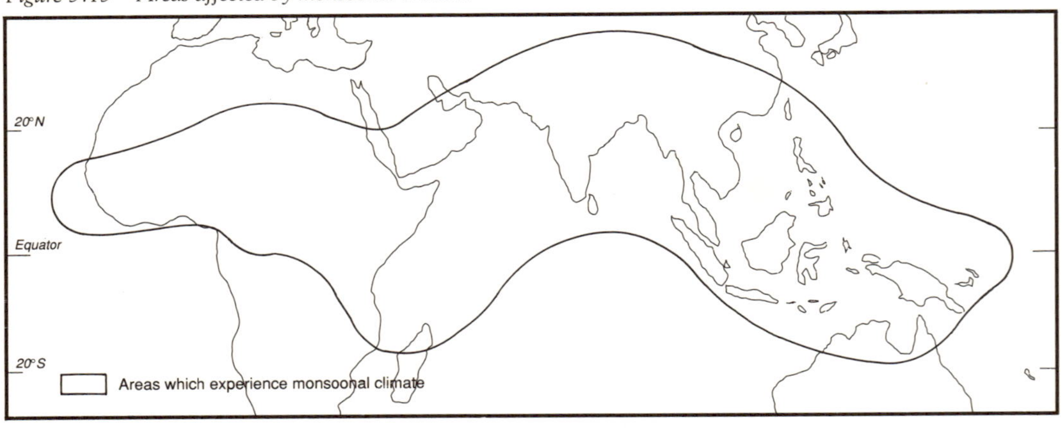

jet stream and cause it to interact with the monsoon circulation. Over north-west India and west Pakistan the location of the subtropical jet results in upper-level convergence and forces air to subside throughout the year, suppressing the rain-producing properties of the summer monsoon and leading to a desert-like climate. Between longitudes 70°E and 100°E the opposite effect occurs. The subtropical jet enhances the monsoon circulation.

The African Continent straddles the equator and has significant consequences for the tropical circulation in that region. In summer in the Northern Hemisphere heating of the north African deserts causes the pressure to fall in the same way as in Asia. But this is also the time of the southern winter and a high-pressure region forms over southern Africa resulting in a massive flow of air from south to north across the African continent. This flow influences the atmospheric circulation almost 1000 km to the east over the Indian Ocean. Air flows in a huge ring or circle over the Indian Ocean. Cool air is drawn towards northern Africa from the northern edge of the semipermanent Indian Ocean high to the south-east. As the air flows northwards it is deflected into a south-westerly as it crosses the equator. It then flows along the coast of Arabia and across India reaching the Thailand–Indochina peninsular as the summer south-west monsoon.

Tropical cyclone One of the most spectacular and destructive phenomena of the tropical regions is the tropical cyclone. Tropical cyclones are known by a variety of names but their technical name is tropical revolving storm. They are known as hurricanes in the Caribbean Sea and surrounding areas and the eastern north Pacific Ocean, while in the western Pacific Ocean and in the Northern Hemisphere they are called typhoons. Elsewhere they are usually called tropical cyclones.

Tropical cyclones occur in all the major oceans except the South Atlantic. Figure 3.16 shows the main formation areas and their average tracks. The average latitude of occurrence in the Southern Hemisphere is 15°S and the average in the Northern Hemisphere is 20°N. Tropical cyclones usually form in summer and autumn and are more likely in the western parts of the tropical oceans. A water temperature in excess of 28°C is usually required for a tropical cyclone to form and it is very rare for them to form closer than 5° either side of the equator.

Tropical cyclones are unable to cross the equator. They derive their spin from the effect of the rotation of the earth via the Coriolis force. This results in tropical cyclones in the Southern Hemisphere rotating clockwise and in the Northern Hemisphere rotating anticlockwise. To cross from one hemisphere to the other it would be necessary for their rotation to stop and reverse but the process of stopping would destroy the cyclone.

The average life of a tropical cyclone is about five days but some have been known to last only a few hours and others have continued to exist for two weeks. During and shortly after formation the cyclone normally drifts eastwards in the general easterly flow of the tropical regions. Usually there is also a poleward drift and eventually the cyclone moves into the region of predominant upper-level westerlies and moves eastwards in the prevailing windstream. The change from westerly drift to easterly drift is known as recurvature. Eventually almost all cyclones drift polewards and are 'captured' by the mid-latitude westerlies. The beginning of the capturing process is indicated by recurvature and the tropical cyclone is usually very short lived after recurvature. It loses its energy source, which is the latent heat stored in the water vapour of the moist air. The air over the cooler waters cannot hold as much moisture as the warmer tropical air and the cyclone is starved of energy. Its thermal structure breaks down, which leads to its total disintegration. On some occasions the thermal nature of the cyclone can be modified. As it disintegrates it may change from the normal

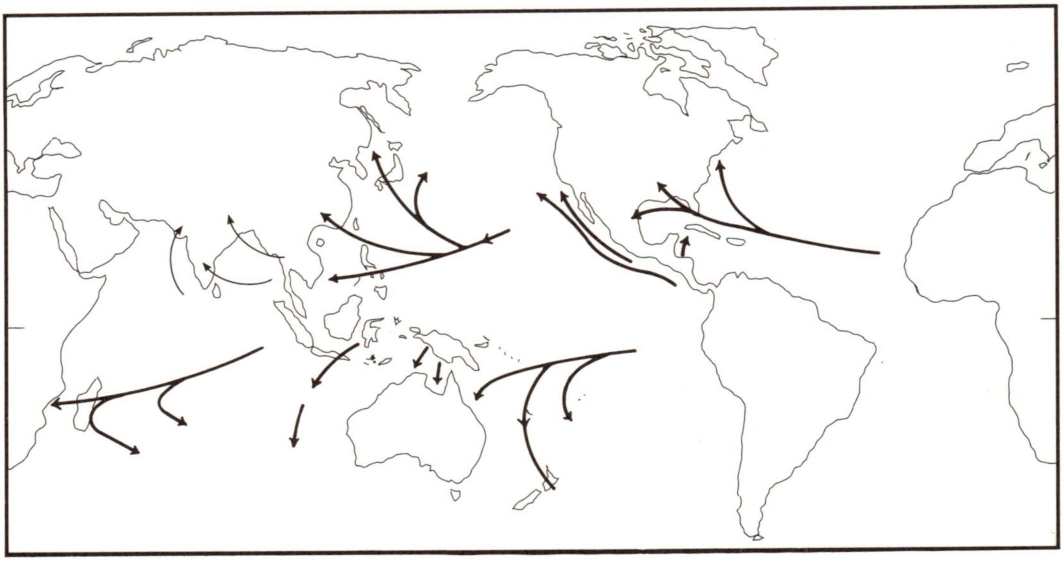

Figure 3.16—Main formation areas of tropical cyclones and their average tracks.

warm-cored structure to the cold-cored structure of the normal extra-tropical cyclone. On such occasions the low reintensifies and continues the life cycle of a normal low or extra-tropical cyclone. A more detailed description of the structure of tropical and extra-tropical cyclones is given in Chapter 4.

Theoretical Wind Circulation of the Atmosphere

A detailed explanation of the cause of all the features of the mean general circulation is beyond the scope of this book but some of the causes of the major features can be understood by considering the atmosphere as a giant heat engine in which the angular momentum of the atmosphere is conserved.

The energy that drives the winds and weather phenomena has its source in the sun and reaches the earth in the form of radiation of varying wavelengths, illustrated in Figure 3.2. The absorption of radiation by the atmosphere causes it to heat up, as described previously in Vertical Structure of the Atmosphere, but the heating is not evenly distributed over the earth. This causes the temperature and density to vary throughout the atmosphere, creating pressure forces which move air thus creating the winds.

To explain the large-scale wind regimes it is necessary to consider the temperature distribution of the atmosphere. The amount of energy striking the earth at the poles is less than that at the equator. The sun's rays just glance the surface of the earth at the poles but at the equator the sun is directly overhead. If the rays are considered to be a cylinder of a particular cross-sectional area, at the surface the area of the earth covered by the 'cylinder' of rays is very much greater at the poles than at the equator. This means the amount of energy striking the earth at the equator for a given area is much greater than at the poles. This difference causes the temperature difference between the poles and the equator.

Over a few years the temperature of the earth, on average, remains almost constant. However, as energy in the form of radiation is continuously

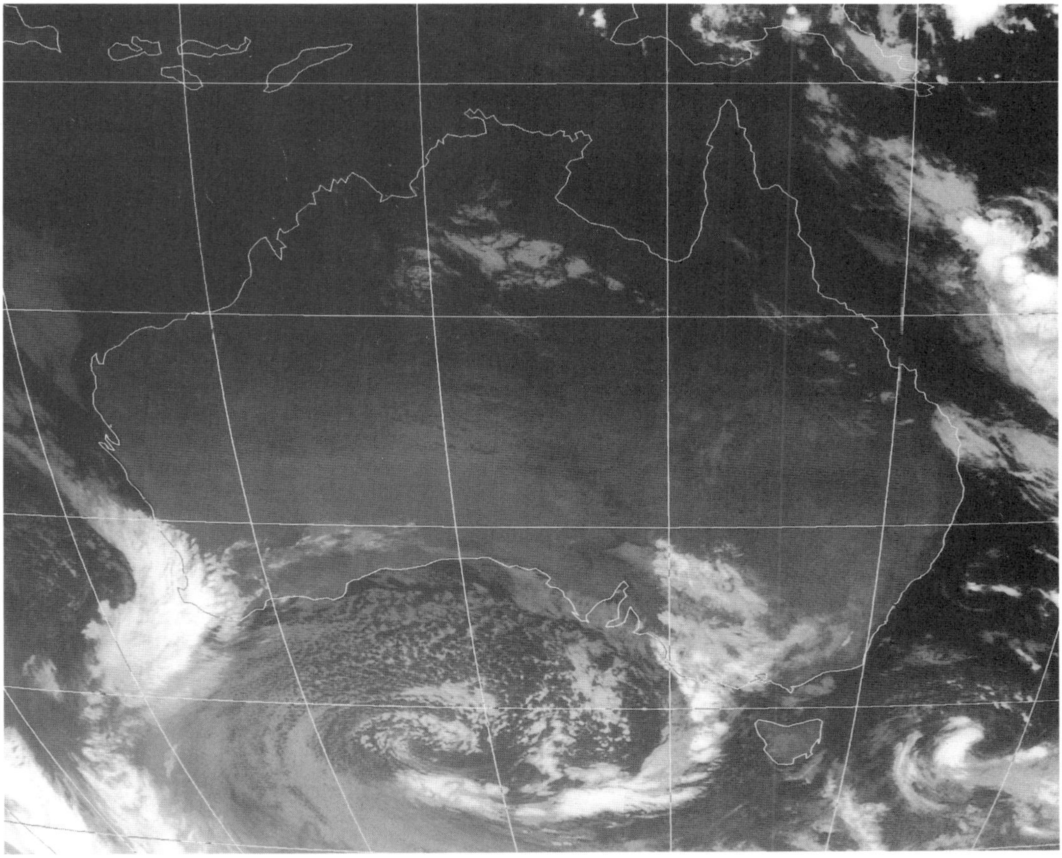

Figure 3.17—Satellite photograph showing infra-red radiation.

received from the sun, the earth must continuously emit energy in the form of radiation to exactly balance that received from the sun. This energy is emitted in the form of infra-red radiation, which is 'seen' or photographed most often by weather satellites, such as that shown in Figure 3.17. The distribution, over the earth's surface, of the energy radiated back to space is such that there is a net loss of energy at the poles and a net gain at the equator. If this continued for a long period of time the equator would become increasingly hot and the poles would become increasingly cold, but this does not happen. The relatively constant temperatures on the earth's surface can only occur if energy (in the form of heat) is transferred from the equator to the poles. The general circulation of the atmosphere together with the ocean currents are the means by which this transfer occurs in the atmosphere.

The air, warmed at the surface of the equator, becomes buoyant and rises until it reaches the tropopause. This acts like a lid because above it the air temperature increases, causing the rising air to lose its buoyancy. Cold air over the poles continues to radiate heat and cools, becoming denser, and sinks. As it does so it moves towards the equator and slides under the warmer air. The air that rose above the equator is pushed towards the poles to replace the sinking polar air and heat is continually transferred to the pole by the warm poleward flowing air. Cold air moving to the equator cools the lower latitudes.

The real atmosphere, however, is much more complicated. The first complication to be considered is the rotation of the earth from west to east. A measure of the rate of rotation is called angular velocity. A solid object that spins at two revolutions per second has twice the angular velocity of a solid object that spins at one revolution per second.

To understand how the rotation of the earth affects the flow of air in the atmosphere, the concept of momentum must first be considered. The momentum of an object is its mass multiplied by its velocity. One of the fundamental laws of nature is that the momentum of an object is conserved (that is, it does not change) unless an outside force acts upon it. This is the reason passengers tend to fly into the windscreen of a car if it stops suddenly. (Seat belts provide a force that stops the passengers hitting the windscreen.) This is an example of linear momentum. A spinning top illustrates angular momentum, which is the product of angular velocity and a measure of the mass of the top. If the top is spun between the fingers it continues to spin because its angular momentum is conserved. In fact, it gradually slows down because friction with the ground provides a force that changes the top's angular momentum. The measure of the mass of the top is the moment of inertia, which is the mass of each particle of the top multiplied by the square of the distance of that particle from the axis of rotation. It is the property of conservation of angular momentum, for example, that makes it possible for ice-skaters to spin very quickly.

Figure 3.18a illustrates a spinning ice-skater with legs apart and arms out wide giving him a moment of inertia of I_a. The skater has an angular velocity Ω_a and angular momentum of magnitude M. In Figure 3.18b the skater draws his arms into his sides and pulls his legs together and, as there is very little friction between the ice and the skates, the skater's angular momentum stays constant. However, the drawing in of his arms and legs reduces the skater's moment of inertia I_b and therefore if the angular momentum is to remain constant his angular velocity Ω_b must increase; that is, the skater must spin more quickly. This is summarised by the expression $M = \Omega_a \times I_a = \Omega_b \times I_b$.

Something analogous to the spinning skater occurs in the earth's atmosphere when the warm air moves towards the poles. In this case the air moves closer to the axis of rotation of the earth, its moment of inertia decreases, its angular momentum is conserved and therefore its angular velocity about the earth's axis must increase. As the rotation of the earth is from west to east, the west to east movement of the air must therefore increase, which causes increasingly strong upper-westerly winds to develop towards the poles.

As the air from all around the globe tries to move towards the poles it has to push against the air already there, which causes the air to 'pile up'. But as the pressure at the base of the atmosphere is just the weight of the air above the surface, the

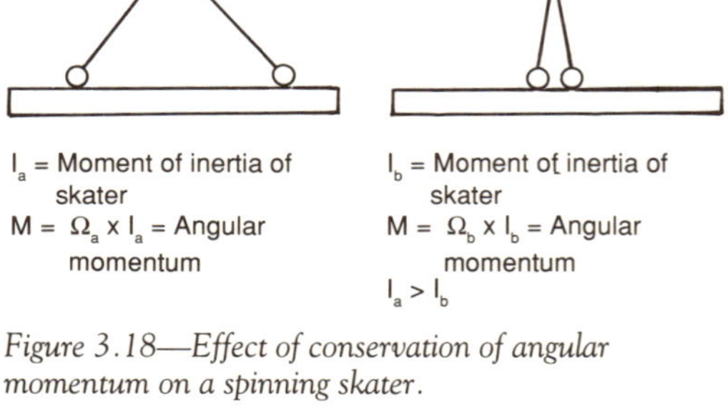

Figure 3.18—Effect of conservation of angular momentum on a spinning skater.

piling up of the air therefore causes an increase in the surface pressure. This effect causes surface pressure to increase with latitude and leads to a surface high-pressure belt, which directs some of the surface air towards the pole and some towards the equator. This compensates to some extent for the piling up process at upper levels. As the air piles up it cannot escape upwards because the temperature structure of the stratosphere causes it to act like a lid and the internal pressure forces created push air down towards the surface. These processes result in a balance of forces that maintains some piling up of air with a resulting high-pressure belt and high-level subtropical jet stream around the mid-latitudes.

The air that reaches the surface and then returns to the equator loses much of its westerly speed because of friction with the earth's surface. Using the same reasoning used to explain strong westerly winds aloft, conservation of angular momentum requires air moving back towards the equator to have an easterly component. However, for the low-level winds friction is also an important force and slows the wind so that the easterlies returning air to the equator near the surface are not as strong as the westerlies, which are generated by the air moving towards the poles at high levels where friction effects are negligible.

The air that was forced down to the surface, but continued on to higher latitudes, because of the conservation of angular momentum, continues to gain westerly speed. However, friction at the surface stops these speeds increasing as much as wind speeds at higher altitudes.

Figure 3.3 illustrates the above effects. The high-pressure area is known as the subtropical ridge. The surface return flow to the equator forms the trades and the flow that continues towards the poles at the surface forms the belt of temperate westerlies that are sometimes referred to as the 'Roaring Forties'. The strong westerly winds at high altitudes above the subtropical ridge comprise the subtropical jet stream.

The deserts of the world occur under the subtropical ridge because of the large-scale sinking motion that causes the air aloft to warm and prevent the formation of rain-producing cloud.

Physical Models of the Atmosphere

The general circulation of the atmosphere transports heat from the equator to the poles and maintains the earth at an almost constant average temperature. But, because the earth is rotating, the process of transporting heat to the poles also results in the transport of angular momentum. It has been shown that these two factors allow some of the features of the general circulation to be explained but the theoretical explanation of the positioning of the subtropical ridge, the existence of highs, lows, high-latitude troughs and ridges, fronts and the polar front jet is beyond the scope of this book. However, the principles involved can be illustrated by the use of physical models of the atmosphere. It is necessary to consider the effects that different speeds of rotation of the earth have on the general circulation and this can be done using the dishpan experiment.

This experiment consists of a container of water with ice in the centre with an outer rim that can be heated. Heating the water at the outer rim and cooling it at its centre is a crude representation of the essential features of one hemisphere of the earth. In addition it is possible to spin the whole apparatus, so simulating the spin of the earth. By spinning the dishpan at increasing speeds the circulation of the water changes and at a certain speed, depending on the characteristics of the dish, the flow is very similar to that of the earth shown in Figure 3.3. Figure 3.19 illustrates the flow patterns for increasing speeds of rotation.

In these figures the length of the strokes represents the speed at which the water particles are travelling. In practice this is achieved by taking a time exposure photograph of aluminium particles floating on the water. The camera is fixed to the dishpan and rotates with it. From the discussion above it would be expected that the

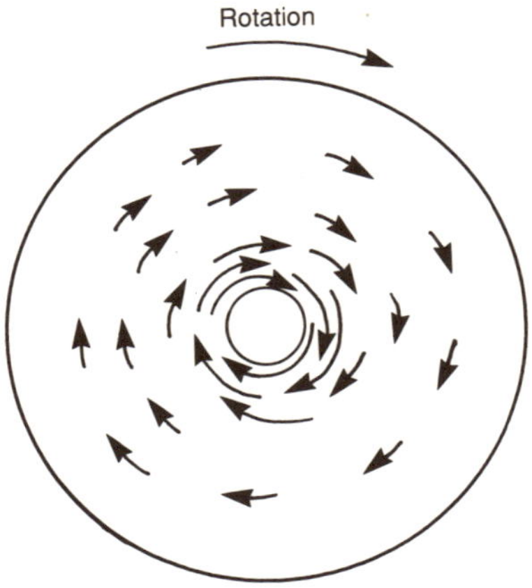

3.19a —Low rate of rotation illustrating strong 'westerly' current around the 'south pole' (the ice container). Length of arrows represents speed of movement of the flow.

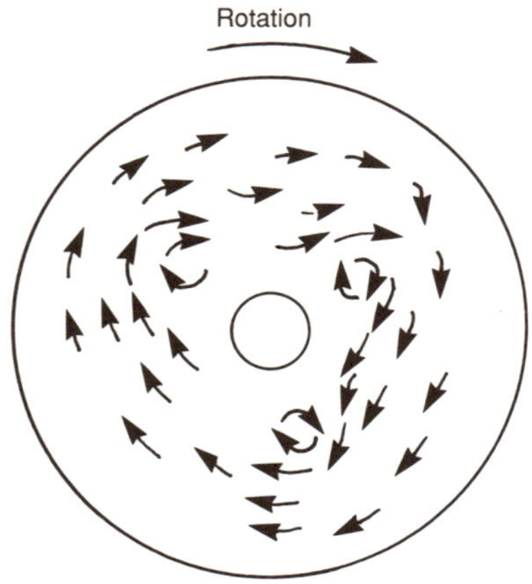

3.19b —Rate of rotation greater than in 3.19a, illustrating horizontal wave motion and large eddies.

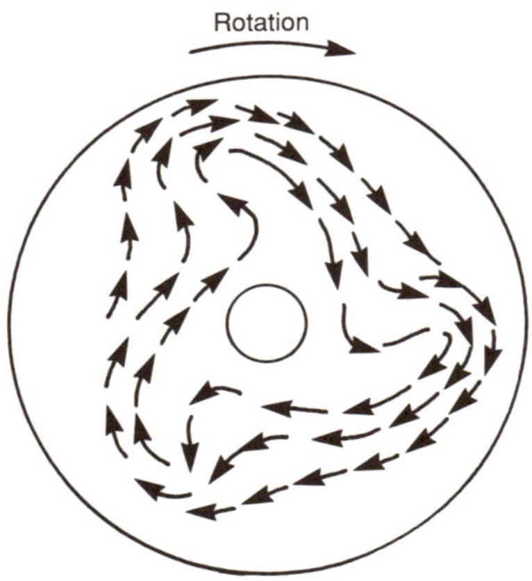

3.19c —Rate of rotation greater than in 3.19b, illustrating tilting troughs and ridges.

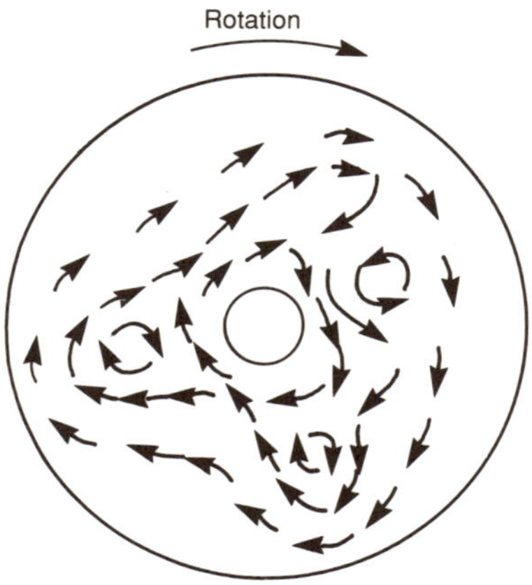

3.19d —Rate of rotation greater than in 3.29c, illustrating unstable flow with cut-off highs and lows similar to the real atmosphere.

Figure 3.19—The dishpan experiment.

conservation of angular momentum would cause the speed of the water to increase in the direction of the rotation of the pan as heat is transported by the water from the rim to the centre. Figure 3.19a illustrates the flow at a low rate of rotation. There is a very strong 'westerly' current (jet stream) around the 'south pole' (the ice container). If the speed of rotation is increased the circulation pattern changes to that illustrated in Figure 3.19b. Instead of flowing smoothly around the pole the strong westerly flow or jet stream breaks down into symmetrical waves and large eddies where the number of waves and eddies depends on the speed of rotation. The increased angular momentum makes it impossible for the vertical meridional circulation alone to transport sufficient heat to the poles. The required increase in angular momentum transport is achieved by horizontal eddies transporting warm water in a north-westerly flow and cold water in a south-westerly current. If the rate of rotation is increased still further the troughs and ridges are tilted as shown in Figure 3.19c and eventually break down into cut-off lows (cyclones) and highs (anticyclones) as shown in Figure 3.19d. This highly unstable flow is very similar to the way the atmosphere behaves.

In summary, the transport of heat and angular momentum required to keep the earth at a constant temperature at its present rate of rotation cannot be achieved by a vertical circulation cell alone. Large horizontal eddies are also required to contribute to the heat transport. Between the subtropical ridge and the equator, meridional transport by a vertical circulation is the main method of transporting heat and angular momentum polewards. South of the subtropical ridge, however, the most important means of transport are the large horizontal eddies that comprise both cyclones and anticyclones. Fronts and the polar front jet are manifestations of strong local temperature gradients generated by the large horizontal eddies.

Between the boundaries of the large-scale eddies (the highs and lows) there are very strong horizontal gradients of pressure and temperature. These correspond to fronts in the real atmosphere. The strong temperature gradients also extend into the upper atmosphere. It can be shown that strong temperature gradients lead to strong pressure gradients which in turn cause strong winds. In the real atmosphere this effect produces the polar front jet at high altitudes above fronts as illustrated in Figure 3.3.

Summary

In this chapter the main features of the general circulation of winds in the troposphere have been described. These characteristics of the circulation have been explained, subject to some simplifying assumptions, by applying the principle of conservation of angular momentum to a rotating earth which remains at a constant temperature.

While this approach is useful for explaining the general circulation, a more detailed consideration of the forces acting on a parcel of air is required to explain the individual characteristics of macroscale and smaller-scale atmospheric phenomena. The next chapter describes some of the more common macroscale (sometimes referred to as synoptic scale) phenomena and examines the forces which determine their characteristics.

4. Macroscale Circulations

The macroscale (synoptic scale) weather patterns are those familiar highs and lows that appear daily on television screens during the weather segment and in newspapers. They typically range in size from hundreds to thousands of kilometres across. The typical weather chart, illustrated in Figure 3.4, is a map of the variations in atmospheric pressure over the earth's surface and is similar to a topographic chart that shows variations in the height of the terrain. The central pressure of a high is higher than the surrounding pressures while the central pressure of a low is lower than any of the surrounding surface pressures. It is the difference in pressure between points on the earth's surface that drives the winds in large swirls or eddies around the centres of highs and lows.

To understand more clearly why the air moves the way it does it is necessary to consider the forces acting on a parcel of air in the atmosphere. The movement of any object, whether a rock or a parcel of air, is completely determined by the forces acting upon it. There are many forces active in the atmosphere but some are of much greater significance than others. To explain the wind circulation of synoptic scale features, four forces need to be considered: pressure force, Coriolis force, centrifugal force and friction.

Pressure Force

The pressure force is the force exerted on a parcel of air because of differences in pressure. It is one of the most important forces in meteorology as well as in our everyday lives. The pressure force keeps our car tyres firmly inflated and enables us to blow up balloons. The greater the difference in pressure between two places the greater the pressure force exerted. Any force has a magnitude and a direction associated with it. The pressure force is always perpendicular to lines of equal pressure and directed towards the low pressure. On weather charts these lines are called isobars; they are the lines that make up the familiar patterns of highs and lows, as shown in Figure 3.4.

Pressure has many units of measurement. The unit usually used in meteorology is hectopascal (hPa). A standard atmosphere has a surface pressure of 1013.2 hPa.

Coriolis Force

This force is the result of the rotation of the earth on its axis. The rotation of the earth makes the stars appear to revolve around the south celestial pole. A merry-go-round can be used as an analogy to the rotating earth. If you imagine you are on the merry-go-round, the surroundings appear to revolve around the centre of the merry-go-round. Suppose a ball is thrown by a person on the merry-go-round to someone standing on the ground nearby so that the ball appears to travel in a straight line over the centre of the merry-go-round. For the person on the merry-go-round the ball appears to travel in a curve as illustrated in Figure 4.1. At Time 1 the observer sees the ball exactly in line with the centre of the merry-go-round. At Time 2 the observer sees the ball at an angle A_2 to the left of the centre. At Time 3 the angle between the ball and the centre has increased to A_3 and by Time 4 has increased further to A_4. The ball appears to be curving away to the left of the centre of the merry-go-round. There seems to be a force deflecting the ball, but this impression is due entirely to the fact that the observer is rotating with the merry-go-round.

Similarly, the earth is rotating and objects travelling in a straight line with respect to the fixed surroundings (the stars) will move in a curve from the point of view of an observer on

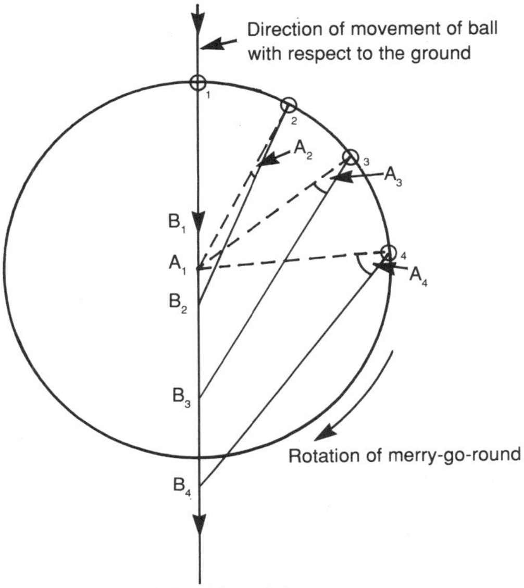

O₁ = Initial position of observer

B₁ = Initial position of ball

A₁ = Angle between ball and observer's fixed point (the centre of the merry-go-round)

Figure 4.1—A merry-go-round as an analogy to the rotating earth to explain the Coriolis force.

the rotating platform, in this case the earth. This is the reason that all objects moving on the earth's surface in the Southern Hemisphere experience a deflection to the left, while in the Northern Hemisphere the deflection is to the right. No deflection occurs at the equator because to an observer the stars do not appear to rotate at the equator. The force attributed to this deflection is called the Coriolis force. It is always at right angles to the direction of movement and its strength is proportional to the speed of movement and the latitude.

Centrifugal Force

This is the force that is utilised by a centrifuge to separate substances of different densities, for example cream from milk. It is also the force utilised by a sling shot. If a stone is attached to a piece of string and whirled around, the string is pulled taut by the centrifugal force. An equal and opposite force (the centripetal force) is supplied by the string.

Friction

The final force of importance in synoptic scale air movements in the atmosphere is friction. Friction or 'drag' in relation to air is caused by the roughness of the surface of the earth. It is analogous to the way sandpaper resists movement as it is rubbed against a piece of wood.

A consideration of these four forces can be used to explain the synoptic scale wind flows illustrated in Figure 3.4.

Geostrophic Wind

The simplest air flow to explain occurs when the isobars are straight, as shown in Area A of Figure 3.4. If it is assumed that the friction is negligible (a reasonable assumption for altitudes above about 700 m) and there is no centrifugal force (the isobars are straight), then the only forces acting on a parcel of air are the pressure force and the Coriolis force.

The movement of a parcel of air initially at rest is shown at various stages in Figure 4.2. The pressure force causes it to initially accelerate towards the lower pressure (Stage 1 in Figure 4.2) but as it does so it experiences a Coriolis force to the left of its direction of movement. As pressure force continues to accelerate the parcel the Coriolis force also increases (Coriolis force is proportional to the speed) and the parcel is deflected further to the left, as shown in Stage 2. At Stage 3 the acceleration caused by the pressure force has caused the speed of the air parcel to increase so much that it is moving parallel to the isobars, with the Coriolis force greater than the pressure force. This imbalance (illustrated at Stage 4) then forces air to move towards the high

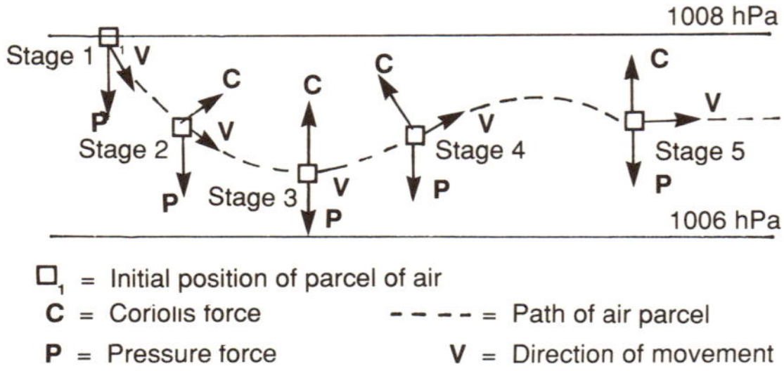

Figure 4.2—Geostrophic flow.

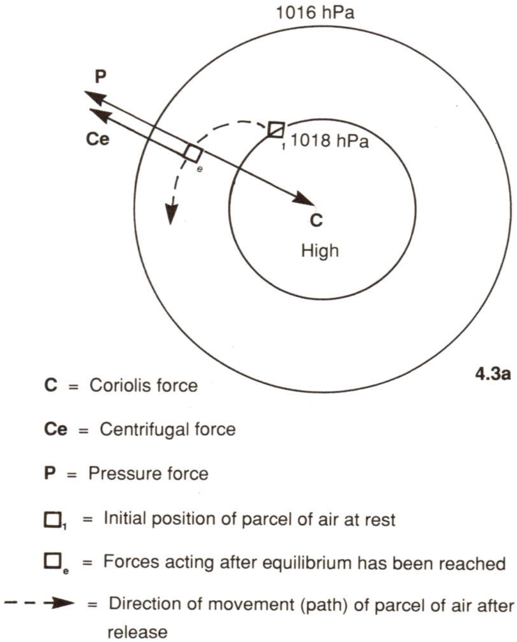

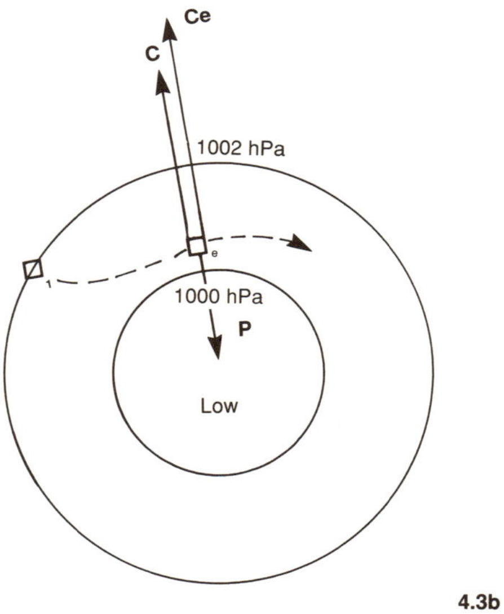

Figure 4.3—Forces acting on a parcel of air when isobars are curved and friction is neglected in the Southern Hemisphere.

pressure and the opposing pressure force causes a deceleration of the air parcel and a corresponding decrease in the Coriolis force, which allows the parcel of air to again move towards the lower pressure. This results in an oscillating motion where the air moves slightly away from, then towards, the low pressure, eventually stabilising (illustrated at Stage 5) to a steady state where the pressure force exactly balances the Coriolis force and the movement of the air parcel (the wind) is parallel to the isobars. As the Coriolis force is proportional to the wind speed, the magnitude of the balancing pressure force determines the wind speed. The pressure force is determined by the pressure gradient (the distance between the isobars). The closer the isobars, the greater the pressure gradient and the greater the wind speed. The wind generated by this balance of forces is called the geostrophic wind.

Gradient Wind

It is clear from Figure 3.4 that isobars are often curved and the assumption that there is no centrifugal force is therefore not valid. In this case the three forces acting on a parcel of air are the pressure force, the Coriolis force and the centrifugal force. This is the situation that applies in highs and lows.

Figure 4.3 illustrates the forces acting on a parcel of air for the curved isobars around a high and a low. The same process as described for the geostrophic wind eventually leads to the parcel of air moving parallel to the isobars except there are three balancing forces: Coriolis, centrifugal and pressure force. In the case of a high the Coriolis force is balanced by the pressure force plus the centrifugal force. Because the Coriolis force is proportional to the wind speed, however, the strength of the wind around a high for a given pressure gradient must be greater than the corresponding wind speed for straight isobars. Furthermore, in the Southern Hemisphere the Coriolis force is always to the left of the wind direction, so it follows that the wind must flow anticlockwise around a high as shown in Figure 4.3a. The technical name for a high is an anti-cyclone.

Air flowing around a low has the pressure force balanced by the Coriolis force and the centrifugal force and results in the wind speed around a low, for a given pressure gradient, being less than the wind speed for straight isobars with the same pressure gradient. Furthermore, because the Coriolis force is to the left in the Southern Hemisphere, air moves around the low in a clockwise direction. The technical name for a low is a cyclone. The gradient wind results when the pressure gradient, the Coriolis force and the centrifugal force are in balance.

Close to the earth's surface the drag of friction becomes significant. Figure 4.4 illustrates the four main forces that act on a parcel of air in the vicinity of the surface. The effect of the drag of friction is to reduce the wind speed for a particular pressure gradient. In the case of straight isobars the reduced wind speed reduces the Coriolis force and the balance between the Coriolis and pressure forces no longer exists. As the pressure force exceeds the Coriolis force there is a net force pushing the air parcel towards the low pressure so that air flows at an angle to the isobars. The angle is determined by the strength of the friction force, which is in turn determined by the roughness of the earth's surface. Over sea the cross-isobar flow angle is typically between 5° and 25° depending on the height of the waves. Over land friction is much greater and the angle of the cross-isobar flow can be up to 50°.

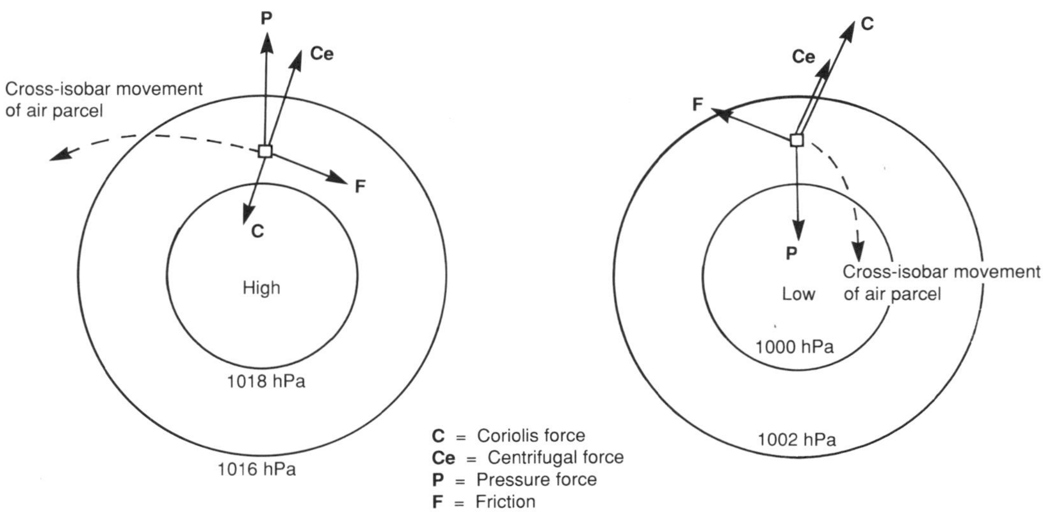

Figure 4.4—The four forces acting on a parcel of air.

The four forces (pressure force, Coriolis force, centrifugal force and friction) explain the surface wind observed in large-scale horizontal synoptic circulations of the atmosphere. Their effect is summarised by Buys Ballot's Law, which states that in the Southern Hemisphere an observer with his back to the wind has low pressure to the right and high pressure to the left. The reverse is true in the Northern Hemisphere.

Hydrostatic Assumption

Consideration has been given above to the forces that act horizontally in the atmosphere but the atmosphere also has vertical extent. In the vertical the force of gravity is an important influence on the behaviour of the atmosphere. Air has mass that is acted upon by the force of gravity and manifests itself as weight. Surface pressure is a measure of the weight of air above the surface and is about 1.033 kg/cm^2.

As pressure is a measure of the weight of air above a certain point, the lighter the air above that point the lower the pressure. Near the top of the atmosphere there is very little air above and therefore low pressure would be expected, whereas at the bottom of the atmosphere the highest pressure would be expected. This reasoning suggests that pressure should decrease with height. This can be confirmed by considering a stationary vertical column of air and the forces acting upon it.

A parcel of air in the column is stationary (moving neither up nor down) but its weight is pulling the air down so there must be an equal and opposite force balancing the weight. This force is the pressure force but as the pressure force is always towards the low pressure it must be directed vertically upward so that the pressure must decrease with altitude. An atmosphere where the pressure force and weight are in balance is said to be in hydrostatic equilibrium. But equilibrium is not always maintained and hydrostatic imbalance can lead to strong updrafts and downdrafts that have a major impact on the weather we experience. Such imbalances result in the strong vertical motion that occurs in thunderstorms and tornadoes. Gentler vertical motions occur in fronts.

Isobaric Surfaces and the Geostrophic Wind

Highs and lows are identified by the pressure patterns seen on weather maps. These pressure patterns are constructed from lines joining points of equal pressure (isobars) on the surface of the earth. But the atmosphere is three dimensional—it has vertical extent and isobars can be regarded as the intersection with the surface of the earth of surfaces of equal pressure, as illustrated in Figure 4.5. In the case of a high-pressure system the surfaces of equal pressure form a dome-like structure similar to the layers of an onion with each layer representing a surface of constant pressure. This representation can be used to extend the interpretation of geostrophic and gradient winds in terms of the slope of pressure surface. Figure 4.5 illustrates the typical vertical structure of the pressure surfaces of a high. In the Southern Hemisphere the winds blow anticlockwise around the high. In terms of the three dimensional structure of the high, geostrophic and gradient winds blow with the downslope side of the isobaric surfaces to their right. This is the three dimensional version of Buys Ballot's Law.

Figure 4.6 illustrates the relationship between the slope of isobaric surfaces and the pressure gradient on a horizontal surface. The two sets of pressure surfaces shown in Figure 4.6a and Figure 4.6b are identical except for their slope. But even though the pressure surfaces are the same distance apart the pressure gradients on a horizontal surface which cuts those surfaces are not the same. It is clear from this diagram that the horizontal pressure gradient in Figure 4.6a is greater than the horizontal pressure gradient in Figure 4.6b. That is, for pressure surfaces a certain distance apart,

Cumulus cloud cruising along the coast of Kangaroo Island, SA. (See Chapter 6.)

Suns rays breaking through a deck of stratocumulus. (See Chapter 6.)

Thickening stratocumulus, Tallangatta, Vic. (*See Chapter 6.*)

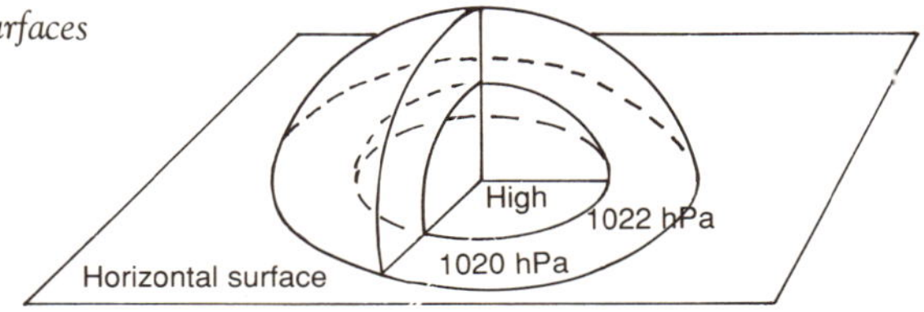

Figure 4.5—Three dimensional pressure surfaces associated with a high.

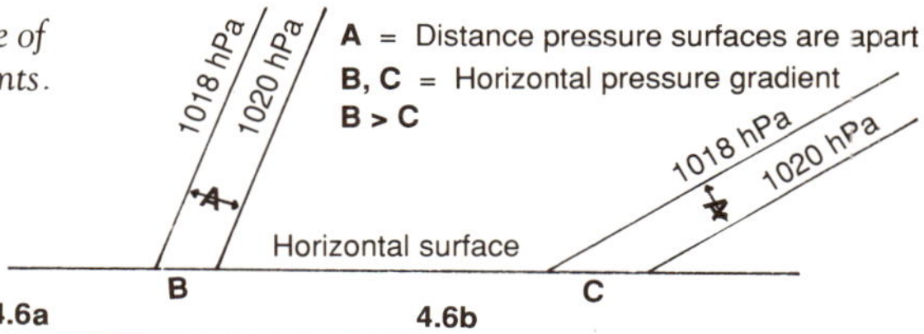

Figure 4.6—The relationship between the slope of isobaric surfaces and horizontal pressure gradients.

the greater the slope of the pressure surfaces the greater the horizontal pressure gradient and therefore the greater the strength of the geostrophic and gradient winds.

If these two relationships between isobaric surfaces and the strength of the geostrophic and gradient winds are combined with the hydrostatic assumption, it can be shown why in general terms westerly winds dominate in the troposphere and why those winds increase in speed with height. This is illustrated by Figure 4.7 which is a description of the pressure surfaces between the equator and the South Pole. The air at the South Pole is much colder and therefore denser than the air at the equator and the hydrostatic assumption would suggest that at the pole the vertical pressure surfaces are much closer together than at the equator.

The two main features of the isobaric surfaces are that their slopes increase with height and that they slope upwards towards the equator. The first feature suggests that winds should increase with height, which generally speaking they do. The second suggests that in both hemispheres the winds should be westerly and this is also observed.

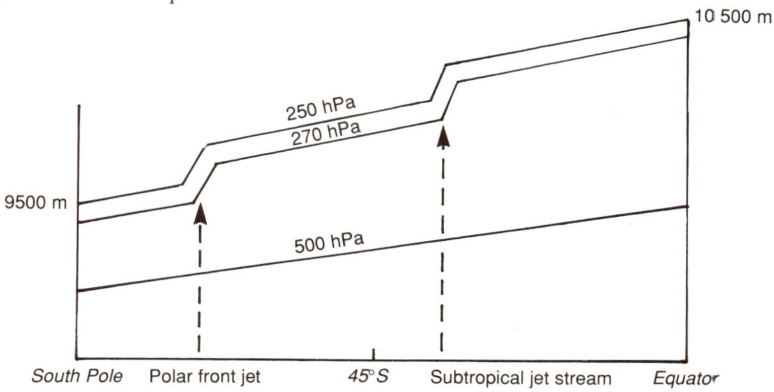

Figure 4.7—Isobaric surfaces between the equator and the South Pole.

Air-masses

In Chapter 3 it was shown that the transfer of heat and momentum polewards results in large horizontal eddies transporting cold air towards the equator and warm air towards the poles: the familiar highs and lows seen on the daily weather map. It has also been shown that in highs the horizontal winds spiral outwards from the centre as shown in Figure 4.8. Assume that initially the temperature at A is 25°C and the temperature at B is 15°C and the distance between A and B is 100 km. If the winds are moving away from the centre at, for example, 10 km/h, after 24 hours the air parcels that were at A and B are now at C and D, which are 580 km apart. In this way the difference in temperature across a high becomes less as time progresses so that after a period of several days the temperature and humidity of the air in the high has become almost uniform over a very large area. Such a large region of air with almost uniform temperature and humidity is called an air-mass. There are many classification schemes for air-masses and the four used in this book are polar, tropical, maritime and continental. These classifications are not mutually exclusive, and they can occur in various combinations each having different properties, for example a polar maritime air-mass. These properties are described in more detail below. Figure 4.9 shows where each type is usually found.

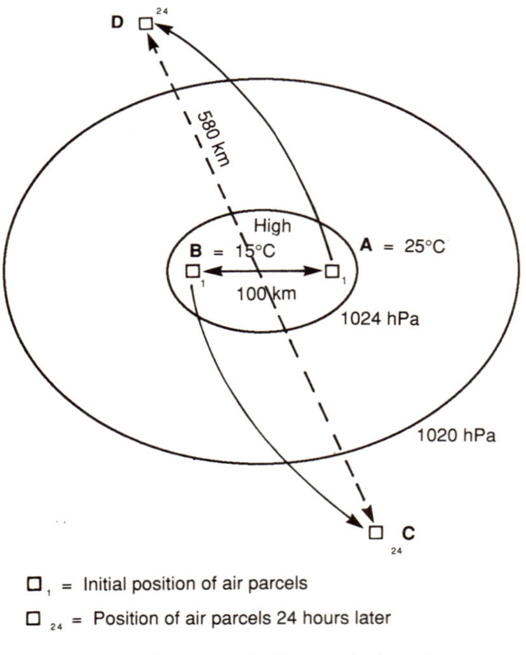

Figure 4.8—The relationship between highs and air-masses.

Continental Polar Air-masses

Continental polar air-masses form during the winter months over large land areas such as the Antarctic, North America, central–northern Asia and Greenland. Clear skies result in the air near the ground cooling by radiation and contact with the ground. At the same time the air dries by sublimation. As the surface air cools it becomes denser and contracts and air rushes in from aloft. The contraction causes the surface pressure to increase leading to the formation of a high. The presence of the high-pressure area tends to maintain the air-mass characteristics. As the air close to the ground cools by conduction much more rapidly than the air above, and because the air aloft is sinking and being compressed and warmed, a large vertical temperature gradient is created. Surface temperature can be 20–30°C colder than air temperatures at altitudes of 2–3 km.

Continental Tropical Air-masses

Continental tropical air-masses form over large landmasses during the summer months. They are found typically over Australia, southern and northern Africa, central Asia, and at times northern America. Air near the ground is heated to very high temperatures and the lack of nearby moisture sources causes the air to be very dry.

Maritime Tropical Air-masses

Maritime tropical air-masses occur over equatorial ocean regions. As there is an abundant water

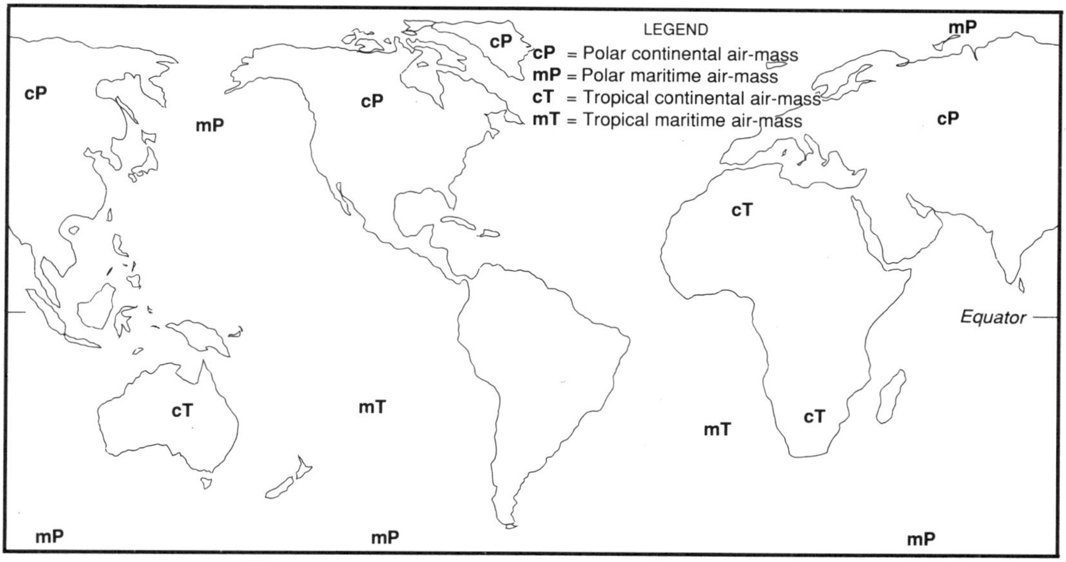

Figure 4.9—Locations of the main air-masses across the world.

supply over the oceans these air-masses tend to be very moist but they are not as hot as the continental tropical air-mass. The sea has a greater capacity to store and conduct heat and does not heat up so rapidly or as much as the ground.

Maritime Polar Air-masses

Maritime polar air-masses are restricted to the polar oceans in both hemispheres. As in tropical areas there is also an abundance of water and these air-masses are moist. The ability of the water to conduct heat also prevents the sea from cooling to such low temperatures as those experienced in continental areas in winter, and also results in the air in contact with the polar oceans being not as cold and moister than the air of the polar continental air-masses.

Weather Associated with Synoptic Features of the Weather Chart

Much of the variation in the day-to-day weather is caused by the passage of synoptic scale features of the atmosphere. Fronts, highs and lows, tropical cyclones, troughs and ridges are all common occurrences in various parts of Australia. To understand the weather that is associated with these systems it is necessary to understand their three dimensional structure.

Structure of Fronts and Associated Weather

It has been shown that high-pressure areas tend to develop and maintain large air-masses with almost uniform surface temperature and humidity characteristics. Similarly low-pressure areas tend to magnify small temperature and humidity differences.

Figure 4.10 shows an air parcel at D with a temperature of 25°C and an air parcel at C with a temperature of 15°C; D and C are 300 km apart. If it is assumed that the air is spiralling in towards the centre at 5 km/h, after 24 hours the parcels of air are located at B and A. The change of temperature with distance between B and A is much greater than the rate of change between D and C. In short, the wind flow of a low increases

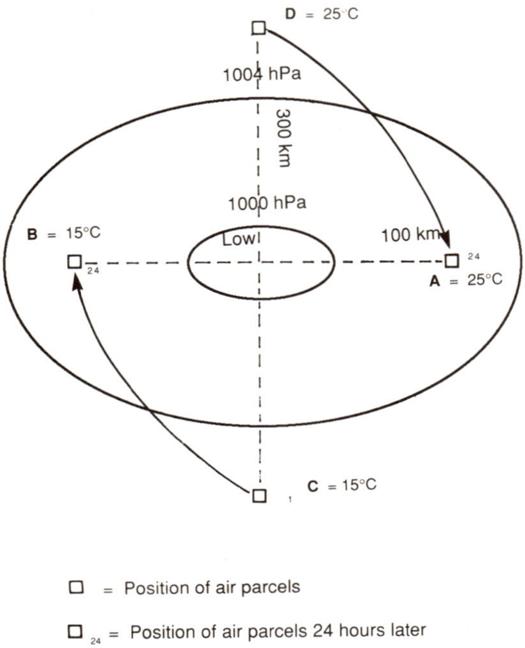

Figure 4.10—The relationship between lows and fronts.

temperature contrasts in the atmosphere.

In Chapter 3 it was shown that the transfer of heat polewards is carried out by pools of cold air moving equatorwards and pools of warm air moving polewards. This leads to sharp boundaries between the cold and the warm air, which can be magnified by the process described in the previous paragraph.

A front is the narrow boundary zone between two air-masses with wind, temperature, humidity and weather varying rapidly across it. Fronts can be classified into three main types; the cold front, the warm front and the occluded front. The differences between these three types of front result from their differing vertical structures and the relative movement of the air associated with them. Figure 4.11b shows an idealised schematic representation of a cold front. Its main characteristic is the vertical shape of the frontal surface that is in the shape of a 'nose' of cold air forcing itself under warmer air ahead of the front. This causes the air ahead of the front to rise and in doing so it cools and, if water vapour is present, as it usually is, cloud will form. There is a great deal of variation in the rate of rise of the warm air ahead of the front and it is this rate of rise that largely determines the distribution of cloud as the front passes over at a particular point. The slope of the cold air varies but is usually in excess of one in a hundred and near the surface the typical nose shape is caused by the effect of friction on the advancing cold air, which retards its movement.

The cold front The actual structure of a cold front is more complicated than that shown in Figure 4.11b. An intensive study of summertime cold fronts over Australia has indicated the complex structure shown in Figure 4.12. The front is a transition zone that may extend for 300 km from the main boundary of the cold air to the boundary of the warm air and may contain several discontinuities of pressure, wind, temperature and humidity. Discontinuities are often associated with convective cloud.

A form of cold front, or change, which is of considerable importance in New South Wales is the southerly buster (sometimes called 'southerly burster'). These rarely originate as a classical front over the Southern Ocean and they are often associated with small-scale (mesoscale) lows. These are considered in more detail in Chapter 5.

The warm front Figure 4.11b shows a schematic representation of a warm front. It has the same general structure as a cold front but moves in reverse. Instead of the cold air advancing to replace the warm air, the warm air advances and replaces the retreating cold air. This causes a difference between the vertical structure of these two types of front. Typically the slope of a warm front is much more gentle than that of a cold front, usually less than one in a hundred. Because the warm air is rising over the cold air and the cold air is retreating, the typical nose of the cold

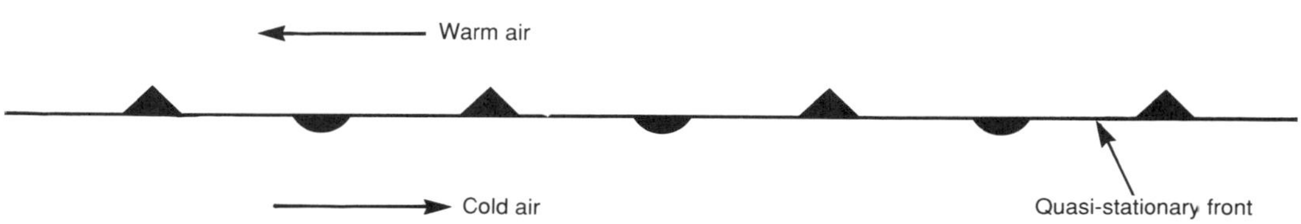

4.11a Initial time

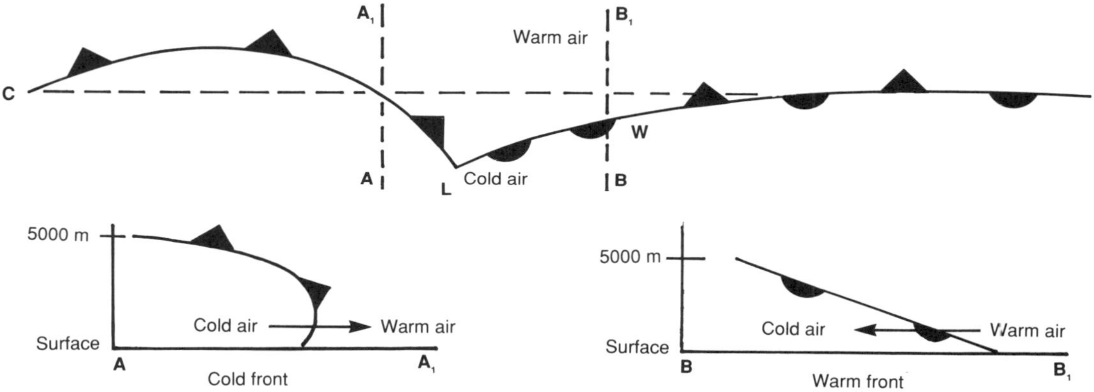

4.11b 12 hours later

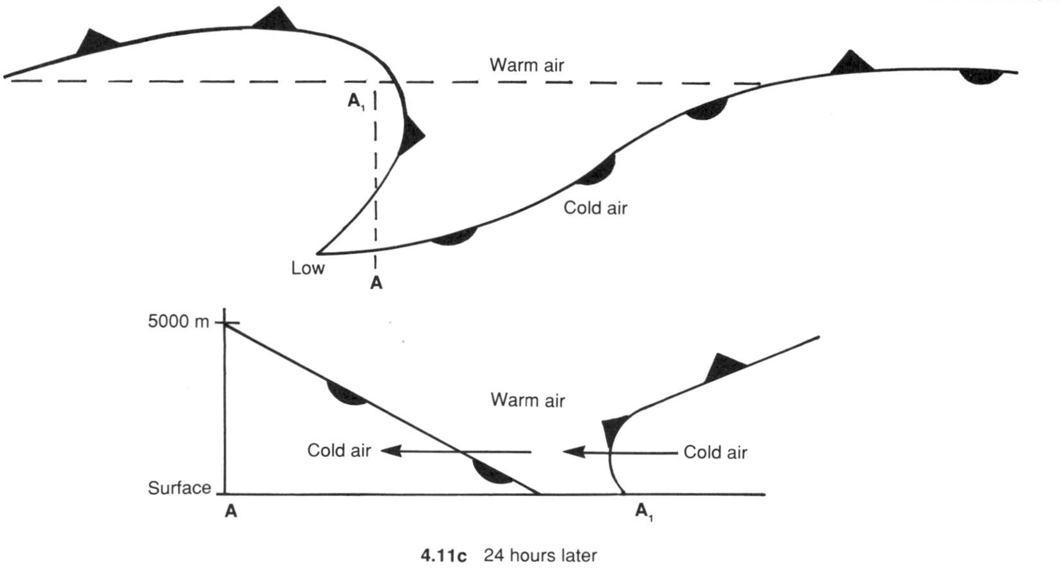

4.11c 24 hours later

Above and overleaf: Figure 4.11—The life cycle of a low and associated front during a 36-hour period.

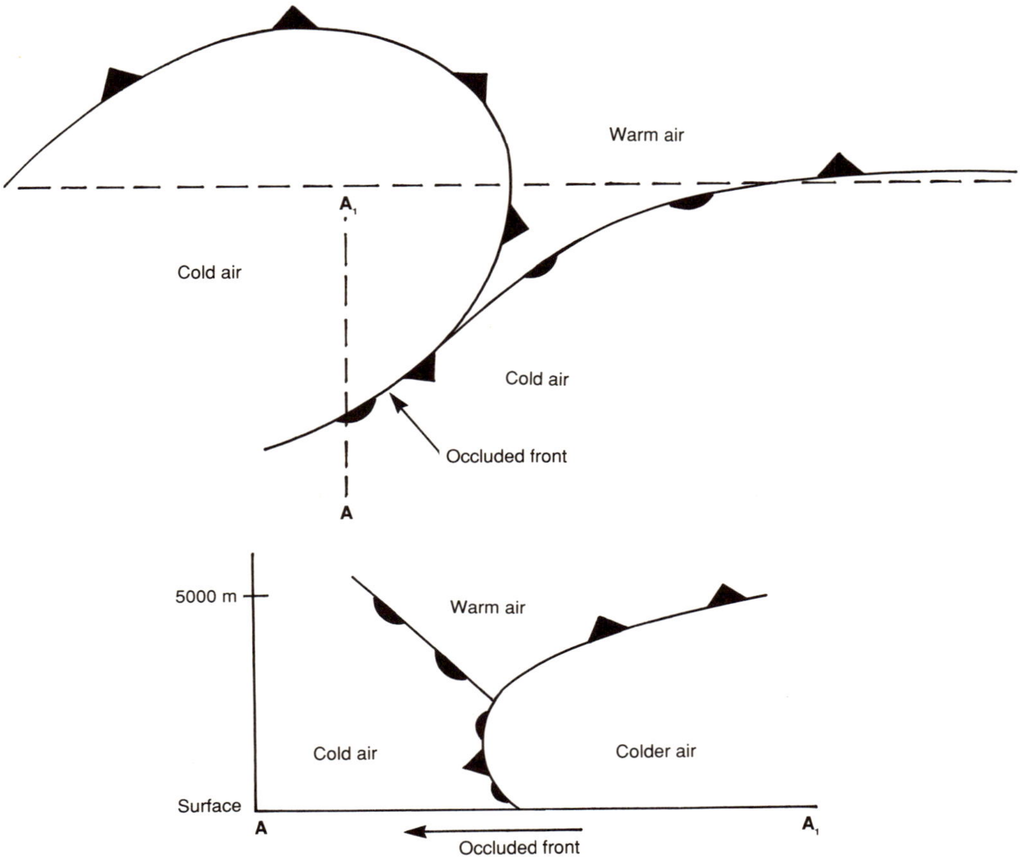

4.11d 36 hours later

front caused by friction with the surface is not present and the front has more of a wedge shape. As the slope is more gentle than that of a cold front, a warm front is usually associated with widespread steady rain rather than the heavy convective rain forced by the more vigorous vertical motions that are caused by the advancing cold air of a cold front. In the Australian continent warm fronts occur much more rarely than cold fronts. However, satellite photographs do indicate their presence over the Southern Ocean.

The occluded front The occluded front occurs when a cold front overtakes a warm front. As with the warm front described previously, occluded fronts are quite rare over the Australian continent but can sometimes be seen over the Southern Ocean on satellite photographs. Lows (or extra-tropical cyclones) are associated with the boundaries of air-masses and are intimately connected with fronts. As the atmosphere is dynamic its features are continually changing and both fronts and cyclones evolve through a clearly identifiable life cycle. The formation of an occluded front can be described as part of the life cycle of an extra-tropical cyclone. Figure 4.11 describes the life cycle of a low and associated front over a 36-hour period. A quasi-stationary front is the boundary of two air-masses, Figure

4.11a, and the effect of the circulatory motion of the cyclone is such that the cold air bows outward into the warm air-mass while the warm air pushes towards the cold air field. This process creates a warm front indicated by LW and a cold front indicated by LC with vertical cross-sections as shown in the cross-section AA_1 and BB_1 in Figure 4.11b. Figure 4.11c illustrates the situation 12 hours later. The action of the circulatory motion of the low has forced the cold air into the warm air-mass and the warm air has advanced into the cold air-mass. If the cold front is moving faster than the warm front, the gap between the two fronts becomes narrower. The vertical cross-section through AA_1 is shown in Figure 4.11c. Another twelve hours later, illustrated in Figure 4.11d, the circulation of the low has caused the cold front to overtake the warm front. The vertical cross-section through AA_1 shows the warm air lifted upwards away from the surface. This is the typical structure of an occluded front. If the air to the rear of the advancing front is colder than the air being displaced it is called a cold occluded front and if the reverse is true it is called a warm occluded front.

Frontal slope A characteristic of all fronts is that they slope with height. The three characteristics that affect the slope of a front are the temperature (density) difference between the cold and warm air, the relative wind speed of the two wind flows and the amount of friction the surface of the earth exerts on the lower layers of the air.

The polar front jet Using a simplified model of the isobaric surfaces of the Southern Hemisphere (Figure 4.7) we explained why westerly winds predominate and usually increase with height. On a global scale the cold dome of air over the poles is sinking and flowing equatorwards, forcing the warmer, less dense air of the lower latitudes upwards over the cold air. This has the effect of concentrating the changes in temperature and density along the narrow boundaries of fronts. This is illustrated in Figure 4.7 by the relatively gentle slopes of the isobaric surfaces between the two sharp kinks. The kink near 55°S is entirely the result of the narrow frontal boundary. From the theory discussed earlier the large slope of the isobaric surfaces would be expected to produce very strong westerly winds with a maximum speed at the top of the troposphere. Such winds do in fact occur and are referred to as the polar front jet stream. They are associated with any frontal boundary. The second kink is associated with the subtropical jet stream, which is discussed in Chapter 3. It is not associated with frontal activity at the surface but has its origin in the transfer of

Figure 4.12—The structure of summertime cold fronts over south-eastern Australia.

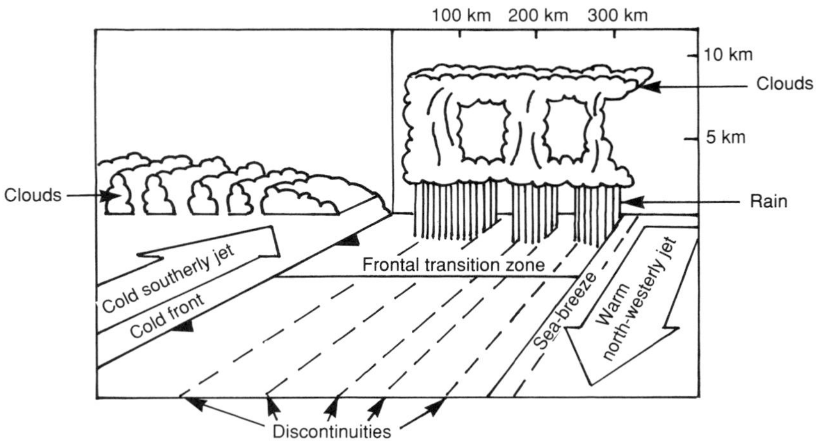

angular momentum towards the pole. However, a sharp kink in the isobaric surfaces at the tropopause would be expected with strong westerly winds.

Forecasting Frontal Weather

Fronts are most active in the high and mid latitudes polewards of the subtropic ridges and it is rare, especially in summer, for northern Australia to experience the passage of a front. However, in the southern parts of Australia fronts are a much more common occurrence.

Fronts often do not occur as sharp boundaries between the warm and cold air as illustrated by the classical model (Figure 4.11). They are more likely to consist of a transition zone, which may be up to several hundred kilometres wide, separating the warm and the cold air as illustrated in Figure 4.12. This causes a great variation in the sequence of cloud and weather experienced during the passage of a front. Topography can also have a strong influence, for example on the windward slopes of the Great Dividing Range cloud, rain and drizzle may take much longer to clear following the passage of a front than on the leeward side. There are, however, some common characteristics which can sometimes provide a guide for the prediction of the approach of a front and cooler weather.

A typical sequence of cloud and weather associated with the passage of a front is described in the table below. The temperature is dependent on the time of year.

48 hours prior	Small cumulus or clear sky.	Fine; north-east wind
24 hours prior	Possibly medium cumulus; cirrus invading the sky from the west	Fine; northerly gusty winds
12 hours prior	Overcast cirrus or cirrostratus; large cumulus	Possibly some showers; strong north-westerly winds
6 hours prior	Overcast cirrus or cirrostratus; some altocumulus, large cumulus and some cumulonimbus	Some showers, possibly lightning to west and south-west; strong north-westerly winds
Time of front	Cirrus, altocumulus, altostratus, large cumulus and cumulonimbus	Showers, squalls and storms; wind backing to the south-west
After front	Cumulus, stratocumulus and altostratus clearing	Showers and rain clearing; cooler southerly or south-easterly winds

Vertical Structure of Lows

There are two types of low-pressure system. One has the coldest air at its centre and occurs mainly in the high and mid latitudes. They are the common lows seen on the television weather maps over the Southern Ocean and southern Australia. The technical name for such a low is an extra-tropical cyclone.

The other form of low is warm cored. In Australia tropical cyclones are the most common form of this type of low, which is usually restricted to the northern coastal parts of the continent. But there is evidence to suggest that some of the destructive lows that form near the coast of New South Wales and Queensland are also warm cored, although they are not usually given the name tropical cyclone. The dissimilar vertical structure of the two types of low-pressure system is the reason for their different destructive power.

Figure 4.13 shows cross-sections through a cold-cored and a warm-cored low. The important difference is the change in the shape of the isobaric surfaces with height. In the case of the cold-cored low the air at the centre is denser than the air near the edges, which results in the isobaric surfaces being packed closer together in the centre as shown in Figure 4.13. Contrasted with this is the shape of the isobaric surfaces of a warm-cored low. Because the air in the middle of the low is less dense than the surrounding air the isobaric surfaces are most widely spaced in the centre and bulge out as illustrated in Figure 4.13b.

In the cold-cored low the slope of the isobaric surfaces increases with height, which implies that the wind also increases with height because the strength of the geostrophic wind is proportional to the slope of the isobaric surface. This means that the winds associated with a cold-cored low are at a minimum at the surface and increase with height. The reverse is the case with a warm-cored low. The slope of the isobaric surfaces decreases with height and eventually reverses. It follows therefore that the maximum cyclonic winds occur at the surface and reverse direction, becoming anticyclonic, in the upper atmosphere. It is because the maximum winds of the warm-cored low occur at the surface that tropical cyclones cause such destruction.

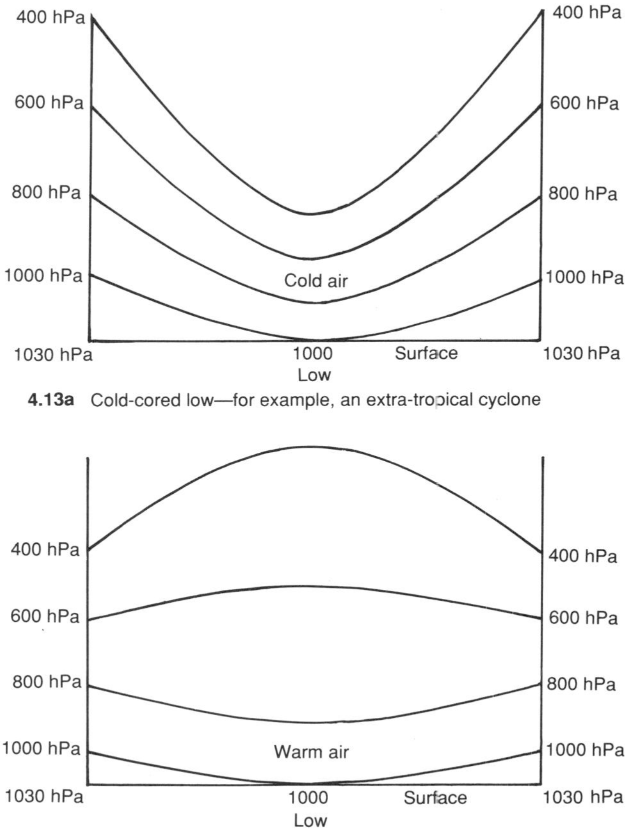

4.13a Cold-cored low—for example, an extra-tropical cyclone

4.13b Warm-cored low—for example, a tropical cyclone

Figure 4.13—Temperature structure of warm-cored and cold-cored lows.

Vertical Structure of Extra-tropical Cyclones

A low or extra-tropical cyclone does not always occur as a closed circulation (an eddy) throughout the whole depth of the troposphere. In the middle and upper layers of the atmosphere, instead of circular flow as at the surface the wind usually flows in large wave-like patterns as illustrated in Figure 3.5. This wave-like flow forms patterns of troughs and ridges. The middle- and upper-level troughs and ridges and lower-level highs and lows interact to reinforce or weaken one another. This is illustrated schematically in Figure 4.14.

It was shown earlier in this chapter that, for a particular pressure gradient, the wind speed around anticyclonically curved isobars (a high) are greater than the wind speed around cyclonically curved isobars (a low). For the wave pattern in Figure 4.14 this causes the piling up of air (called convergence) to the east of the upper ridge. The increased amount of air causes the pressure to rise at the surface ahead of the ridge and air is forced downwards towards the surface, reinforcing the high. Similarly there is a net loss of air (called divergence) to the east of the trough, which causes the pressure to fall at the surface ahead of the trough, reinforcing the low. This in turn creates forces which cause air to be drawn upwards from the lower levels to replace the net loss of air occurring aloft over the low. The vertical motion causes a cooling of the ascending air as its pressure falls and eventually it may form cloud and produce rain.

The pattern of convergence and divergence

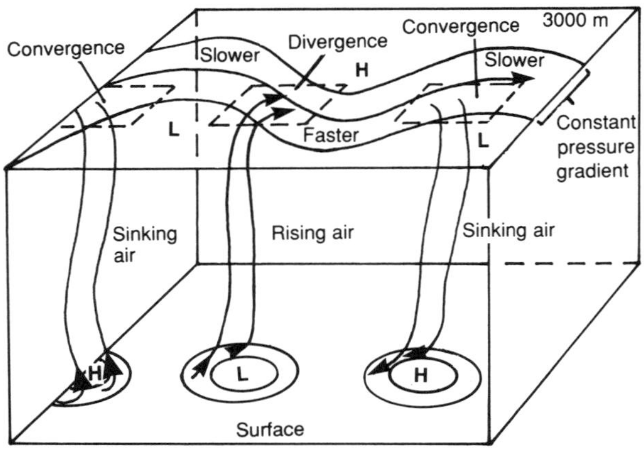

Figure 4.14—The pattern of convergence and divergence caused by wave-like flow in the upper atmosphere.

caused by the wave-like flow in the upper atmosphere is a very important factor in determining the strengthening and weakening of highs and lows. Lows and highs usually go through a definite life cycle. The upper and lower patterns are not always as strongly reinforcing as those illustrated in Figure 4.14 and to some extent may exist independently. A weak shallow low may be present on the surface without any marked upper pattern, for example it may be associated with a quasi-stationary front. On the other hand, a jet stream and upper trough, without any marked associated surface pattern, may be some distance upstream. However, as the trough approaches and the divergence area moves over the low centre, its vertical motion is increased. At the same time it is stretched vertically and the speed of rotation is increased in much the same way a skater increases the speed of his spin by drawing in his or her arms and legs. As the spin increases the temperature contrast between the eastern and western sides increases and produces a definite slope that helps maintain the low. This process is illustrated in Figure 4.15. As the low matures the contrast between the temperatures decreases as the cold air is swept right around the low and becomes occluded. The mechanism that maintained the vertical slope is lost and the low is no longer under the area of high-level divergence and the low slowly disintegrates. The jet stream moves on as the upper wave pattern slowly propagates downstream. This pattern of growth and decay is common over the Southern Ocean especially in winter.

Sometimes the result of such a life cycle is the shearing-off of a pool of cold air in the middle levels of the atmosphere, which may not be apparent at the surface. Such pools of cold air sometimes drift northwards over Australia causing widespread rain over southern Australia.

Cold Cut-off Lows

The mechanism of intensification of a cold cut-off low is similar to that described above but

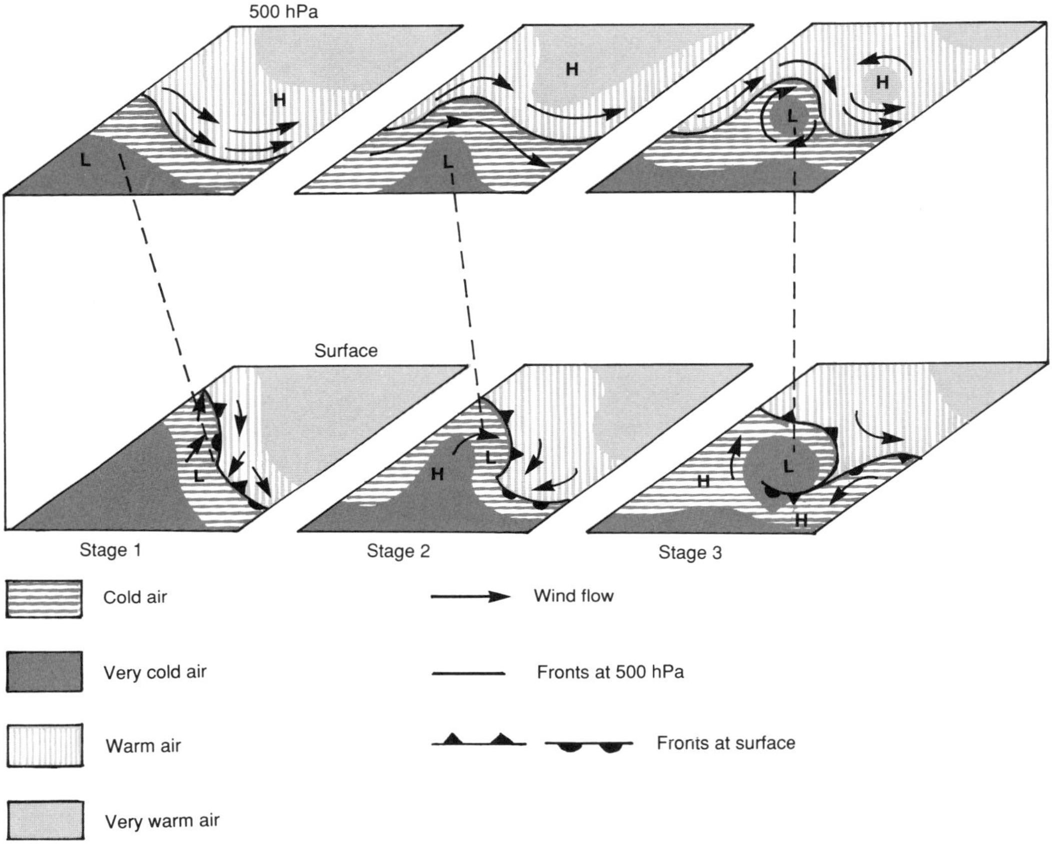

Figure 4.15—The life cycle of an extra-tropical cyclone.

often the closed isobars do not occur at the surface until late in the development of a cold cut-off low, and sometimes not at all. The vertical motion, however, is still sufficient to produce widespread rain.

Cut-off lows provide a significant proportion of the spring rainfall in the wheat-growing areas of western Victoria and southern New South Wales. Rain-producing cut-off lows occur on average slightly more often than once per month from August to November and produce approximately 30 per cent of the total rainfall during that period.

East Coast Lows

East coast lows are a phenomena that occur over southern Queensland and eastern New South Wales usually between latitudes 25°S to 40°S. They occur typically in autumn or winter with an average frequency of one or two per year. They are characterised by their small size and often extremely rapid development. Figure 4.16 is the typical synoptic pattern from which they develop and is known by various names. Sometimes it is called an easterly or tropical dip, or a blocking pattern, and it usually occurs about ten times per year. Only a small proportion of easterly dips or

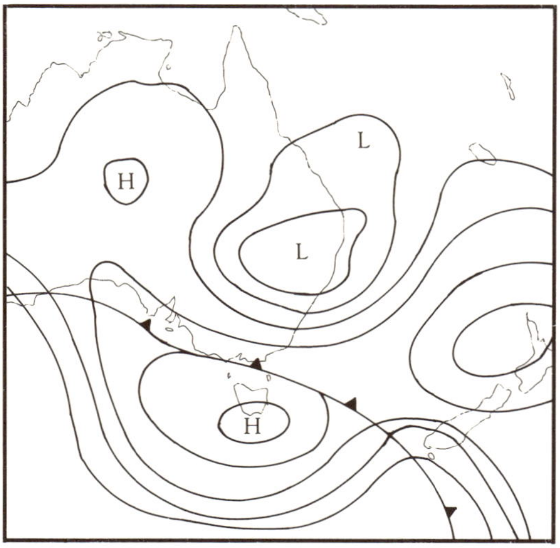

Figure 4.16—A typical synoptic pattern which precedes the development of east coast lows.

blocking patterns result in the development of an east coast low.

The occurrence of easterly dips is most likely in late winter and early spring. They are also observed to occur in Africa and South America but are much more common in Australia.

East coast lows are classified into three types according to where they form within the easterly dip. The first type forms to the west of the trough line. The second type forms on the trough line and the third type forms to the east of the trough line. Such lows often develop very rapidly and have been responsible for very strong winds and floods along the east coast from southern Queensland to the Victorian border.

While there are three distinct types, all have certain characteristics in common. The formation of severe east coast cyclones usually occurs at night near the coast in a region of strong oceanic temperature gradients. Night-time formation is preferred as continental cooling enhances the temperature gradients along the coast and a strong temperature gradient near the surface seems necessary to maintain the strength of a low. If east coast lows move away from the coast, they rapidly weaken. They usually form in the divergent poleward exit region of the subtropical jet and just downstream of a mid-level cold pool. There is usually significant convection and upslope precipitation on the poleward side of the low. The severe forms of east coast low are usually warm cored in the lower troposphere. As already explained, this results in a wind speed maximum at low levels; in fact, spiral bands are formed in the cloud pattern and a distinct eye occurs just as in a tropical cyclone. Wind speeds often reach hurricane force.

Lows following the pattern of the first type form a small hurricane-like vortex. They are typically only about 100 km across. However, they can be very intense causing hurricane force winds in excess of 150 km/h. Such lows usually form on the central or northern sections of the Australian east coast when a deepening easterly dip is located over the continent. They tend to move southwards and usually stay within about 50 km of the coast and have been known to closely hug the east coast over tracks of 1000 km. Because of their small size they can easily slip through the observing network undetected.

Lows following the pattern of the second type are somewhat larger than the first type. They form within the easterly dip as it reaches the coastline. Development occurs very rapidly with the bulk of the pressure falls occurring within six hours. They are usually associated with anti-cyclogenesis to the south leading to very strong pressure gradients and winds along the coast and very heavy rainfall. The six heaviest rainfalls recorded at Nowra since 1900 have all been caused by this type of east coast low. Their peak intensity and formation time is biased towards the morning hours. The autumn and winter months show by far the highest frequency of this type of low and their occurrence is much more common than either the first or third type east coast lows.

Lows following the pattern of the third type form on the western side of the easterly dip. Like the first type they are very small, about 100 km across, and very difficult to detect. Their development is very rapid with hurricane-force winds being produced within six hours of formation. Their life cycle, however, is correspondingly short. The low and its associated weather often completely disperse within twenty-four hours of formation. These lows are much rarer than the second type lows.

North-west Cloudbands

North-west cloudbands are a feature of the synoptic scale weather chart over the Australian region. They often stretch from the Timor Sea near Indonesia across northern Western Australia through central Australia to the east coast, a distance of 5000 km. The cloudband is usually quite narrow compared to its length. A typical band is about 5° longitude wide. Figure 4.17 is a satellite photograph of a typical north-west cloudband.

At its source the band consists of low-level convective cloud. Cloud tops increase in height towards the south-east end of the band with stratiform cloud becoming more widespread. The cloud base also increases to the south-east if no significant rainfall occurs. However, if precipitation occurs, cloud forms in the lower layers of the atmosphere under the main cloudband and results in a cloud of great vertical extent within the band.

In Chapter 3 the Walker circulation and the Southern oscillation were described. There are also areas of varying convective activity along the intertropic convergence zone and the Indonesian region is an area where there is usually considerable convective activity. It is this region that provides the source moisture for the formation of the cloudband.

Upper-level troughs embedded in the westerlies of the mid-latitudes are a common feature of the atmospheric circulation and on

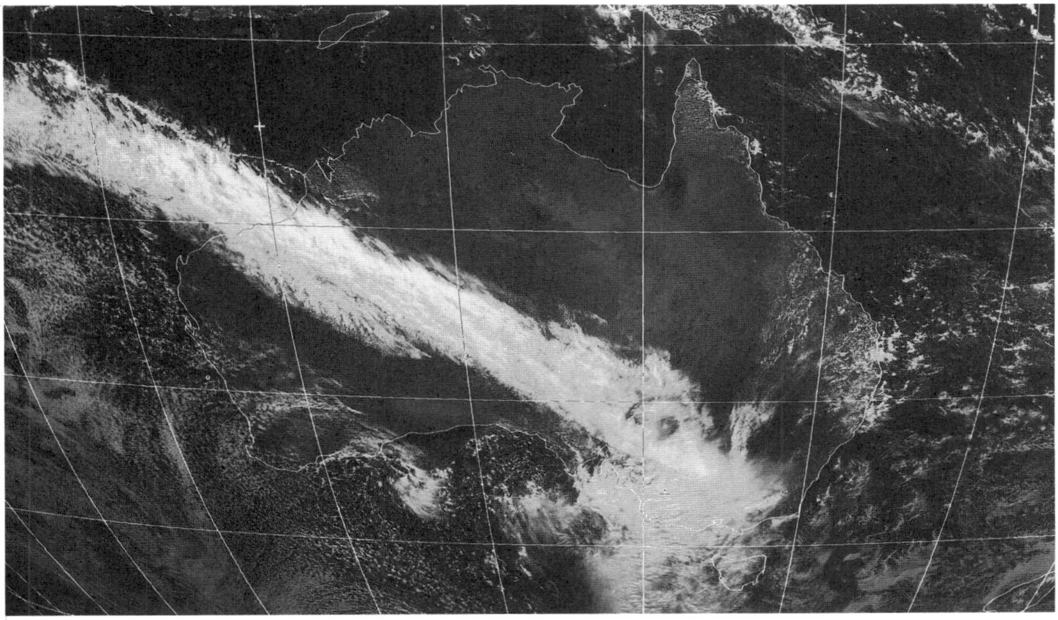

Figure 4.17—Satellite photograph of a mature north-west cloudband taken by the Japanese geostationary satellite GMS–1 *using visible light.*

occasions such troughs extend well into, and are well defined in, tropical regions. The approach of such a system to Western Australian longitudes heralds the likely formation of a north-west cloudband. Typically in these circumstances an anticyclone is located over eastern Australia and its orientation is such that the moist air from over the Indonesian–Timor Sea area is advected over north-west Australia. The moist air is cooled as it is forced to rise over the cooler and drier air of the approaching trough. As it cools, moisture is condensed out of the air and a cloudband is formed which is orientated north-west to south-east across the continent.

The amount of uplift experienced by the moist air is dependent on the speed and strength (amount of uplift) of the approaching trough as well as the stability of the moist airstream. The amount of rainfall produced by the cloud depends on the amount of moisture contained in the airstream and the strength of the vertical motion caused by the uplift. Such cloudbands on occasions produce significant rainfall over the regions traversed by the band.

The cloudband has a well-identified life cycle. The system disintegrates when the moisture source is lost and this occurs when the upper-level trough moves too far eastwards to allow the moist source air to be forced to rise over the cooler drier air in the trough. On some occasions the loss of the moisture source results in the complete disappearance of the cloudband but this is quite rare. It is more usual for the cloud to disintegrate into a disorganised mass or to become integrated into the frontal cloud at higher latitudes, which is associated with the original mid-latitude trough.

North-west cloudbands may form at any time of the year but they are most frequent during May, June and July. Typically they exist for one to four days and most have disintegrated after six days. On rare occasions they have been known to exist for longer than eight days.

Summary

The significant forces which shape the nature of macroscale (or synoptic scale) circulations are the pressure force, Coriolis force, centrifugal force, friction and gravity. These forces have been shown to determine the structure and behaviour of such commonly observed features of the circulation as highs, lows, fronts, troughs and ridges and their effect on the Australian weather has been discussed.

While synoptic scale features can be used to describe the general characteristics of weather and climate over broad areas, significant local variations occur. These are caused by the effect of forces which vary considerably over small areas and produce local or mesoscale circulations which are superimposed on the larger macroscale systems. The description of mesoscale systems and the forces which drive them are the subject of the next chapter.

5. Mesoscale Circulations

There are many forces that act upon a parcel of air. The large-scale circulations that have been considered in previous chapters are controlled by forces that apply throughout the whole area of the circulation. However, there are other forces that have very localised effects, and which are the result of the roughness and shape of the local topography, vegetation types or changes in temperature and roughness at the land–sea boundary.

Although these forces may not strongly influence the general nature of large-scale wind circulations, they are of considerable importance in determining local weather conditions and wind flows such as sea-breezes and land breezes, and mountain and valley winds.

The Sea-breeze

The sea-breeze is a thermal circulation. It is driven by the temperature difference between the water and the land. The vertical circulation of the sea-breeze can be explained by considering changes in the horizontal pressure gradient. These are caused by imbalances in the vertical pressure force and gravity created by the temperature difference of the land and sea surfaces. Figure 5.1 illustrates the changing balance of forces that occurs throughout the life cycle of a sea-breeze.

The sea has a much greater capacity to absorb heat than the land and this is the reason the land heats up during the day more quickly than the sea. In the early morning, when land and sea temperatures are the same, there is no difference in pressure between land and sea. This is illustrated in Figure 5.1a which shows the pressures at the surface and 1000 m as 1000 hPa and 900 hPa respectively.

As the sun rises (Figure 5.1b) the land heats up and for simplicity it is assumed that the temperature of the sea air remains constant. The increasing

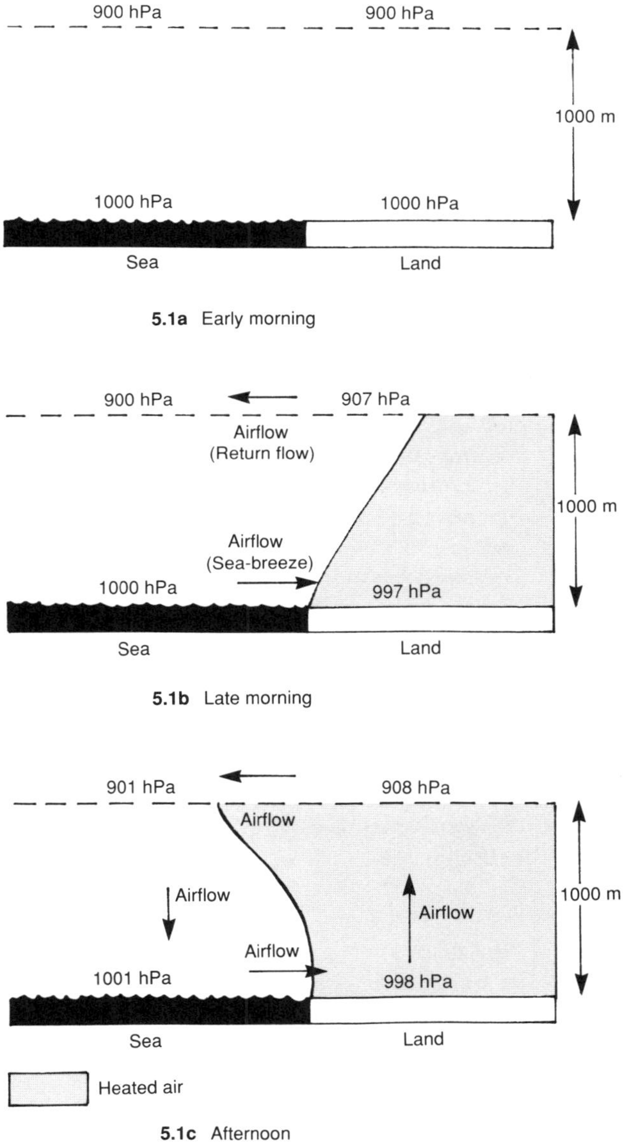

Figure 5.1—Life cycle of a sea-breeze.

temperature of the land causes the air above it to expand and become less dense. This causes the weight of the air above the land to decrease and, because surface pressure is a measure of the weight of air, the surface pressure decreases. This is indicated in Figure 5.1b; the pressure at the surface is reduced from 1000 hPa to 997 hPa. Because the air in the column from the surface to 1000 m has become less dense and therefore lighter, the vertical pressure gradient between the top and bottom of the column that supports the weight of air in the column is also reduced (see Chapter 4, Hydrostatic Assumption) so that a pressure gradient of only, for example, 90 hPa in 1000 m is required to support the weight of the air instead of 100 hPa as required in Figure 5.1a. Simple arithmetic gives the pressure at 1000 m over the land as 907 hPa. It is clear from Figure 5.1b that there is a horizontal pressure gradient from the sea to the land at the surface and from the land to the sea at 1000 m. The resulting air flow at the surface is the sea-breeze.

The net effect of only the horizontal flow of the sea-breeze at the surface and the return flow illustrated here at 1000 m results in a loss of air at the surface over the sea and at 1000 m over the land, and a gain of air at the surface over the land and at 1000 m over the sea. This causes further imbalances in the pressure field and drives compensating vertical motions with sinking air over the sea and rising air over the land as illustrated in Figure 5.1c.

When the air is forced to move towards or away from the land it experiences a Coriolis force that, being to the left in the Southern Hemisphere, tends to cause the wind direction to turn anticlockwise (to back) as the sea-breeze goes through its life cycle during the day.

The opposite effect occurs at night when the land surface cools to below the temperature of the nearby sea. The vertical circulation reverses and the surface air flows from the cooler land towards the warmer sea. The land breeze is usually more gentle than the sea-breeze.

Both the sea-breeze and land-breeze circulations are superimposed on the prevailing synoptic circulation. In cases where this synoptic circulation is very strong, for example, during strong hot north-westerlies in Sydney, the thermal forces may not be sufficiently strong to overcome the pressure forces of the synoptic circulation, and the vertical sea-breeze circulation cannot form at all. Depending on the relative strength of the synoptic pressure force and the locally induced thermal pressure force, there may be an anticlockwise turning (backing) of the surface winds along the coast or no change in direction at all.

The sea-breeze is a well-known phenomenon in coastal areas of Australia, especially during spring and summer. Its direction varies according to the orientation of the coastline.

The Southerly Buster

The southerly buster (or southerly burster) is a well-known phenomenon of coastal regions in south-east Australia and marks the sudden onset of strong southerly wind squalls near the coast. The winds originate from over the sea and often replace hot north-westerlies. Similar phenomena occur on the eastern sides of New Zealand, South Africa, South America and also North America.

The winds are most gusty just after the change and frequently reach at least 55 km/h; speeds of up to 135 km/h have been recorded. Temperature changes are often dramatic, especially if the buster arrives during the afternoon. A fall in temperature of 10°–15°C in a few minutes is common.

It is rare for precipitation to accompany a southerly buster but quite often the leading edge is associated with a spectacular roll cloud. When this occurs, it is orientated perpendicular to the coast. On some occasions there is no cloud associated with the change and its abruptness can be quite hazardous to low-flying aircraft and small boats.

The southerly buster is the result of the interaction of a cold front with the local top-

A photograph of the morning glory in the Gulf of Carpentaria. (See Chapter 5.)

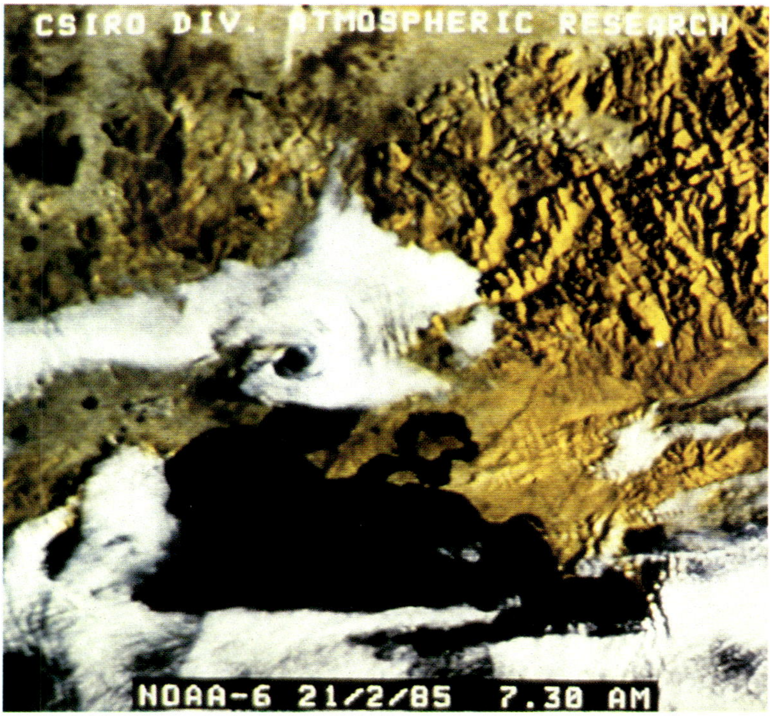

A false colour NOAA–6 satellite photograph of a Spillane eddy over Victoria made visible by fog. (See Chapter 5.)

Cloud capping at Macquarie Island, between New Zealand and Antarctica. This photograph shows a good example of orographic lifting. (See Chapter 6.)

Roll cloud on the leading edge of a southerly buster. (See Chapter 5.)

ography. But not all cold fronts result in the formation of a southerly buster, for example it is rare for a cold front moving in from the Southern Ocean to result in the formation of a southerly buster. They are more often the result of a wind change that occurs ahead of a major front and subsequently develops. Such changes are often shallow and become trapped by the mountain range that runs parallel to the south-east Australian coast. Theoretically it can be shown that in these circumstances the speed at which the front moves depends on the temperature difference between the air behind and ahead of it and as a general rule the faster the front moves, the greater the temperature difference. The temperature difference is greater on the coastal and inland plain than over the ranges.

In 1985 John Colquhoun, a Sydney meteorologist, conducted a survey of southerly busters at Sydney Airport between 1974 and 1983 in the months of September and March inclusive. He found that of the 95 occurrences, 62 per cent occurred between 1 p.m. and 9 p.m. local time. They were most frequent in December (2.3 per year) and November (1.7 per year) and least frequent in September and March (0.7 per year). For 29 per cent of occurrences the maximum gust speed was 75 km/h or more. Gusts of 95 km/h or more were recorded for 1 per cent of occurrences of the southerly buster.

Topographically Generated Winds

Katabatic winds are caused by forces that are the result of temperature differences induced by the local topography. They are most strongly developed when the synoptic pressure gradient is small such as during anticyclonic weather.

In mountainous or hilly regions during the day differential warming of the landscape occurs. North-facing slopes receive more direct radiation (in the Southern Hemisphere) than south-facing slopes. During the afternoon, depending on the steepness of the valleys, west-facing slopes may receive more heating than east-facing valleys. The differences in heating received by various aspects of the topography set up pressure gradients similar to those created by the different heating rate of the land and sea that results in the formation of a sea-breeze. Because of the usually complex shape of terrain, the pattern of pressure forces and the resulting wind flows are more complex than the sea-breeze.

To simplify our discussion, consider a symmetrical valley lying in a north–south direction. During the day, air on the slopes and on the floor of the valley will be heated more than air over the centre of the valley, as illustrated in Figure 5.2. The air at points marked A will be much warmer than the air at the point marked B. Using reasoning similar to that used to explain the sea-breeze, it would be expected that the pressure on the floor of the valley would be greater than the pressure over the slopes. Such a pressure distribution will produce the wind flow as shown in Figure 5.2, causing air to flow up the valley walls. The air flowing away from the floor of the valley will be replaced by air sinking from above the valley floor and to maintain continuity a closed circulation will be established. The upslope flow is called an anabatic wind. In tropical regions these local flows often lead to more precipitation along the slopes of the valley than on the valley floor.

The net effect of this circulation is to heat the air within the valley to a higher temperature than the air at the same level over the surrounding plain or the air above the valley further downstream. With analogous reasoning to that above this temperature differential will cause a pressure gradient that will force an up-valley flow of the air within the valley. It is referred to as a valley wind and fills the whole valley. To replace the air flowing up the valley and maintain continuity, an anti-valley flow occurs above the valley and the anabatic flow up the valley sides is superimposed on the valley flow.

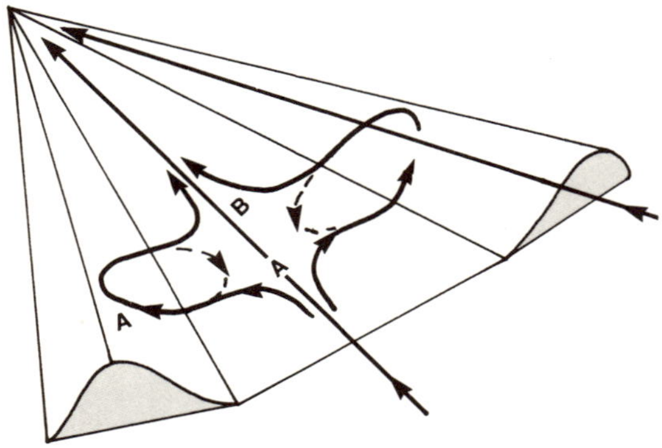

Day

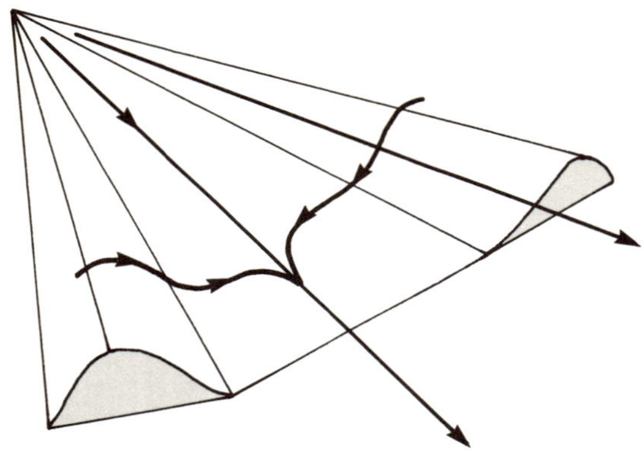

Night

Figure 5.2—Winds generated by the heating of a valley during the day and cooling of it at night.

At night cooling of the valley produces a reverse circulation. The emission of long-wave radiation from the valley walls and floor cools the land and the air close to it. The cool air then slides down the valley wall under the influence of gravity. This downslope flow is called a katabatic wind. Air from above the valley floor flows towards the valley walls to replace the air that slides down the walls and a circulation, the reverse of the daytime situation, is set up across the valley. The cool air of the katabatic winds meets on the valley floor and under the influence of gravity flows down the slope of the valley floor to create the so-called mountain wind. It is the reverse of the valley wind that occurs during the day. The anti-mountain wind, the reverse of the anti-valley wind of the day, is the return flow that replaces air lost from the top of the valley because of the downslope valley wind.

Katabatic winds are variable in speed and are often less than 4 km/h though much stronger flows can occur over snowfields and icefields where the cooling effect may operate during both day and night. In the Antarctic, katabatic flows, especially near the coast, may be 500 m thick and are very strong. Often they will exceed 95 km/h and persist for several weeks.

Katabatic flows in hilly and mountainous areas have important consequences for agriculture. They may lead to the formation of frost pockets on the floors of valleys, especially in areas where the mountain wind may be dammed by tall vegetation or a constriction in the valley. If the temperature conditions and humidity of the air are such that the temperature of the cooled air is less than the dew point, fog will occur on the floors of the valley.

Downslope Winds

Downslope winds are a common phenomena throughout the world. Like katabatic winds their driving force is gravity. But unlike the katabatic flow the synoptic pressure gradient has an important role to play in their formation.

Downslope winds occur on the lee side of mountains. There are many famous examples of downslope winds from around the world such as the föhn in Alpine Europe, the bora of Yugoslavia, the mistral of the north Mediterranean coast, the zonda of Argentina and the chinook of North America. In Australia the best known downslope winds are the Adelaide gully wind and the scarp wind of Perth.

Downslope winds may gust to more than 185 km/h causing considerable damage. Typically they occur at night and are marked by a sudden

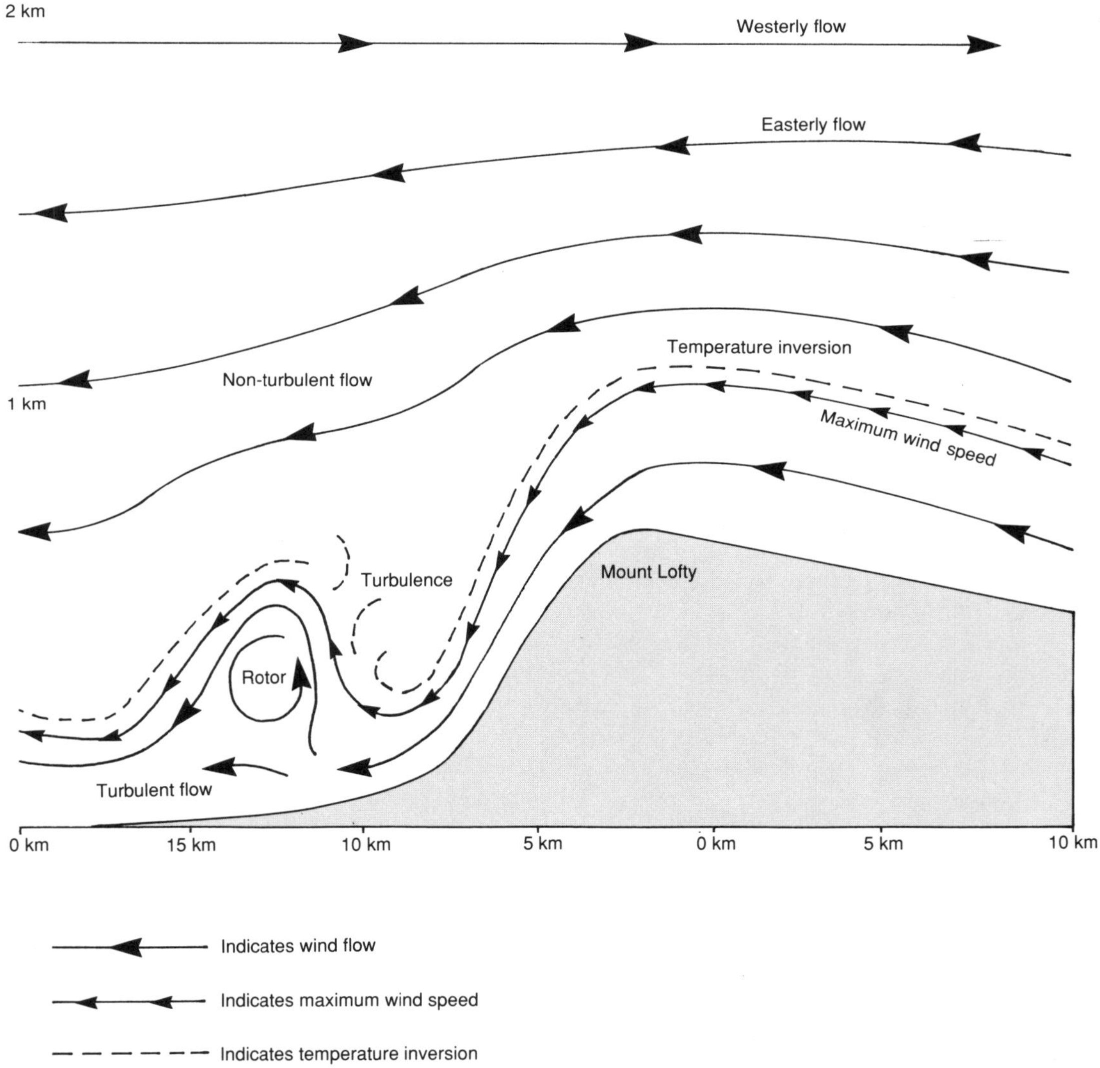

Figure 5.3—A schematic representation of the Adelaide gully wind.

onset. Wind direction is steady but the strength is extremely variable over a short period of time. The occurrence of downslope winds is usually associated with topography that is ramp-shaped; that is, on the windward side the slope is gentle and on the lee side the slope is relatively steep.

Various theories have been put forward to explain downslope winds. An investigation into the Adelaide gully wind by Grace and Holton (1988) suggests that in suitable conditions, air close to the ground is forced to rise by a prevailing easterly synoptic flow pushing it up the gently rising slope on the western side of the Mount Lofty Ranges. When this air reaches the crest it is considerably cooler than its environment. As the air flows over the crest it rapidly accelerates down the steep slope on the western side of the range under the influence of gravity. The energy of these downslope winds (their speed) can be accounted for by the amount of energy expended by the prevailing synoptic flow in forcing the boundary layer air up to the crest of the range. The winds are often quite strong in the Adelaide area and gusts of up to 110 km/h have been reported under such conditions. Figure 5.3, based on a study carried out by Grace and Holton (1988), illustrates schematically the Adelaide gully wind flow.

Spillane Eddy (Melbourne Eddy)

Horizontal gyres (or eddies) induced by topography are a common feature of atmospheric circulation. A marked example of such a gyre is a relatively common feature in Victoria where it is known as the Spillane eddy after the scientist who first identified it.

It occurs when a very stable east to north-east air flow impinges on the Australian Alps. If the flow is not strong enough to rise over the Alps the pressure forces created by the topographical features are such that a large gyre is generated over central Victoria as the air is forced around the mountain barrier. The gyre has about the same horizontal scale as the obstacle that creates it.

The average barrier height of the Alps is approximately 1 km with a peak height of about 2 km. The typical conditions required for the formation of the Spillane eddy are a light to moderate north-easterly geostrophic wind flow impinging onto the Alps and a low-level stable layer in which the potential temperature increases about 10°C in a layer from 0.5 km to 1 km, or 15°C from the surface to about 2 km. In these conditions an eddy forms in the wake of the Alps over central Victoria south of the westward extension of the Great Dividing Range and it has a diameter of about 100 km. The theory of such eddies suggest they should be shed from the Alps with a period which depends on the wind speed. For north-easterly winds impinging on an obstacle of the scale of the Alps, speeds of less than 15 km/h would result in a shedding period in excess of 15 hours. In fact eddies are rarely shed because they usually have a life of less than 15 hours. They are established when the low-level stable layer forms late in the afternoon or evening and are obliterated when surface heating during the morning destroys the surface layer.

Because the eddies gain their energy from low-energy synoptic flows, they are associated with quite benign weather conditions with no precipitation. However, on occasions they do make a considerable impact on the accumulation of air pollution in the Melbourne region. They occur in a stable low-level atmosphere which prevents the vertical escape of pollutants. In addition the circulatory nature of the eddy allows the pollutants to accumulate as air may pass over a pollutant source more than once. A satellite photograph of a Spillane eddy over Victoria appears on page 111.

Eddies such as the Spillane eddy are a common low-level mesoscale feature and occur all over the world. They are often formed off the west coast of Africa in the wake of the Atlas mountains and off the coast of California.

The North Australian Cloud Line

Mesoscale cloud lines that are not associated with major synoptic weather systems such as tropical cyclones, confluence zones in the low-level wind field, fronts or monsoonal depressions, exist in tropical areas of Australia. They exhibit considerable variety both in their shape and in their movement and can be classified into three types.

Type 1

Type 1 consists of long thin cloud lines. The clouds that form the line are generally small cumuli but isolated large cumulus and cumulonimbus cloud with precipitation also occur at times.

The length of the cloud line is often in excess of 500 km while the width is generally less than 150 km. The cloud lines may consist of single straight lines or of several arcs, which may be 100 km in length. Occasionally there may be two or more parallel lines travelling at different speeds.

Type 1 cloud lines occur most frequently in the region of Cape York Peninsula and the western part of the Top End. They form almost exclusively during the morning and afternoon and move westwards at speeds ranging from 15 to 55 km/h.

A limited climatology carried out in 1987 by Drosdowsky and Holland for September to April from 1982 to 1983 and from 1985 to 1986 suggested that type 1 lines are most frequent in September and October (about nineteen per month) and least frequent in January, February and March (about three or four per month).

The morning glory The morning glory is a particular variety of the type 1 cloud line, see photograph on page 111. The Garrawa Aboriginal people who live near the south coast of the Gulf of Carpentaria call it *kangólgi* and it is credited with increasing the supply of bird life. This may reflect the fact that it occurs most frequently in October, just prior to the wet season. It is a wind squall or a succession of wind squalls, accompanied by a pressure jump and quite often by a long roll cloud or series of roll clouds. The cloud line is very spectacular, stretching from horizon to horizon but having a width of a few kilometres at the most. The cross-section of the cloud line is very uniform. The vertical extent of the cloud is not well known but it probably does not exceed 2500 m and only rarely does the cloud produce precipitation.

The morning glory is a wave-like structure known as an undular bore, which is propagated along the top of a shallow stable layer near the surface, underlying a deep neutral layer. It is similar to a water wave generated by the horizontal movement of a paddle. There appear to be several mechanisms that approximate the paddle. One such mechanism is the collision over Cape York Peninsula of the afternoon sea-breezes from both coasts, which results in an increase in the depth of the cooler, denser air under the inversion. This creates a dome of dense air that collapses, forcing a wave to be created on the top of the stable layer. The wave is then propagated westwards over the Gulf of Carpentaria along the top of the stable layer. A similar disturbance may also be initiated by the katabatic flow down the western slope of the range which runs down the eastern side of the peninsula.

Type 2

Type 2 lines consist of extensive areas of cloud, which may be either stratiform or convective and up to 400 km across but with a sharp leading edge. These cloud lines were found by Drosdowsky and Holland to be equally frequent for each of the months September to April with about five or six occurring each month. Their preferred area and time of formation and the speed of movement are very similar to type 1 lines but the type 2 lines tend to persist for longer and move further westwards before dissipating. A satellite photograph of a typical example of this type is on page 118.

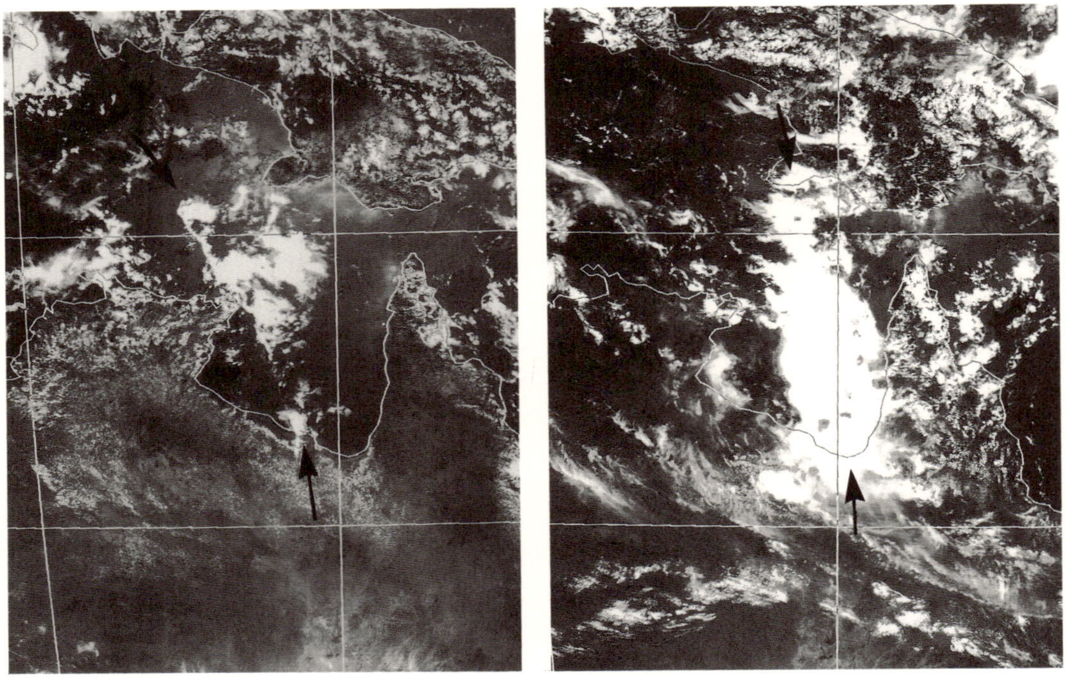

Satellite photographs of a type 2 (left) and type 3 (right) cloud line (marked by arrows) taken by the Japanese geostationary satellite using visible light.

Type 3

Type 3 cloud lines consist of deep cumulonimbus convective systems with a leading edge at least 2° latitude in length. They show a greater variability in the times of formation than type 1 or 2 lines. Some varieties of type 3 lines may form at any time of the day but they have a tendency to decay late in the afternoon or during the evening. Their preferred area of formation also shows a wider distribution than type 1 or 2 lines. A satellite photograph of a typical example of this type appears above.

Summary

In this chapter local or mesoscale circulations have been considered. These largely result from variations over a relatively small area of frictional forces and surface heating rates caused by peculiarities in the local terrain. Although the general circulation, the macroscale and the mesoscale circulations have been treated separately they in fact constitute a continuum and constantly interact with one another. The driving energy of the entire atmospheric system is the sun. Its energy is absorbed initially at the molecular scale and through the interaction of the various scales of motion of the atmosphere energy is transferred to and drives the large planetary scale circulations. These in their turn lose energy to the smaller-scale circulations and this energy is eventually dissipated by frictional forces.

Atmospheric circulations result in regions of rising air and sinking air and when air rises it cools and moisture may condense out to form cloud. The different scales of atmospheric circulations produce different types of cloud. These are discussed in the next chapter.

6. Clouds

These often spectacular shapes in the sky have long excited the curiosity and fascination of humanity. A children's game, which has existed down the ages in many civilisations, involves studying the clouds and then inventing situations for them; here a giant seahorse travels across the horizon; there a chariot is drawn by two white horses; a huge fish pursues a school of smaller sprats overhead. Only the imagination limits the possibilities when you stare at the moving kaleidoscope above.

Although broad statements can be made about certain clouds producing specific types of weather, clouds cannot be used in isolation to forecast the weather as there are too many exceptions to the rule. Clouds are visible evidence of the presence of water vapour in the atmosphere. Under favourable conditions the water vapour condenses into minute liquid water (or ice) droplets, so tiny that they fall very slowly.

Basically the following sequence of favourable conditions must be followed for cloud formation: lifting, cooling and condensation. If a parcel of air is lifted, its pressure decreases and it therefore expands. As it expands it cools and if there is sufficient water vapour present in the parcel, condensation will occur and cloud becomes visible. If this process occurs at very high altitudes, water vapour will change to ice crystals rather than to liquid water. This produces special types of distinctive cloud that are easily identified. For this sequence to develop, however, the first part of the process, lifting, must begin and this can be produced by several different mechanisms.

Convection

When the sun shines on the ground, particularly in the summer months, the air in contact with the ground is heated and begins to rise. As a parcel of air begins to rise it starts to cool; when it reaches the same temperature as the air surrounding it, the parcel of air stops rising. By this time another parcel of air near the ground has begun the cycle again and we have 'pulses' of air rising intermittently before becoming part of their environment. These pulses of rising air are examples of convective heating and are a major mechanism for atmospheric lifting and cloud formation. The type of cloud generally produced is called convective and is mainly part of the cumuliform group of cloud.

Cumulus cloud is localised and usually occurs in clumps or heaps across the sky. Indeed the word *cumulus* is Latin for 'heap' and this is a good description of the cloud type. The height of this type of cloud is determined by how quickly the heated air parcel can cool and reach the temperature of the surrounding air. However, if the temperature of the surrounding air cools off with height at a faster rate than the air parcel can lose its heat, then the parcel will always be warmer than its surroundings and will therefore keep rising. In this situation conditions are said to be unstable and convective clouds will tend to grow extremely tall and perhaps reach the thunderstorm stage.

Orographic Lifting

The atmosphere can also be lifted when air passes over rising terrain and the photograph on page 112 is a good example of this. It shows cloud capping at Macquarie Island.

Another special case of terrain 'lifting' producing cloud is the lenticular cloud, which is produced by the phenomenon of mountain waves. Mountain waves are produced when we have a strong airflow at right angles to a mountain range. If a stable layer exists in the mid-troposphere, standing waves that may extend 100 km or so downstream of the mountain range are produced in the airflow.

If sufficient moisture is present clouds that extend in long bands parallel to the mountain range on the downstream side can form. These clouds usually exist around the 5–7 km level in the atmosphere, but they can be higher. They are normally referred to as altocumulus lenticularis because of their lens-like shape. Clouds of this type are commonplace over south-eastern Australia, particularly during the winter months when strong westerly flows frequently occur. Figure 6.1 is a satellite photograph which shows an example of mountain waves over eastern Australia.

Similar phenomena are often generated by the Flinders Ranges in South Australia, the Great Dividing Range of Victoria and New South Wales, as well as the mountains of western Tasmania.

Air-mass Lifting

This type of lifting produces widespread cloud that may cover large areas of the continent at any one time. As explained in Chapter 4, Structure

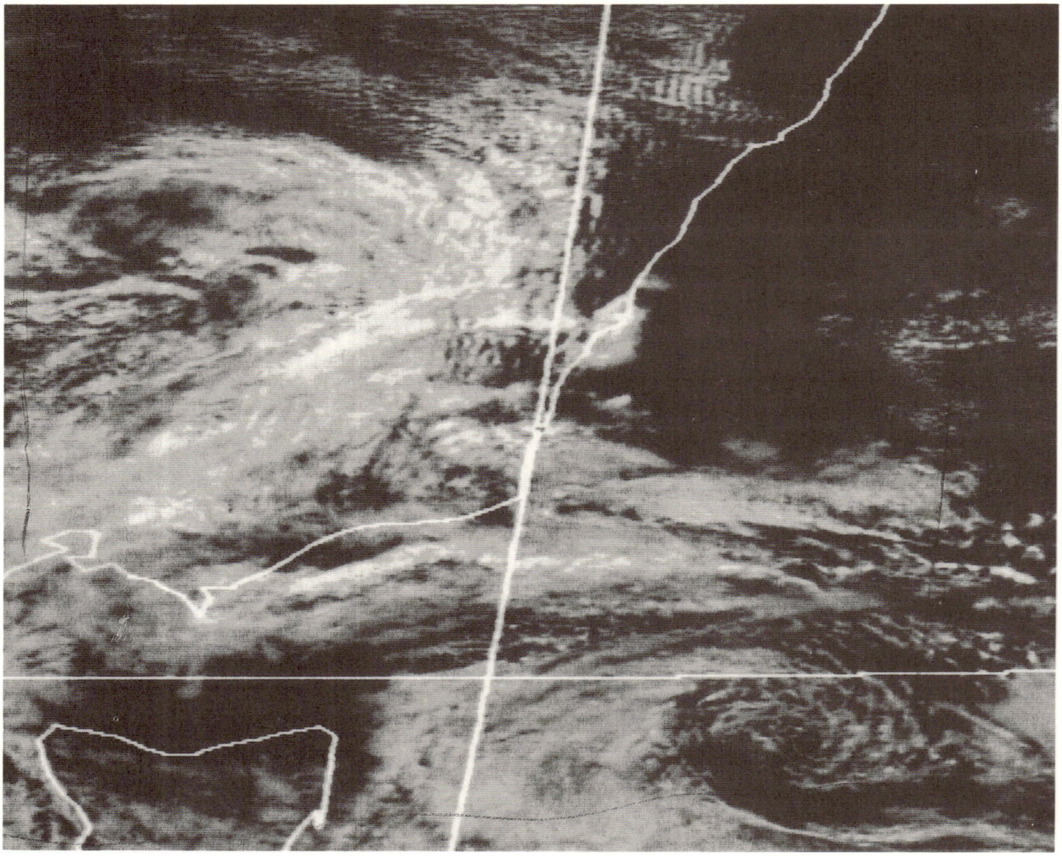

Figure 6.1—Mountain waves over eastern Australia.

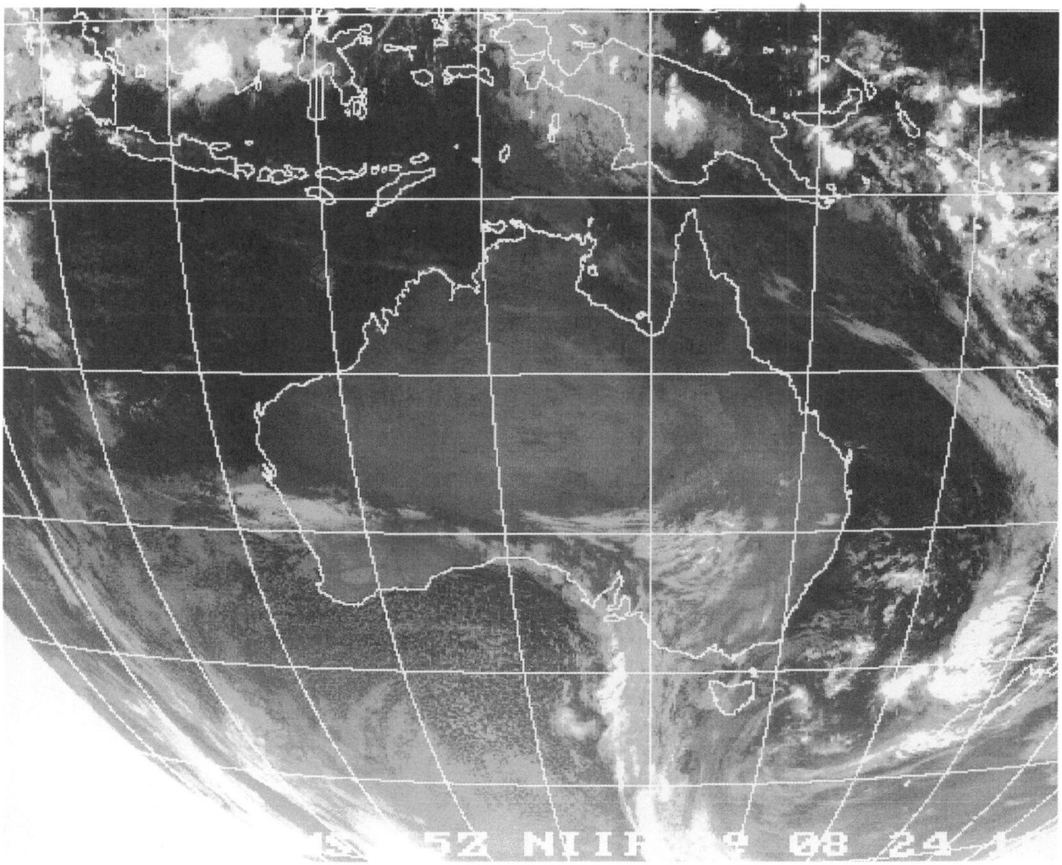

Figure 6.2a—Satellite photograph showing a cold front approaching Adelaide.

of Fronts and Associated Weather, a cold front will produce widespread atmospheric lifting.

A cold front can be thought of as a wedge of cold, dense air thrusting into the air-mass ahead of it. This causes the existing air-mass to ride up the face of the cold air, producing yet another variation of lifting, cooling and condensation. Cloud so produced can be diverse in nature and will depend on the temperature difference between the two air-masses, the stability of the surrounding atmosphere and the pattern of the upper atmosphere in the area. Extensive stratiform (layer) cloud can result, but cumuliform clouds may also be produced. If conditions are unstable, thunderstorm activity may also be present..

Figure 6.2a is a satellite photograph and Figure 6.2b is the equivalent synoptic chart. It shows a cold front moving across Australia. The cloudmass is extensive and is being produced by air-mass lifting of the type described. The position of the cold front as marked on the synoptic chart corresponds approximately with the trailing edge of the cloudmass on the satellite photograph. This is frequently observed with the approach of a front; first there is increasing high cloud that thickens, perhaps with rain developing, and finally a change in the wind usually with a pronounced temperature drop as the air-mass changes. A

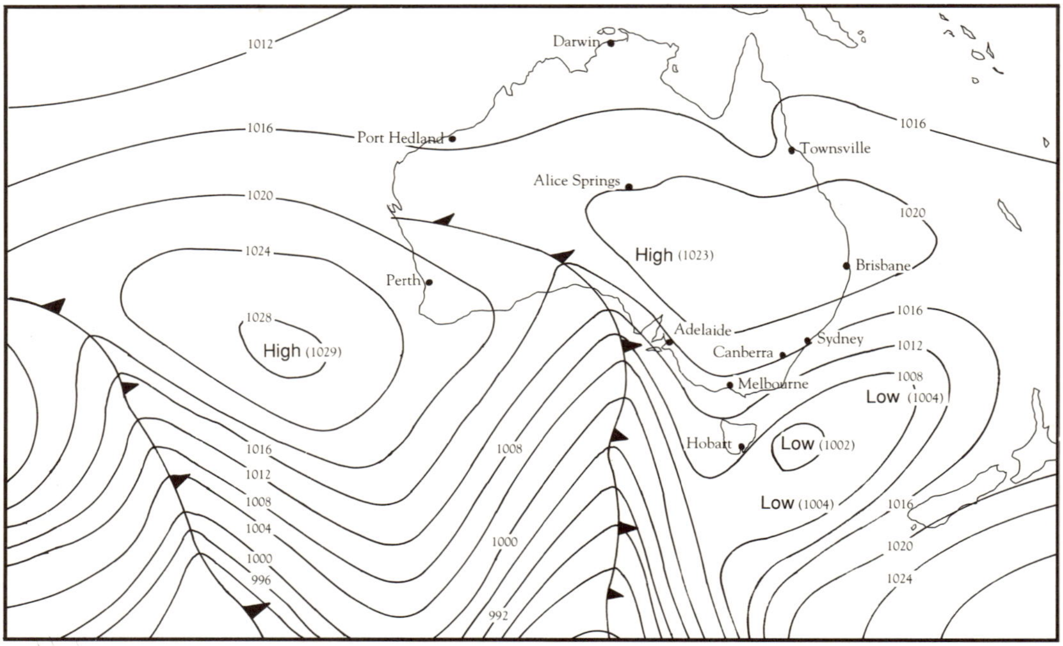

Figure 6.2b—Synoptic chart showing a cold front approaching Adelaide.

warm front also produces extensive cloud by the uplift of air over a large area. In Figure 6.3, however, the cold air is stationary, and the warm air rides over the top, creating uplift along the interface.

Warm fronts are usually high-latitude phenomena. They are commonplace in Europe, North America and the USSR but are far less frequent in Australia. This is because a large block of stationary cold air is required for the development of a warm front and this mainly occurs over snow-covered landmasses.

Mechanical Friction

The final way in which cloud is produced is by mechanical turbulence of wind with the ground. As the wind blows over the ground, turbulent eddies occur which provide the necessary lifting to produce cloud formation. This mechanism is very similar to orographic lifting.

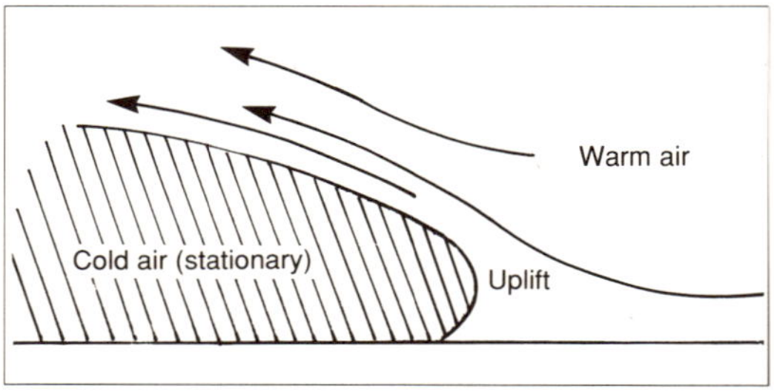

Figure 6.3—Air-mass lifting.

Cloud Types

As seen in Chapter 3, the atmosphere has several layers based on a temperature variation. Clouds occur mainly in the first 10 km of the atmosphere, which is the troposphere.

Clouds between the surface and the 2.5 km level are known as low cloud and include stratocumulus, cumulus (tops of this cloud may reach into the next level) and stratus. From 2.5

to 6 km, clouds are known as middle level and consist of the alto group, namely altostratus and altocumulus. Above 6 km, the clouds consist of tiny ice crystals because they are normally well above the freezing level at this height. These are known as high clouds and consist of the cirroform group, that is cirrostratus and cirrocumulus.

Low-Level Clouds

Stratus This is the lowest cloud in the atmosphere. It can sometimes be so low that it obscures the tops of tall buildings or hilltops. Drizzle or light rain is sometimes associated with this cloud type and it can produce areas of poor visibility similar to those resulting from a fog.

Stratocumulus Probably the most frequently observed cloud in the Australian sky, it consists of ragged clumps scattered about with no particular organisation or pattern evident. It does not grow to any great depth and does not produce any shower activity.

Cumulus This is similar to some extent to stratocumulus, except that cumulus clouds are taller and tend to have a more organised structure. Cumulus is termed a low-level cloud and to base it is generally between 0.7 and 2 km, though the cloud tops may be well into the middle level.

If the tops of the cloud are above the freezing level of the particular air-mass, ice crystals will occur in the upper reaches of the formation and this may produce precipitation (called a shower), which tends to be localised rather than widespread. If a temperature inversion exists at a particular level in the air-mass, this will impede the cloud growth. If this inversion is below the freezing level, shower activity is suppressed.

Precipitation from stratiform clouds, as we shall see, tends to be widespread and this is called rain. Both showers and rain can, under certain conditions, be heavy. The main meteorological difference is the extent of the area affected.

Rainbows are usually associated with showers from cumulus clouds. They are caused by sun rays on rain droplets as they fall, causing refraction of the sunlight similar to that produced by a prism.

Cumulus clouds that extend into the middle levels and produce showers are usually called towering cumulus. When showers have formed, these towering cumulus can be detected and located by weather radar. In certain cases, clouds of this type grow further in height and become cumulonimbus or thunderstorm clouds.

Cumulonimbus

This is the 'King of Clouds' and extends from the low layers of the atmosphere to the top of the troposphere. Typical summer thunderstorms in Australia reach heights of 10 km or greater.

Figure 6.4 is a satellite photograph which shows thunderstorm activity over Australia as bright white blobs; this view is of course looking down on the top of the cloud and is very different to the view we are accustomed to from below. It does give some idea, however, of the massive size of these systems, with a cluster of three or four covering several hundred square kilometres.

The amount of energy stored by a cumulonimbus cloud is enormous, and is of the same scale as a small atomic bomb. The main difference is that a thunderstorm cloud takes an hour or two to release its energy over a fairly extensive area; a nuclear device releases its energy in an instant over a localised area. The shape of a thunderstorm cloud provides some idea of the forces operating within it.

Once in operation, the cumulonimbus cloud becomes an awesome circulating engine of moving air. Fast-moving updrafts are surrounded by violent downdrafts that may bring heavy showers, or even hail, over the surrounding countryside.

A feature of the cumulonimbus cloud is that it has a comparatively flat top supported by curving sides, so that the shape resembles a blacksmith's anvil. In fact, the flat top section of the cloud is known as 'the anvil' for this reason.

The flat shape of the anvil is determined by atmospheric temperature. The troposphere is about 10 km, and within this region the atmos-

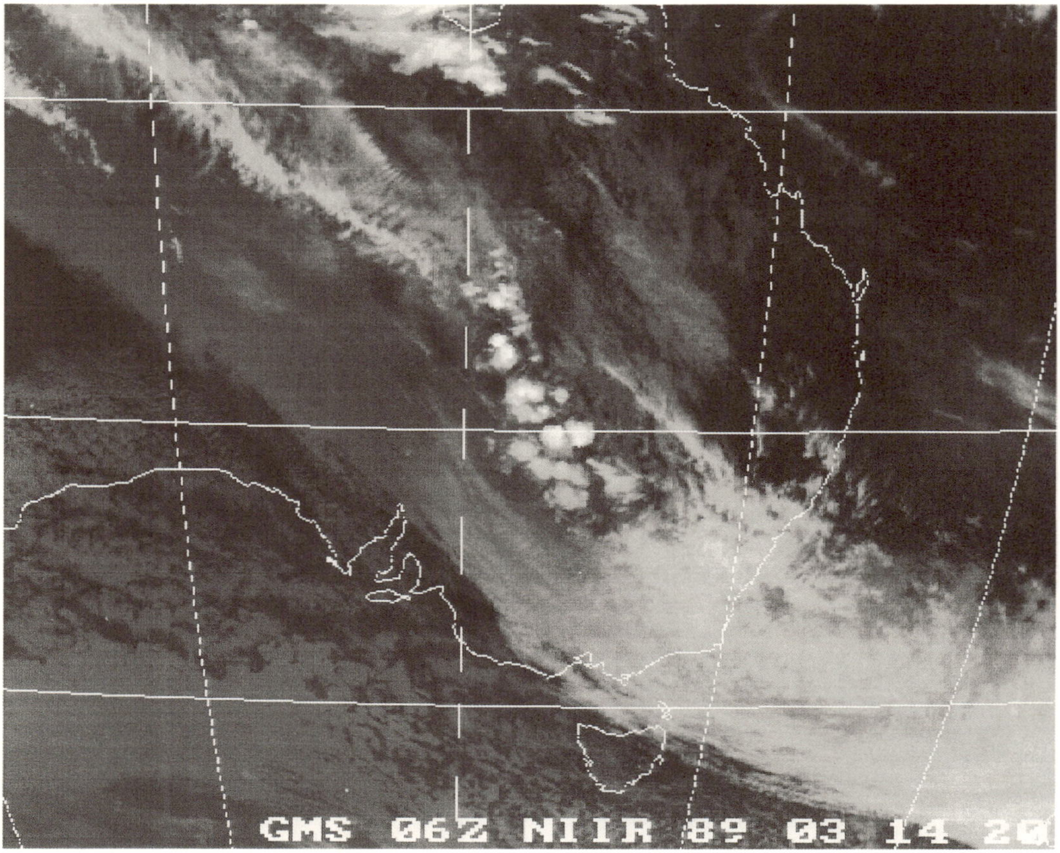

Figure 6.4—Satellite photograph showing thunderstorm activity over south-eastern Australia.

pheric temperature tends to decrease with height. After the stratosphere, the atmospheric temperature remains fairly constant with height for a distance. The interface between the troposphere and the stratosphere is termed the tropopause and is therefore a temperature inversion in the atmosphere. Thunderstorms do not generally penetrate this inversion but instead tend to flatten out beneath it.

A fully mature thunderstorm extends to the top of the troposphere. With severe thunderstorms, in which there is a very strong updraft driving the system, the cloud can sometimes punch through the tropopause for some distance, producing a bulge on the top of the anvil. This is called overshooting.

This phenomenon is not common in Australia but when it does occur, heavy hail or even tornadic squalls can follow. These overshoot type of thunderstorms are far more common in the United States and are primarily responsible for the outbreaks of tornadoes that occur over the Midwest during the summer months.

Lightning, thunder and hail are some of the most spectacular by-products of cumulonimbus clouds. It is not known for certain why lightning occurs but it appears that the massive updrafts near the centre of cumulonimbus clouds cause tremendous build-ups of static charge. When conditions are right, the charge will dissipate by throwing a giant spark from one cloud to another, or from the cloud to the ground. This spark is called lightning, and the sharp crack caused by the rapid expansion of air so produced is called thunder. When heard from a significant distance, thunder will sound more like a rolling rumble than a crack.

The approximate distance of a thunderstorm can be gauged by counting, in seconds, from the instant lightning is seen to when the thunder is heard. The total time elapsed is then divided by three. This gives the distance, in kilometres. For example, if 15 sec. passes between lightning being seen and thunder being heard, the lightning flash is about 5 km away. On occasions, the cumulonimbus will be obscured by other, surrounding clouds, and in this case identification can be difficult. However, lightning will produce bursts of static on the radio, and this effect extends out as far as 50 km, providing another method of establishing whether or not cumulonimbus clouds are in the general area.

Hail is another spectacular by-product of thunderstorms. A hailstone begins as a frozen droplet of water that is carried aloft in the updraft area of the thunderstorm. Sometimes as it begins to fall back to earth it will become trapped in the updraft for a second time before falling once again. This process can occur several times with each journey up through the cloud resulting in another layer of ice being deposited on the growing hailstone. A hailstone cut in two reveals a ring-like structure built up of several layers of ice, one upon the other.

While ice crystals are produced in every thunderstorm, only about 10 per cent of thunderstorms will generate hail that reaches the ground. A powerful updraft is certainly required and thunderstorms that produce hail are generally quite severe. Hail can show a considerable variation in dimension from pea size through to cricket ball size in extreme cases. The most damaging effect of large hail on the modern urban environment is the denting of automobiles, which can result in an insurance payout of several million dollars for just the one thunderstorm. To damage an automobile requires hail of about marble size or more and fortunately this is a fairly unusual occurrence in Australia.

As previously discussed, on rare occasions a severe thunderstorm will spawn a violently rotating funnel of air known as a tornado. The detailed reason for the formation of tornadoes is not fully known but they are always associated with the most severe of thunderstorms, and often involve the overshoot phenomenon.

The study of impact damage produced by debris from tornado funnels indicates the possibility of up to 500 km/h wind velocities. Tornadoes are an occasional weather phenomenon in Australia but fortunately most have occurred in unpopulated areas. This contrasts with the situation in the Great Plains area of the United States where tornadoes are an ever present menace to the population during the summer months.

Middle-Level Clouds

Between the 2.5 and 6 km levels are the middle level clouds. These are two basic types, namely altostratus and altocumulus, and can adopt many different configurations.

Middle-level cloud can be thin and wispy as well as being fairly localised. It can also be very extensive and thick in which case widespread rains may result over the affected area. Middle-level cloud will often move in a different direction to low cloud because wind speed and direction usually vary with altitude.

Altostratus When present as a thick deck of cloud, altostratus is usually associated with cold frontal activity or upper-level disturbances. To an observer on the ground, as a thickening layer of altostratus approaches the light will become progressively dull. The thicker the layer, the greater the chance of rain, and this is why we learn to associate dull light with the likelihood of rain. Altostratus can also arrange itself in waves or ripples across the sky. This can be caused by the formation of mountain waves, or by atmospheric turbulence produced when one layer of air slides over another, producing disturbances at the interface.

Altocumulus This is the cumuliform or heaped version of middle-level cloud. It is normally not a very tall cloud, although on occasion it develops turret-like projections from the cloud tops. This formation is known as altocumulus castellanus and is a sign that the middle levels of the troposphere are undergoing lifting. This, in turn, indicates atmospheric instability, and altocumulus castellanus is often a precursor of thunderstorm development. Altocumulus and altostratus are often mixed together in cold frontal development to produce an extensive cloudband across sizeable areas of the continent.

High-Level Clouds

This classification refers to cloud between 6 km and the top of the troposphere. Because the freezing level for water (0°C) is usually well below 6 km, high clouds are generally composed of tiny ice crystals that float in the atmosphere. As with the other cloud types, high-level cloud is often associated with cold frontal activity or an upper-level disturbance. The anvil of a thunderstorm is also composed of high cloud, and when the thunderstorm has reached the end of its cycle and has collapsed, areas of high cloud cumulonimbus debris often remain and are carried off in the prevailing wind.

In certain weather situations, high speed rivulets of air cut through the existing high-level airstream. These rivulets are called jet streams. Jet streams cause lifting of the upper atmosphere and frequently produce elongated streaks of high cloud across the sky. High cloud is composed of the cirroform groups of cloud with the two main types being cirrostratus and cirrocumulus. *Cirrus* is the Latin word for 'hair', and many formations of high cloud appear similar to fine long hair blowing in the wind.

Cirrostratus This often takes the form of elongated wisps across the sky that were dubbed 'mare's-tails' by the old sailing ship crews. It can also take the form of a semi-transparent veil of cloud across the sky that can produce a large halo effect around the moon at night. This is the reason behind the old saying that a halo around the moon foretells bad weather ahead. As this type of cloud is often produced by adjacent cold frontal activity, some truth is attached to the legend; however, some cold fronts become inactive before reaching the observer, or veer away, so that the saying probably has as many failures as successes.

Cirrocumulus As the name indicates, this is the cumuliform version of the cirrus group. It is probably the most unusual cloud in the Australian sky, often being associated with an upper-level disturbance. In some cases, cirrocumulus can be quite extensive and cover significant areas of the continent. Certain manifestations of the cloud can be quite spectacular, consisting of small rippled elements across the sky. It does not produce any precipitation, but can be the prelude to unsettled weather if it is associated with a developing upper-level disturbance.

Clouds, the visible aggregation of visible water droplets, are one of the most fascinating features of the sky of our planet, and they add a great dimension to its beauty whether viewed from above or below.

7. Meteorological Instruments

The instruments for measuring the various meteorological elements have increased in number and become more sophisticated as our knowledge of the atmosphere has increased. The main elements measured in today's recording of the changing weather patterns are: atmospheric pressure; temperature; rainfall; wind; sunshine; humidity; evaporation; cloud; rainfall patterns; dew point; and sea-surface temperature.

Barometers

The simplest, and probably one of the most accurate methods of measuring atmospheric pressure is with the mercury barometer.

As can be seen from Figure 7.1, the atmosphere exerts a pressure at A and pushes the mercury up the tube to a certain height. This height is measured and the barometric pressure is read as so many millimetres of mercury. This can be converted into the more familiar hectopascals by the use of tables. If there was not a vacuum above the mercury column, and this space was open to the atmosphere, there would be equal pressure pushing down from the inside of the column, and the mercury would fall to the level of that in the bath.

Mercury is used because it is a dense and heavy fluid; water could also be used but the barometer would then have to be about 10 m long to do the same job. This also illustrates a fact about barometric pressure. When you drink a fluid using a straw, it is a common misconception that the fluid is sucked into the mouth. However, the air is actually removed from the straw and the atmospheric pressure pushes the fluid up the straw, as with a barometer.

Another type of barometer is called the aneroid barometer. This works on the principle of having an evacuated corrugated cylinder bolted to a base. Changes of atmospheric pressure will cause deformation of the chamber, which can be used to produce a dial reading; or it can be used to drive a pen that produces a record of the pressure drawn against the time of day. This latter type of instrument is called a barograph.

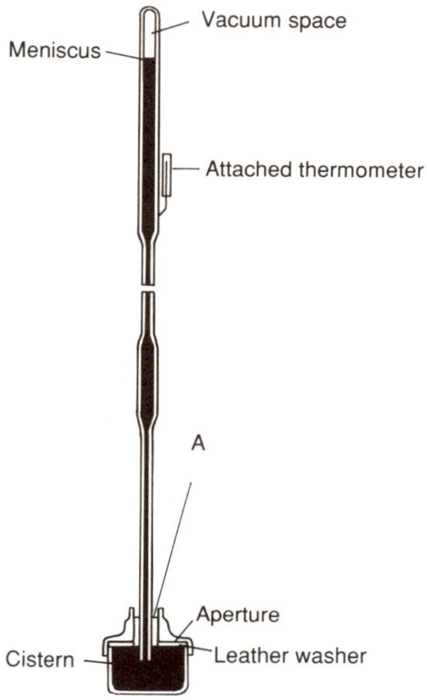

Figure 7.1—The mercury barometer.

The kink in the barograph trace P in Figure 7.2 was produced by a thunderstorm passing over Sydney. Such records are also kept of temperature, humidity, sunshine, rainfall, wind speed and direction. Records of this type are very useful in research and are also called upon from time to time for use in legal matters. If a weather phenomenon has resulted in loss of life, injury or property damage, legal proceedings may follow in which Bureau of Meteorology instrument records of this type are used in court evidence. It is one of the

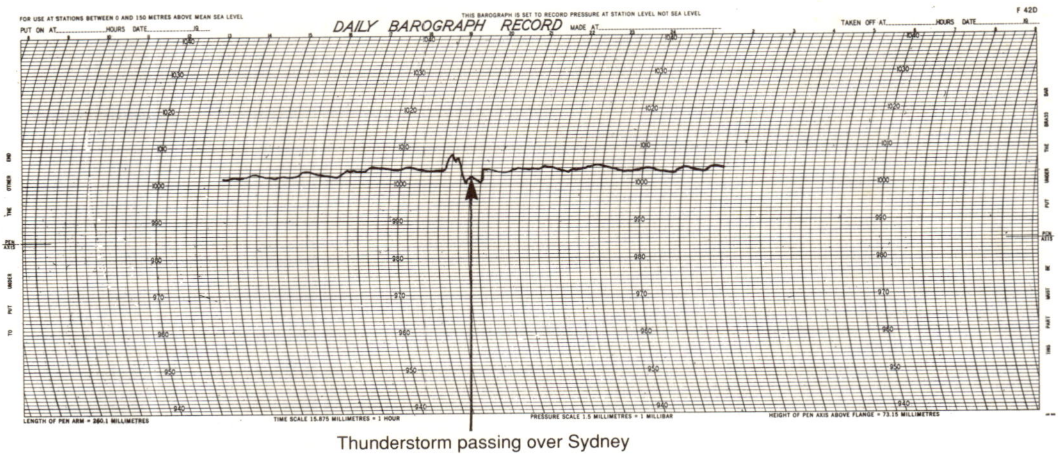

Figure 7.2—Rapid variations in air pressure produced by a thunderstorm passing over the area.

Bureau's functions to ensure that all documentation is archived correctly as part of the official records of the Commonwealth of Australia.

The advantages of the aneroid barometer over the mercury barometer are that it can produce a permanent record and is more readily portable. Transporting mercury barometers is difficult because of the possibility of breakage involving a spillage of mercury. For this reason they are transported in special aluminium protective cases.

Thermometers

The thermometer is probably the most familiar meteorological device and is present in a large number of households. The simplest type of thermometer consists of a bulb filled with a fluid (usually mercury or tinted alcohol) that leads into a very thin tube. As the temperature rises, the fluid in the bulb expands and rises up the tube. If the bulb is dipped in ice water the level of the fluid is marked off as 0°C; when immersed in boiling water, the level achieved is marked off as 100°C. This is the basis of the Celsius scale used in Australia today.

As with the barometer, there is also a recording device for temperature. This is called a thermograph and produces a permanent temperature trace on a sheet of graph paper. This device uses a temperature sensitive element consisting of two strips of different metal (usually invar and brass) welded together and wound in the form of a spiral. The different expansion rates of the two metals causes the spiral to wind or unwind as temperature varies. This movement is translated by the pen arm to the revolving drum and a trace is produced.

Two special types of thermometer are the maximum and minimum thermometers (Figure 7.3) which, as their names imply, measure the maximum and minimum temperature of each day. The principle of these instruments is the same as that of the standard thermometer but some modifications are included that enable maximum and minimum temperatures to be recorded. These thermometers are normally hung at an angle close to the horizontal for the best operating results.

Maximum Thermometer

At first glance this seems like a normal mercury thermometer but there is a constriction in the tube through which the mercury passes. After

The automatic weather station at Marion Reef off the north Queensland coast. (See Chapter 7.)

A drifting buoy on display at the Bureau's 75th anniversary exhibition in 1983. (See Chapter 7.)

Colour radar display showing rainfall intensity. (See Chapter 7.)

An unusual view of Melbourne through a Campbell–Stokes sunshine recorder. (See Chapter 7.)

A pluviograph (rain gauge) and thermometer screen on display. (See Chapter 7.)

maximum temperature is reached the mercury begins to contract but only the mercury below the constriction falls back into the bulb. The rest of the column remains in place, therefore indicating the maximum temperature of the day. After the maximum temperature has been noted, the instrument is reset by shaking the mercury back down so the mercury column is continuous again.

Minimum Thermometer

This is an alcohol-based thermometer that is also very similar to a conventional thermometer, except that a coloured glass index rides inside the thermometer's tube. This index does not readily emerge from the alcohol because of the surface tension effect.

As the temperature falls, the meniscus of the alcohol drags the index towards the base of the thermometer until the minimum is reached. Then the temperature begins to rise leaving the index where it is. The head of the index furthest away from the bulb of the thermometer indicates the minimum temperature for the day in question.

Maximum and minimum temperatures are

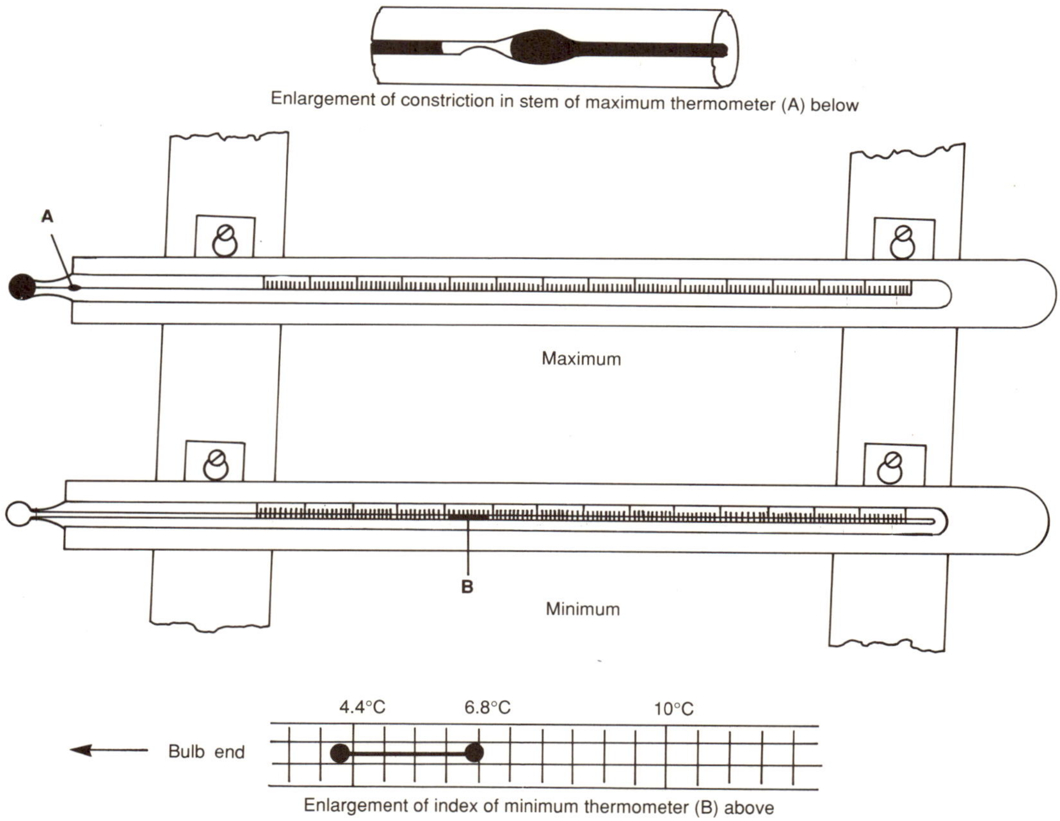

Figure 7.3—The maximum and minimum thermometers.

normally read at 9 a.m. each day when the routine observations are performed. The maximum temperature usually occurs around 3 p.m. daily, and the minimum temperature around 6 a.m. Both these times are approximate and can vary quite widely because of such occurrences as cold fronts, cloud cover and fog.

Rain Gauges

Rainfall can be measured by several different types of instrument. The simplest is commonly called a rain gauge and this is usually a vertical-sided container with some kind of graduated scale attached.

The scale used in Australia is millimetres and this replaced the old points and inches scale that was in use up until the 1970s. If, for example, 25 mm was registered in the gauge, after rain had fallen and providing there was no run-off or absorption of water by the soil, this means the countryside would be covered in water to a depth of 25 mm. This does not occur of course, because the water percolates into the soil and runs off into lower areas.

Because of the distorting effects of nearby objects such as houses, trees and shrubs, it is important that a rain gauge be placed in the open. The general rule for exposure of a rain gauge is that if there is an object of height X in the general area, then the rain gauge should be placed at least 2 x X from the object. This criterion rules out most suburban backyards as official rainfall observing sites, although approximated readings are still useful and interesting to take.

The Pluviograph

As with temperature and barometric pressure, rainfall can be recorded in graph form by a special instrument called a pluviograph. Several different types have been produced but the basic operation can be seen in Figure 7.4.

Rainfall enters the funnel F and pours through the spout S into the chamber C. The float then begins to rise, producing a movement of the pen arm P, which is recorded on the revolving drum D. After a certain amount of rain has been collected in the chamber, a counterweight arrangement (not shown) tilts it and causes the water to empty via the tube T. The pen trace on the drum appears as a series of spaced rises and falls from which the rainfall rate over a given time interval can be deduced.

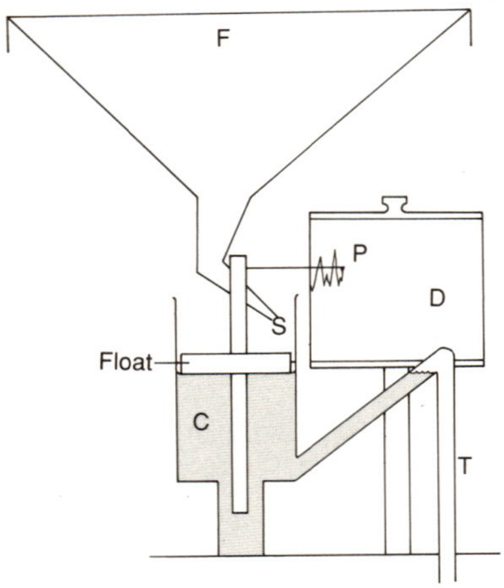

Rainfall enters the funnel F and pours through the spout S into the chamber C. The float then begins to rise, producing a movement of the pen arm P which is recorded as the revolving drum D. After a certain amount of rain has been collected in the chamber, a counterweight arrangement (not shown) tilts it, causing the water to empty via the tube T. The pen trace on the drum appears as a series of spaced rises and falls from which the rainfall rate over a given time interval can be deduced.

Figure 7.4—The pluviograph.

The heavier the rain, the closer the spacing of the lines drawn on the chart. Information of this type is invaluable in constructing drainage systems capable of handling rainfall of various intensities. In urban environments, where a significant proportion of the rainfall runs off rather than percolates, drainage design is increasingly important to prevent loss of life or property damage.

Sunshine Recorders

Several different devices are available to record sunshine hours and sunshine intensity. Pyranometers, for example, measure the actual intensity of the sun's rays by use of complex electronic means. A much simpler and more rugged device, which has been used by the Bureau of Meteorology for many years, is the Campbell–Stokes sunshine recorder (Figure 7.5). It uses the well-known technique of being able to produce a burn on a sheet of paper or cardboard by using a glass lens and the sun.

A piece of cardboard is slid into the bowl. As the sun shines through the glass sphere, a burn is produced in the card. As the sun moves across the sky, the burn travels across the card, which is divided into hours of the day, thus providing a record of the times the sun was actually shining. When a cloud obscures the sun's rays, no burn is produced.

This robust, simple instrument provides a wealth of data that is used in diverse areas such as agricultural crop planning and solar-power design.

Wind Anemometers

Measurement and indication of wind direction and wind speed is a complicated business because of the great variation of both factors in any airstream. A centuries-old technique of indicating wind direction is by means of the weathervane. This employs the use of a pointer of some description, often decorative, which is free to rotate and point into the wind. The points of the compass are often displayed below, indicating the direction from which the wind is blowing.

Measuring the wind speed is a much more complex matter and many different techniques have evolved. An instrument currently used by the Bureau of Meteorology, which measures both wind speed and direction, is the anemograph (a specialised type of anemometer). This consists of a freely rotating head that points into the wind. The head consists of an open tube A into which the wind blows, causing a pressure reduction in the vertical tube S as shown in Figure 7.6.

This pressure reduction is used to produce movement in a pen arm, which in turn produces a written trace of the wind on graph paper. As with the other automated instruments, this is

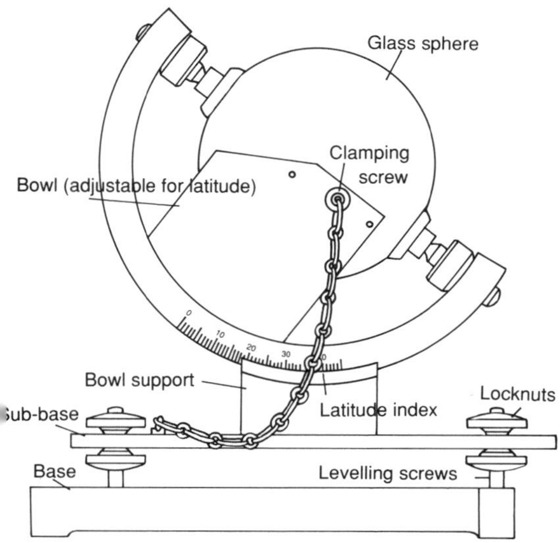

Figure 7.5—The Campbell–Stokes sunshine recorder.

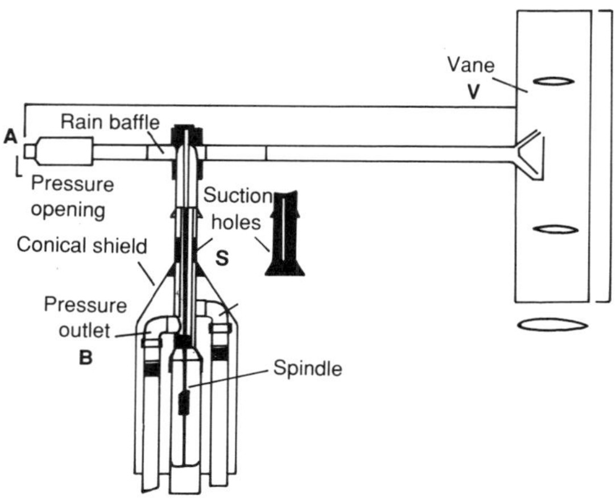

Figure 7.6—Anemograph head.

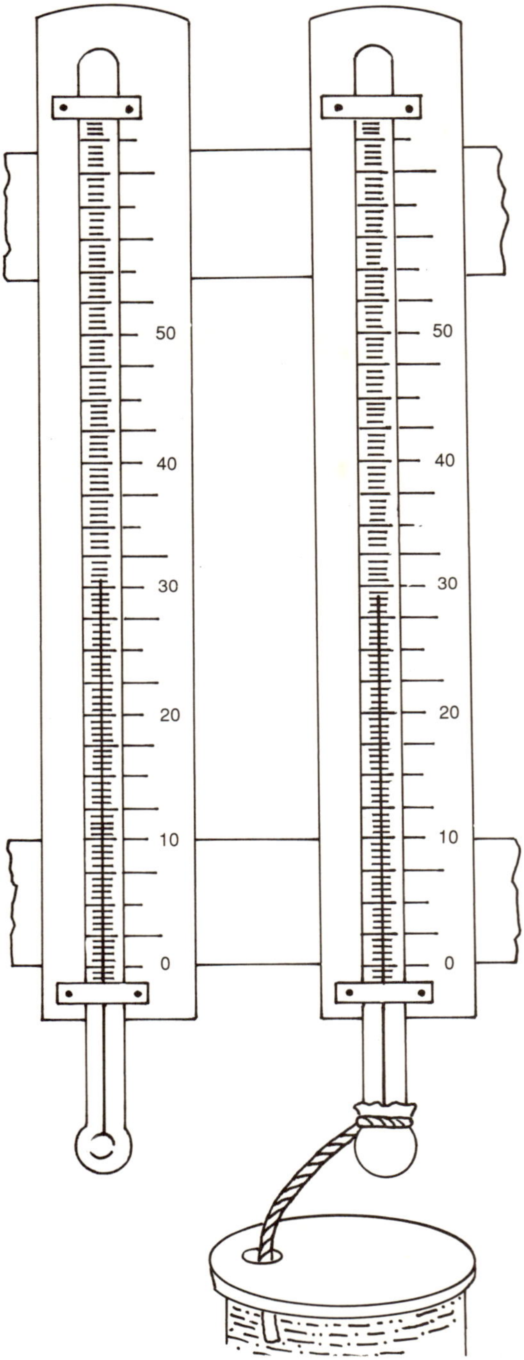

plotted against time, enabling the wind speed to be recorded continuously throughout the day.

Wind direction can also be recorded because of the rotation of the head attached to the wind vane. The maximum wind gust can be readily recorded, together with the time at which it occurred.

Measuring Humidity

There are several different techniques for measuring humidity. The two most common techniques used in Australia are the evaporation method and the hygroscopic method.

The evaporation method makes use of the wet bulb thermometer. The bulb of this thermometer is wound with muslin and kept damp as seen in Figure 7.7. This instrument must be exposed to shaded, free flowing air to give an accurate reading. The temperature it records is the temperature at which evaporation is occurring in the particular air-mass surrounding the thermometer. This is called the wet bulb temperature. A comparison of the wet bulb temperature with the conventional or dry bulb temperature is used to calculate relative humidity tables.

The hygroscopic method makes use of the fact that the dimensions of certain substances vary with the relative humidity of the surrounding air-mass. One such substance is human hair, which changes in length according to variations in the relative humidity of the air. The hair hygrograph uses this principle to produce a trace of relative humidity on a timed revolving drum, similar to several of the other automatic instruments.

Straight hair is preferable to curly hair to produce a trace because it has a more uniform reaction to humidity variations. (The difference between straight and curly hair lies in the cross-section. Straight hair has a circular cross-section while curly hair has an elliptical one.) For accurate recording the hair must be free of grease and

Figure 7.7—The dry bulb (left) and wet bulb thermometers.

Figure 7.8—Inside view of a Stevenson Screen.

dirt and accordingly should be cleaned on a regular basis.

Exposure of the Instruments

How are these instruments, designed to measure the individual meteorological elements, exposed to the atmosphere? Usually the thermometers (wet bulb and dry bulb) and possibly a thermograph, are housed together with the maximum and minimum thermometers in a device called a Stevenson Screen. This is a louvered cabinet with a double roof, all constructed of wood, which allows the sampling of free flowing, shaded air around the thermometers. The inside view in Figure 7.8 shows a typical display of instruments and how they are arranged in a Stevenson Screen.

The Evaporimeter

Evaporation is measured by means of an instrument called an evaporimeter, which is merely a circular tank of water in which the level is carefully monitored on a daily basis. Measurements can be made in various ways, such as comparing the water level with a measured scale on a daily basis or using flotation measurements. Adjustments to take rainfall into account must also be made. For example, if the following levels are recorded:

Today's water level: 75 mm.
Rainfall for previous 24 hours: 5 mm.
Total: 80 mm.
Yesterday's level: 76 mm.

The amount of evaporation for the 24-hour period was 80–76 = 4 mm.

In many country areas, the evaporimeter must be covered with a wire mesh, called a bird guard. This is because in times of hot weather, or water shortage, the evaporimeter becomes attractive to wildlife and birds or other animals sometimes quench their thirst from the instrument.

Observations of Cloud

Observing cloud types from the ground has developed into an art form over the centuries. As shown in Chapter 6, various categories have been identified and named and their approximate height above ground level is well known.

It has only been in recent times that we have been able to rise above the clouds and obtain an overall picture of the cloud patterns that travel about our planet. This has really been made possible with the advent of the weather satellite.

The first specialist meteorological satellite was launched in the United States on 1 April 1960 and was named *TIROS 1* (Television Infra-Red Observational Satellite). This was the forerunner of a family of increasingly sophisticated 'weather eyes' in the sky, that have perhaps provided more information about weather systems than any other device so far. At present Australia generally receives three-hourly, hourly and sometimes half-hourly satellite photographs from the Japanese Geostationary Meteorological Satellite (GMS), which is located about 35 700 km above the equator directly north of Australia. Its orbital speed is the same as the rotational speed of the earth, so it remains at a fixed point above the earth's surface.

This type of deployment is different from an orbiting satellite, which is at a much lower altitude (typically between 800 and 1500 km). The geostationary satellite has the great advantage of being able to take a series of photographs at the same point, so any subsequent cloud movement is readily monitored.

By photographing a sequence of such images over a period of, for example, six months, and then playing the result through in the form of a 'movie loop', spectacular results can be achieved. Such loops have proved immensely constructive in increasing our knowledge of the mechanics of the atmosphere.

Meteorological satellites also provide invaluable data from areas in which no surface data exists. This is particularly important in the Southern Hemisphere, which is predominantly ocean and is a 'sparse data' region. Two different types of photographs are available, namely visible, which is a normal daylight photograph, and infra-red, which senses heat patterns produced by the earth–atmosphere system and can be taken day or night. The satellite itself is around 3 m high, weighs 250 kg and is powered by solar cells.

Astonishingly reliable, satellites are capable of running for several years without any attention, automatically taking their pictures and transmitting them back to earth. There have been three GMS satellites to date, and the current satellite was launched in 1984 (GMS3). Satellite photography has proved to be a whole new branch of meteorology, and interpretative techniques are still being developed to enable more information to be gleaned from each photograph.

Radar

During World War II, radar (Radio Detection and Ranging) was discovered and used to locate aircraft. The principle was simple and can be followed in Figure 7.9.

A powerful radio beam is emitted from a transmitter R and reflected back upon encountering the solid object at O. This reflected signal is received at the dish D and produces a display on a cathode ray tube screen, giving bearing and range. It was soon noted that not only solid objects such as aircraft and topography produced 'echoes' on the screen, but also showers and rain areas. Some idea of rain intensity could also be obtained, because heavy rain reflected most of the available signal, whereas light rain reflected

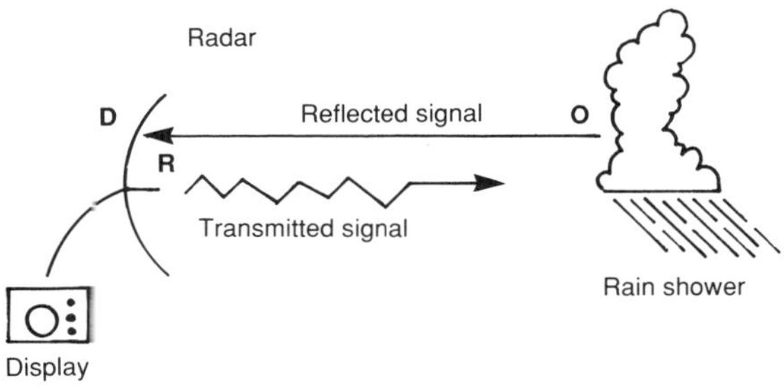

Figure 7.9—Principle of weather radar.

less. The 'brightness' of the screen echo was therefore a comment on how heavy the rain was along the radar beam.

In more recent times, the rainfall has been displayed by means of colour on the radar screens with certain intensities corresponding to certain colours. Red is frequently assigned to the highest rainfall rates and is often observed in relation to thunderstorm activity involving heavy rain or hail. This sort of display is particularly useful in tracking severe thunderstorms and short-term warnings of hail are possible in some cases. For the automotive industry, where enormous damage can be done by such hailstorms, even a warning of half an hour can be valuable.

Radar has also proved very important in the accurate tracking of tropical cyclones near the Australian coast in cases where overlying cloud makes identification of the centre of the system difficult.

Drifting Buoys

Another comparatively recent technological breakthrough has been the use of drifting ocean buoys to collect and transmit various meteorological data. One of the main problems with weather forecasting in the Southern Hemisphere is the fact that the great majority of this part of the world is ocean, from which very little information is forthcoming. Reports from ships and aircraft are vital in this area and now drifting buoys, which are free to move about according to the ocean currents, can also be used. Various meteorological elements can be measured by the buoys, but the two most usual ones are atmospheric pressure and sea-surface temperature. Atmospheric pressure is particularly useful to the meteorologist in chart analysis as drawing isobars across ocean areas where there is no data is fraught with a fair amount of guesswork. Buoys enable a more accurate isobaric analysis to be obtained and this in turn is beneficial to the forecast produced. They are usually 'married' to an orbiting communications satellite that tracks the buoy, receives its data and transmits it back to the receiving station.

Automatic Weather Stations

These consist of a collection of meteorological instruments that take all their readings automatically and then transmit the information to a central agency. Automatic Weather Stations (AWSs) normally transmit information on temperature, rainfall, wind speed and direction, humidity, sunshine and barometric pressure. They can be programmed to collect and transmit at three-hourly intervals but can also be remotely 'interrogated' at any time if unusual weather is expected in the area.

In the long run, stations of this nature are more cost effective than the construction and maintenance of stations requiring staff, although the latter will always be necessary for balloon flights and consultative services. The AWS will play an increasing role in the collection of meteorological data going into the next century.

Balloon Flights

Hydrogen-filled balloons towing aloft electronic packages are used to probe the upper atmosphere and transmit back to earth such data as pressure, temperature and dew point at the various altitudes.

This type of balloon gives vital information of the stability of the atmosphere, which is an important ingredient of everyday forecasting.

Balloons towing aluminium radar reflectors can be tracked, either by weather radar or by hand-operated theodolite, and assuming a certain rate of ascent, the winds at various heights can also be calculated. This is very important in monitoring the upper-level winds which profoundly affect the surface weather systems. Temperature sounding balloons consist of a 'train', comprising a radar reflecting panel, a parachute and the electronic package that records and transmits the data required. This package is called a radiosonde. The train is suspended by cord beneath a hydrogen-filled weather balloon and pulled aloft, being tracked by radar as it rises. As the balloon gains altitude, the atmospheric pressure around it decreases and its size grows accordingly. Eventually, after reaching heights of up to 20 km, the balloon bursts, and the train drops back to earth by parachute, having already transmitted its data back to the receiving station.

These instruments are the main means of monitoring the atmosphere and have been evolving and becoming increasingly sophisticated with time. Further progress is anticipated in the area of meteorological instrumentation in the immediate future, particularly with the next generation of weather satellites which will be able to more accurately monitor temperatures at various heights in the atmosphere and also monitor sea-surface temperatures.

Great progress has been made from the days of Galileo with his thermometer and Torricelli with his invention of the barometer using a mercury column.

Figure 7.10—Balloon trains such as this are sometimes found around the countryside. The unit descends to earth after the balloon bursts at great altitude. The components are, from left to right, parachute, radar reflector and radiosonde.

8. Weather and Society

Effects of Weather on Society

From early times it was believed there was a link between weather and human behaviour and this idea has been increasingly supported in recent times. The effect of weather on the human condition comes under the loose title of biometeorology and it covers such diverse aspects of life as physical disease, stress, discomfort and behavioural patterns.

One of the earliest treatises on the subject was written by the Greek physician Hippocrates in about 400 BC, and was entitled *On Air, Waters and Places*. In this treatise, Hippocrates noted the effect of wind and temperature on human reactions, and also the effect of the seasons on disease epidemics. As with the development of forecasting the weather, biometeorology did not progress greatly beyond the teachings of the ancient Greeks for several centuries.

A serious biometeorological study was undertaken soon after the American Civil War by the eminent Philadelphian physician Dr S. W. Mitchell who was interested in the effect of weather on war wounds and limb amputations. He observed that falling barometric pressure, together with rising temperature and humidity, frequently produced neuralgic pains in amputees. This observation was reinforced some seventy years later in an experiment performed by German meteorologist Otto Hoflich. He studied the correlation of the pains experienced by a World War II soldier, Claus Thurkow, with the prevailing weather situation. Thurkow had lost his right arm during the war, and under instructions from Hoflich, kept a detailed diary on the dates and times when he experienced pain in the stump of his arm. The results were similar to Mitchell's conclusions regarding Civil War veterans.

Over the years, similar correlations have been found between weather and such diverse ailments as arthritis, rheumatism, bleeding ulcers and coronary thrombosis. Explanations for some of these phenomena have been suggested. Our 'feeling' for the weather is transmitted via the skin as it expands and contracts, and as the pores open and close. If the skin is scarred, by a war injury for example, the scarred sector will have different expansion rates to the surrounding 'normal' zone. It is believed that this differential expansion can trigger a pain signal from the area. Deformed skin, such as a corn or wart can produce the same effect.

Similarly, in medical conditions that produce inflammation of the connecting tissues, such as bursitis and fibrositis, barometric pressure changes may cause changes in the internal fluid pressure and, therefore, pain. As we all know, the weather directly affects our comfort and prolonged uncomfortable conditions can produce unpleasant effects for the individual and society.

Heat waves, for example, have been linked with increasing domestic violence, but this may be an indirect effect, caused in the main by increasing alcohol consumption. The large-scale race riots of the 1960s in the United States also seemed to coincide with prolonged hot weather spells that increased people's irritability and discomfort. Some interesting work has been performed recently in the United States by A. G. Barnstow of the United States Climate Analysis Centre. It pointed to the possibility that males are more weather sensitive than females and psychologically troubled people are more affected by the weather than 'normal' people. For these studies, weather situations were compared with the number of telephone calls received by a local Crisis Centre.

Similar links have been discovered between weather and suicide as well as behavioural problems in school children. With all these relationships, there are, of course, certain difficulties in measuring moods and feelings in humans and it is easy to misinterpret cause and effect. Obviously, in these cases weather is not the 'cause' as such, but it may be a trigger that precipitates the result.

Heat and cold discomfort have been measured in controlled environments and general guidelines have been agreed upon for various combinations of temperature, humidity, wind speed and sunshine. Generally, wind flow produces a cooling feeling as it tends to carry heat away from the body. Increasing humidity, on the other hand, produces apparent warming. This is because the human body cools itself by the evaporation of perspiration, and the higher the humidity, the less the evaporation for a given temperature. Extremes of heating and cooling discomfort can be very dangerous to the human body and in severe cases cause permanent tissue damage or even death.

Extreme heat discomfort results in hyperthermia and usually follows prolonged exposure to hot humid weather, or from heavy physical exertion in similar conditions. The advent of the 'fun run' in Australia in the early 1970s has resulted in numerous recorded cases of hyperthermia due to people overexerting them-selves in hot humid weather, usually in full sunlight. In these cases, the heavy work performed by the muscles results in a heating up of the body at a faster rate than the atmosphere will allow the body to cool off by sweat evaporation. The core temperature of the body then rises steadily until collapse and tissue damage may result.

At the other end of the heat discomfort scale is hypothermia, and this occurs when heat is lost from the body faster than it can be manufactured. This is normally experienced in cold, low-humidity conditions when there is a significant wind blowing. This has the effect of carrying heat away from the body, which then attempts to manufacture more heat, only to be further cooled by the wind. The first reaction of the body is usually to begin involuntary muscle movement to generate more heat; we interpret this as shivering. Hypothermia is not common in Australia, although it does occur with cross-country skiiers and occasionally with poorly prepared bushwalkers who are caught in a cold change.

Several tragedies have occurred in the Cradle Mountain area of Tasmania, which is a popular bushwalking area. Its high latitude makes it subject to extremely cold changes, even during the summer months. Cases have occurred where bushwalkers have embarked in hot weather, being only lightly clad, only to be caught in snow after the sudden passage of a cold front through the area. The Bureau of Meteorology in Tasmania issues bushwalkers' alerts in such situations in an attempt to prevent such tragedies.

With some of the longer fun runs, particularly the 43 km marathon, hypothermia and hyperthermia have been experienced by different competitors in the same race. The fast-moving athletes in the first half of the field are more prone to the overheating condition of hyperthermia, while the tailenders may suffer hypothermia, particularly if there is some sort of cold change during the race. This is because the latter group may not be travelling fast enough to produce body heat at a rate similar to the speed at which it is being lost to the environment.

As well as weather producing various sensations of comfort and discomfort on the human body, it also plays indirect roles in the transmission of various diseases. A good example of this is the common cold. Epidemics of the virus-caused disease tend to peak during the winter months in Australia. It is commonly believed that the virus functions better in cold weather, however experimentation does not support this. Control groups of people have been exposed to both cold and virus, while other groups have been exposed to the virus only. The percentage of people who became infected was similar in both groups.

Why does the disease peak during winter? It is

thought that the reason is a secondary one. During cold weather, people will choose an afternoon at the shopping centre or the picture theatre rather than a trip to the beach; school children may choose to stay indoors at lunchtime and people will catch the bus rather than walk. In other words, during cold weather people tend to spend more time in close proximity to other people. This is the perfect environment for the spread of the cold virus and provides a good example of how weather can indirectly affect the spread of a disease.

Another well-known example is malaria, which is spread through a population by a particular type of mosquito. For the mosquito to be able to multiply, a substantial rainfall is required for its breeding cycle and temperatures also have to be ideally warm. This defines a 'malaria climate', which covers the tropics and many parts of the subtropics as well.

A different variety of mosquito transmits the yellow fever virus and this species is found in Australia roughly north of a line from Gosford (central New South Wales coast) to Fremantle on the Western Australian coast. Anyone returning to Australia from a yellow fever country such as South America or Africa must stay south of this line until a certain period has elapsed as a safeguard against spreading the disease.

Another interesting cause and effect involving the weather was noted in Vietnam when it became apparent that outbreaks of the bubonic plague corresponded almost precisely with dry weather. In the rainy season the rats that carried the plague with their fleas were killed off in large numbers as their riverbank burrows were flooded. But in the dry season their numbers grew rapidly, allowing the disease to reach epidemic proportions.

Perhaps the most surprising weather correlations concern the beginning and end of life itself. Statistical tie-ups between the weather and heart attacks have been demonstrated, and usually involve conditions experienced with the approach of a cold front. Obviously weather is not the primary cause in this case but perhaps the falling barometric pressure can trigger the onset of an attack in a person whose heart is already critically poised because of disease.

Paradoxically, similar weather conditions appear to also precipitate the beginning of life with a clear correlation appearing between falling barometric pressure and the onset of spontaneous labour in childbirth. A certain amount of speculation has taken place as to why this relationship should occur. One suggestion is that if pre-frontal conditions (such as falling barometric pressure) trigger labour and the average labour period is twelve hours, then the baby would be born after the front had passed and when the weather had improved. In a natural environment, this could mean a maximisation of survival. Another speculation is that if labour is begun as the weather begins to deteriorate, then predators are less likely to be outdoors to menace the mother at this time of great vulnerability.

The effect of weather on drugs administered to the human body has also been studied. In many societies, particularly Western societies, drugs are prescribed and administered on a scale unprecedented in human history. Evidence has emerged that indicates the effect of certain drugs depends to some extent on the weather. This in turn could affect the dosage levels recommended. However, the exact cause and mechanism of this phenomenon is not yet known.

With all this kind of evidence now emerging, it is clear that the human species is intimately connected with the weather, not only in the obvious external sense, but at far deeper and less expected levels. The late Helmut Landsberg, who is known as the father of modern climatology, once wrote: 'And all of us will have to reckon with the fact that the atmospheric environment plays a major role in our pursuit of happiness,' ('Weather, Climate and You', *Weatherwise*, October 1986).

Perhaps in weather forecasts of the future we

will be able to look forward to comfort predictions, psychological alerts and gynaecological warnings, as well as actual weather predictions.

Weather on the Rampage

By world standards, Australia's climate is fairly mild and equable, but as with other continents, there are occasions when weather goes on the rampage. Because of Australia's sparse population many severe weather events go unnoticed or are rated unimportant. But when such an occurrence takes place over a township or particularly a capital city, it makes headlines and is propagated throughout the nation.

Some of the most famous incidents of more recent years are recalled in this chapter with photographs from newspaper sources and the Bureau of Meteorology.

The Great Sydney Hailstorm— 1 January 1947

New Year's Day 1947 was a typical Sydney summer's day; hot and sultry with a ruffle of sea-breeze along the coastal suburbs. Many Sydney-siders sought to cool off at the beach and big crowds had gathered at the famous surfing areas of Bondi, Coogee, Maroubra and Manly.

Clouds began to develop during the day and it became obvious that afternoon thunderstorms were building on the Blue Mountains to the west of Sydney. However, no-one could have foreseen the ferocity of the weather developing. Around mid-afternoon a thunderstorm moved across from the west, building in intensity as it fed off the hot humid air lying over the Sydney basin. Reaching maximum intensity, it then slowed to the left, rolling towards the north-east and passing along a line extending roughly from Revesby to Bondi.

Sydney has never seen the like of the hail produced by this thunderstorm. Tennis ball-sized stones smashed tiled roofs, pummelled cars and caused widespread injuries to the beach crowds caught in the open with no shelter available. Many cars of that era had canvas tops and there were several reports of the hail slicing through and injuring the passengers within. The roof of the concourse at Central Station was all but destroyed and many streets in the area were rendered impassable by the mounds of hail which persisted in shaded areas for several hours.

Estimation of hail size is always a fairly subjective business, usually prone to exaggeration, but in this case there is no argument. An Earlwood dentist, astonished by the size of the hail falling, seized two large stones and, using dental impression compound, took moulds of them. Plaster of Paris was then used to produce replicas, and these provide solid evidence of the size of the hail on that afternoon.

Flash Flooding in Melbourne— February 1972

Elizabeth Street in Melbourne was constructed over an old creek-bed and despite the gradual laying of greater capacity drainage systems, periodic flooding has occurred over the years. A major flood swamped the thoroughfare in 1863 resulting in the old creek running once again and even inundating Princes Bridge.

One of the most spectacular Elizabeth Street floods occurred in 1972 when a slow-moving thunderstorm brought some 75 mm of rain to the area in one hour. The streetscape became a raging torrent more than a metre deep, washing over cars, around trams and into shopfronts, before quickly abating. The height of the flood was captured brilliantly by a Melbourne *Age* photographer and gives some idea of the fury of the floodwaters.

Brisbane Floods—January 1974

Floods in the Brisbane area are certainly not a rare event with some thirty-seven flood incidents being recorded since 1841. One of the worst floods this century occurred during January 1974 when a prolonged rain situation caused devastating floods in and around Brisbane from the 25th to the 29th.

A Melbourne Age photographer captured the fury of the floodwaters during the 1972 Melbourne floods.

Cyclone Wanda caused severe flooding in Brisbane in January 1974.

The trouble began with Tropical Cyclone Wanda which crossed the Queensland coast near Double Island Point on the night of 24 January, dumping around 200 mm of rain over the city during the next eighteen hours. This completely saturated the soils of the general area, meaning that any future falls would tend to run off the ground rather than percolate into it.

Cyclone Wanda then moved inland as a rain depression, but this had the effect of forcing the monsoonal trough southwards and this triggered two more intense rainfall events over the next three days. During the period 25–29 January Brisbane recorded 656 mm of rain resulting in 6700 homes being flooded. The damages bill came to around $200 million.

As well as the obvious physical damage, the flood had a heavy social impact with many people discovering, too late, that their insurance did not indemnify them against flooding and so financial ruin was added to the general devastation.

The official report on the incident compiled by the Director of Meteorology, Dr W. Gibbs, noted: 'Some people have been permanently affected, both physically and mentally, by the shock of the flood and its aftermath.'

Gales on the New South Wales Coast—May 1974

During the early hours of 25 May 1974, one of the events most dreaded by forecasters took place along the New South Wales coast near Sydney. A tiny low-pressure cell, probably not much more than 100 km across, suddenly developed in the southerly flow that was already established along the southern New South Wales coast.

This small circulation, spinning rapidly in a clockwise direction, formed just off the coast from Sydney and then whirled northwards, staying close to shore as it did so. As it passed Sydney Heads it impelled 70 to 80 knot southerly winds straight into Manly Cove causing great havoc and property damage, including partial demolition of the famous Fun Pier.

By the time this rogue eddy reached the coast off Newcastle it was at its most powerful, and the Nobbys Head Signal Station recorded wind gusts to around 165 km/h, which is a respectable figure for a tropical cyclone.

Probably the biggest single disaster associated with this storm was the wrecking of the large freighter *Sygna* at the height of the storm. The vessel was driven ashore in huge seas near Newcastle. In several quarters this storm is referred to today as the 'Sygna Storm', and it remains one of the most intense blows along the New South Wales coastline in recent times.

Cyclone Tracy—December 1974

One of the most devastating natural disasters in Australia's history, Cyclone Tracy struck Darwin in the early hours of Christmas morning 1974. Although other cyclones have caused greater loss of life, mostly involving unprepared fishing fleets, none has matched Tracy for sheer destruction. Sixty-five people were killed and the damages bill exceeded $100 million. Ninety per cent of Darwin's buildings were either substantially damaged or totally destroyed by winds that were measured at 217 km/h (they may have been greater but the anemograph was ripped away by the gales). To add to the wind damage, torrential rains caused flooding.

The devastation was so tremendous it was suggested that the Australian Government should cut its losses and not even bother rebuilding the city but just totally abandon the site.

The Sandon Tornado—13 November 1976

Tornadoes are violently rotating funnels of air which are associated with severe thunderstorm activity. They are fortunately not common in Australia, but occasionally a thunderstorm will become sufficiently intense to produce a tornado. Such a happening occurred on 13 November 1976 at Sandon, Victoria. Scattered thunderstorm activity was reported over south-eastern Australia

The 'Sandon Tornado' hit Victoria in 1976. Fortunately, tornadoes are not common in Australia.

on that day which became very intense and tornado reports began to come in from an area to the north of Melbourne.

The tornado, which became known as the 'Sandon Tornado', caused some $2–3 million dollars worth of damage, as well as tragically taking the life of a couple motoring through the area. Their car was lifted from the road and carried some 100 m away, killing the couple from impact injury.

Analysis of wind damages gave windspeed estimates of around 170 km/hr for this tornado.

Melbourne Dust Storm—8 February 1983

Melbourne is no stranger to dust storms. From the earliest days of European settlement the great walls of dust moving in from the north-west have been the occasional summer visitor, especially in times of drought.

In the nineteenth century an English visitor to Melbourne, Richard Henry Horne, sent an account of such an event to *The Times* in London:

> It was a fine summer morning in Melbourne on Sunday the 19th of December 1852, but about midday the air became very hot, and oppressively so about two o'clock. Having occasion to visit an encampment in the bush to the northward of the town, I rode up leisurely in that direction. I had not proceeded far when the hot gusts became more frequent and in less than five minutes, there came a gale of wind, bringing with it a long, streaming volume

> of hot, stinging dust, so dense that, when I could venture to peer up from beneath the broad rim of my hat, I could not see a yard in advance, nor could I see below my horse's ears.

Undoubtedly one of the most spectacular dust storms occurred on 8 February 1983 with strong north-westerly winds moving ahead of a cold front. Leading up to this event was probably the worst drought over south-eastern Australia since European settlement. It lasted through 1980 and 1981, culminating in 1982 with much of Victoria and southern New South Wales having their lowest yearly falls on record. This resulted in a very sparse vegetation cover over north-western Victoria and a great deal of dry exposed red dust in the Mallee Region in particular. This dust was whipped into a fast-moving wall that swept across the city of Melbourne and was dramatically captured on film from the Bureau of Meteorology by the Public Relations Officer, Trevor Farrer, in a photograph that was to win worldwide exposure.

Ash Wednesday Bushfires, Victoria and South Australia— 16 February 1983

The unprecedented drought years of 1981 and 1982 had left much of south-eastern Australia tinder dry coming into early 1983, and when dry northerly winds ahead of a cold front pushed Melbourne temperatures up to 43°C on 16 February, only a spark was needed.

In the worst fires seen in Australia since Black Friday, 13 January 1939, large tracts of bush in Victoria and South Australia erupted into unstoppable infernos, causing the death of seventy-one people and a damages bill of over $200 million. Several townships, including Cockatoo, Aireys Inlet and Macedon, were almost totally destroyed, and in the worst single incident, twelve Country Fire Authority volunteers were burned to death in Upper Beaconsfield.

South-east Australia, the French Riviera and California are the three most bushfire-prone areas in the world, and the sad events of February 1983 served as a sharp reminder of the need for constant vigilance during the long hot Australian summer.

In 1983 Victoria and South Australia suffered the worst bushfires seen in Australia for over forty years. (See Chapter 8.)

These moulds, taken by a Sydney dentist, are testimony to the size of the hailstones which fell during the Great Sydney Hailstorm of 1947. (See Chapter 8.)

A combination of cirrostratus and cirrocumulus clouds. These cloud formations are usually associated with cold fronts or jet streams. (See Chapter 6.)

Sometimes, particularly in the winter months, high speed rivulets of air form in the upper atmosphere. These jet streams cause lifting of the upper atmosphere and frequently produce elongated streaks of high cloud across the sky. (See Chapter 6

Stratocumulus at sunset, Broken Hill, NSW. (See Chapter 6.)

High cirrostratus. This cloud type can take the form of a semi-transparent veil of cloud across the sky that can produce a large halo effect around the moon at night. (See Chapter 6.)

Cirrostratus clouds in rippled bands. (See Chapter 6.)

9. Climate and Climatic Change

In previous chapters the forces which drive the atmosphere and create our weather and climate have been considered. A wide variety of phenomena occur in the atmosphere and some of the more notable features, especially those which affect the Southern Hemisphere and in particular Australia, have been described. In this chapter the present climate and its associated weather is placed in the context of the climate history of the earth over the last 4700 million years.

Climate is often thought of as being an unchanging characteristic of a particular place. While this concept may be reasonable over the period of a human lifetime, in the context of longer periods it is inadequate. The climate does change and to address the question of climate change it is first necessary to define climate.

Definitions of Climate

The Meteorological Glossary defines climate in the following way.

> The climate of a locality is the synthesis of the day-to-day values of the meteorological elements that affect the locality. Synthesis here implies more than simple averaging. Various methods are used to represent climate, for example both average and extreme values, frequencies of values within stated ranges, frequencies of weather types with associated values of elements. The main climatic elements are precipitation, temperature, humidity, sunshine, wind velocity, and such phenomena as fog, frost, thunder, gale, cloudiness, grass minimum temperature, and soil temperature at various depths may also be included.
>
> Climatic data are usually expressed in terms of individual calendar month or season and are determined over a period (usually about 30 years) long enough to ensure that representative values for the month or the season are obtained.
>
> There has been some discussion in the literature about the appropriate period of time which should be used to determine climatic data. Instead of the 30-year period ... GARP [The US Committee for Global Atmosphere Research Program] in their 1975 report *Understanding Climatic Change* has suggested that 'climate state' should be determined over a period of time 'considerably longer than the life span of individual synoptic weather systems (of the order of several days) and longer than the theoretical time limit over which the behaviour of the atmosphere can be locally predicted (of the order of several weeks). We may thus speak, for example, of the monthly, seasonal, yearly, or decadal climatic states.

The appropriate period over which weather elements should be measured to define climate depends to a large extent on the use that is to be made of the data. Landsberg (1975) has suggested that when studying climatic change only those changes in terrestrial climate that result from changes in solar emission of an aperiodic nature (or if periodic in nature, of 10 000 years or longer), or changes in insolation received by the earth because of long period changes in orbital elements, should be considered. He suggests that other variations in climate should be referred to as 'climatic fluctuations'.

In trying to come to grips with the problem of determining a suitable time period for defining climate, Gibbs, Maher and Coughlan in *Climatic Change and Variability, A Southern Perspective* (1978), have suggested that, in the absence of climatic change as defined above by Landsberg, the following practical definition is suitable for the Australian context.

> The climate of a particular locality is, for practical purposes, best described by a synthesis of:
>
> (i) the frequency distributions of all meteorological elements at that place over as many years as are necessary to obtain a set of statistics sufficient to delineate the frequency distribution with the precision required;
>
> (ii) a description of the variation in time (systematic or otherwise) of those elements;
>
> (iii) information about serial correlations within the time series of each element, and in the occurrence of particular meteorological phenomena;
>
> (iv) information about the correlations between the time series of the different elements.
>
> In relation to (i) above, the necessary length of record may differ from one climatic element to another. With weather as variable as in Australia, rainfall records for 150 years and temperature records for 50 years or more may be considered necessary to adequately determine and describe the climate.

Scales of Climate

In Chapter 3 the time and space scales of various atmospheric phenomena were described. This subdivision of space scales can also be applied to climatic classifications. The three common subdivisions are microclimate, mesoclimate and macroclimate.

The microclimate deals with meteorological phenomena with a horizontal scale up to about 100 m, a vertical scale of about 10 m and a time scale of about 30 seconds to about 5 minutes. The vertical variations in these phenomena are largely the result of the nearness of the ground causing, for example, turbulence and frictional drag. Horizontally, variations are caused by changes in slope, aspect, soil moisture and soil nature, and vegetation types and height.

The mesoscale climate is a description of meteorological phenomena with a horizontal scale of between 1 and 100 km, a vertical scale of between 1 and 10 km and a time scale of between 1 and 10 hours. The mesoclimate is sometimes referred to as the local climate. The local features that are considered to determine the local climate are ground, soil type and vegetation cover. These features vary slowly over time.

The macroscale climate is concerned with the broad features of climate that are governed by large-scale atmospheric circulation systems. The horizontal scale of such phenomena varies from the smaller synoptic circulations of the order of 500 km to the large-scale planetary waves with a length of 5000 km. They extend vertically through the whole troposphere and have a characteristic vertical dimension of about 10 km. The typical life cycle of such meteorological phenomena varies from about 100 hours for a synoptic scale system to about 400 hours for planetary long waves. Regional macroclimatology deals with seasonal variations in weather phenomena and general tendencies caused by the large-scale topographic features of the globe such as the distribution of the continents on the earth's surface, and the presence of large elevated regions, for example the Himalayan Mountains, the Tibetan Plateau, the Andes in South America and the Rocky Mountains in North America.

Physical Basis of Climate

The energy that drives the earth's climate system comes from the sun in the form of solar radiation, which interacts with the five components of the climate system. These components are the atmosphere, the oceans, the land surface, the cryosphere (mainly the glacial and sea ice) and the biosphere. Each component not only absorbs energy from the sun but also interacts with the other components so that energy flows from one component to the other.

Although the atmosphere absorbs and traps radiation, the absorption is not uniform over the planet. The atmosphere redistributes heat from the surface to the upper atmosphere and from the equatorial regions to the poles and in so doing it also transports angular momentum. It is this process that creates the familiar large-scale weather systems.

The oceans contain most of the water on the planet and there is a continual exchange of moisture, energy, momentum and chemical compounds, such as carbon dioxide, between the oceans and the atmosphere. Probably the most significant feature of the oceans from a climate perspective arises from their enormous capacity to store and redistribute the heat supplied by the absorption of incident solar radiation.

Almost half the solar radiation absorbed by the earth's atmosphere system is absorbed in the tropical oceans. The total mass of the oceans is about 280 times greater than the atmosphere and has a heat capacity about 1200 times that of the atmosphere. This enormous difference means that the oceans have a very large thermal and mechanical inertia compared with the atmosphere, which causes the oceans to be a very sluggish component of the climate system. They have the effect on the climatic system of a giant flywheel compensating for and smoothing out short-term fluctuations of the other components of the climate system. The ocean currents are largely driven by the winds. The enormous mass of water contained in the currents transports great amounts of heat towards the poles and makes a large contribution to the maintenance of the global energy balance. The upper levels of the ocean interact with the lower levels of the atmosphere on time scales of months to years. Deeper ocean waters have thermal adjustment times that take place over centuries so that while the ocean may not have a particularly important role in the day-to-day weather, in the long term it is a very important component of the climate system.

Moisture is an important source of energy for many meteorological phenomena such as tropical cyclones and thunderstorms, which are largely driven by the release of latent heat contained in water vapour. There is an active interchange of carbon dioxide between the oceans and the atmosphere, with large amounts of carbon dioxide being dissolved in the oceans. Carbon dioxide is an efficient absorber of infra-red radiation and, although it forms only a small proportion of the gasses that make up the atmosphere, it plays a significant role through the absorption of long-wave radiation.

The distribution of landmasses over the surface of the earth has a profound effect on the distribution of ocean currents and hence the transport of heat polewards. Landmasses, particularly those with high plateaus and mountain ranges, can also block and redirect atmospheric heat transport. They also play an important role in transferring heat from the surface of the earth to the lower atmosphere where it is redistributed throughout the troposphere by convection. Although some solar radiation is absorbed by the land, a significant amount is reflected back to space. The albedo (or reflectivity) depends on the surface characteristics, for example more radiation is reflected by snow-covered land than forest areas, and leads to imbalances in heat distribution over the surface of the earth. Changes to land surface characteristics cause long period fluctuations in climate. Subsidence and uplift form new plateaus and mountain ranges that affect atmospheric flows, and cause changes to albedo because of changes in vegetation and snow cover. On a still longer time scale continental drift causes significant redistribution of landmass over the surface of the earth.

Continental icesheets, snow deposits, mountain glaciers and sea ice comprise the cryosphere. The continental icesheets of Iceland and Antarctica comprise nearly 80 per cent of the

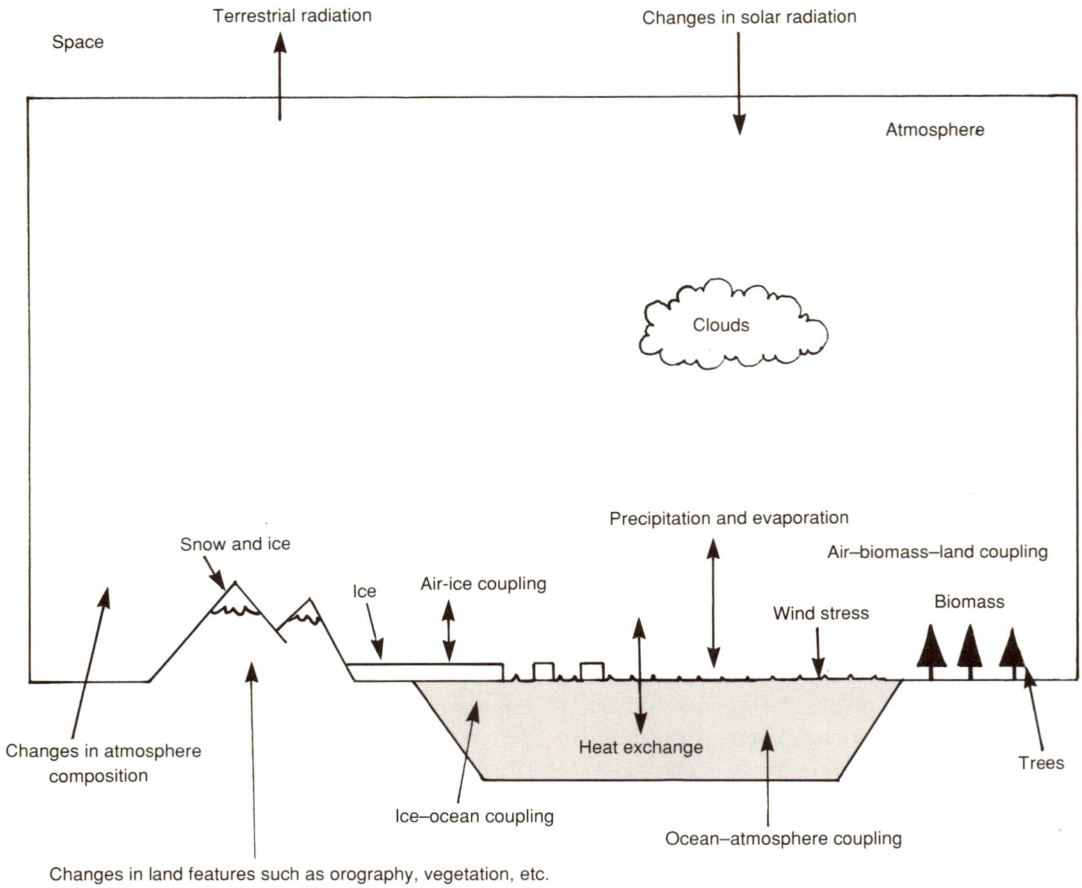

Figure 9.1—Interactions of the components of the climate system.

earth's supply of fresh water and appear to play an active part in the world climate system involving glacial surges that set in motion changes in sea level, sea-surface temperatures and also surface albedo. Solar radiation reflected into space is not available to produce the heat that drives the climate system. Sea ice also acts as an insulator preventing the loss of energy from the ocean during the cold polar winters and so has an effect on the availability of energy to the atmospheric system.

The biomass has a climatic effect through its influence on the chemical composition of the atmosphere. It plays an important role in the carbon dioxide budget of the atmosphere and ocean and in the production of aerosols. It also has a role in determining the chemical balance of other constituent gases and salts. Natural changes in vegetation occur over periods ranging from seasons to thousands of years and are responses to changes in temperature, radiation and precipitation. These changes result in alterations to surface albedo and roughness, evaporation and ground hydrology.

It addition to these natural causes the activities of humanity during the last two hundred years have had a dramatic effect on the biomass. The destruction of large areas of forest has altered, at least locally, the availability of moisture via evapotranspiration, as well as changing the albedo and ground hydrology of vast areas. Humanity has also had a direct effect on the climate system by the substantial increase in atmospheric carbon dioxide caused by the burning of fossil fuels and the destruction of forests. More recently, the use of chlorofluorocarbons has been implicated in the partial destruction of the ozone layer, which has reduced considerably the absorption of ultraviolet radiation in the 0.20 to 0.23 micron range.

For the first time man has become a conscious component of the world climate system. Figure 9.1 illustrates the interactions of the components of the climate system.

The energy that drives the entire climate system originates in the sun. The total radiant power output of the sun is about 3.88×10^{26} watts. The radiant energy crossing a unit area normal to the solar beam at the mean sun–earth distance is about 1360±20 watts per square metre and is called the solar constant. The orbit of the earth around the sun is an ellipse so that the distance from the earth to the sun varies continuously. Figure 9.2 shows the main features of the earth's orbit which have an effect on the energy input into the climate system. At the perihelion (the closest point to the sun) the distance from the sun is about 147.1 million kilometres while at the aphelion (the furthest distance from the sun) it is about 152.1 million kilometres, which causes the solar radiation incident on the earth to vary about 3.5 per cent on either side of the solar constant during a year. At present the incident solar radiation is strongest in January.

The axis of rotation of the earth is not perpendicular to the plane of the orbit of the

Figure 9.2—Main features of the earth's orbit.

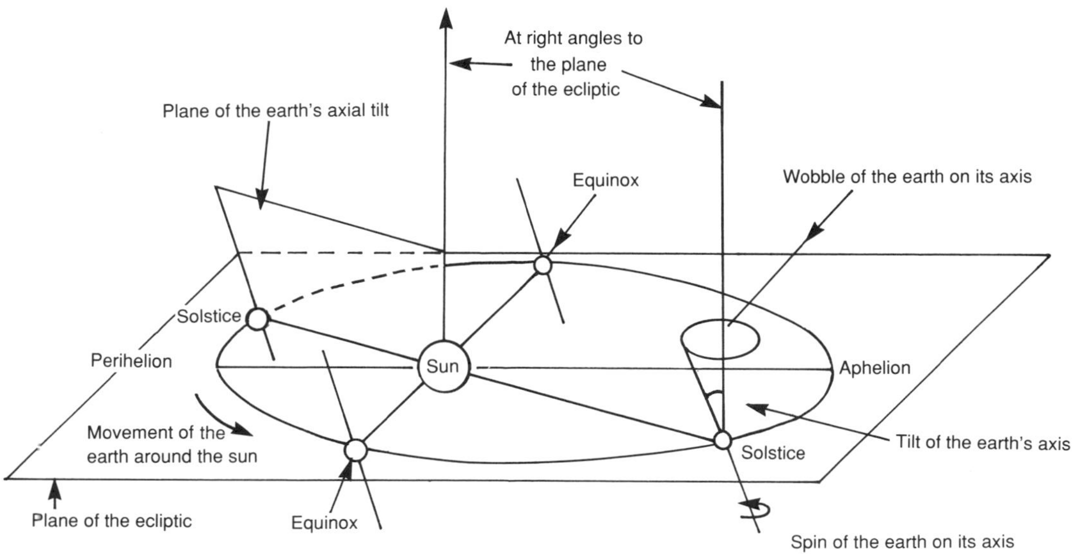

earth around the sun (called the ecliptic). It causes the actual solar energy per unit area reaching a particular place on the earth's surface to vary much more than would be expected from just the eccentricity of the earth's orbit (the difference between the sun–earth distances at perihelion and aphelion divided by their sum). These two effects together cause the seasons.

When the vector from the sun to the earth lies in the plane of the axial tilt, the earth is at one of the solstices (December and June). The equinoxes occur when the sun–earth vector has moved on 90° from its position at the solstices (March and September).

Other characteristics of the orbit change more slowly but nevertheless also cause the amount of solar radiation reaching the earth to vary. The elliptical orbit slowly precesses around the sun in the direction of movement of the earth. Its period is irregular but one revolution averages about 96 600 years. The eccentricity of the orbit also varies as the orbit revolves in space. It, too, has a period of about 96 600 years. A third characteristic that varies the amount of solar radiation reaching the earth is the earth's wobble on its axis. The axis of the earth delineates a cone in space and completes one revolution in about 26 000 years and is the cause of the precession of the equinoxes. The axis precesses in the opposite direction to the orbit around the sun. A fourth characteristic that varies the amount of incident radiation onto a particular place on the earth is the slow change of the obliquity of the ecliptic (the angle of the earth's axis to the plane of the orbit of the earth around the sun). It has a period of about 40 000 years and varies between 24°36' and 21°59'. At present it has an angle of 23°27' and is decreasing.

Variability of Past Climates

During the 4700 million year history of the earth the composition of the atmosphere and the climate has undergone considerable change. Fluctuations in the climate occur on a time scale ranging from periods of a few years through a continuous spectrum up to periods of hundreds of millions of years. Several ice ages have occurred during the earth's history.

An ice age is a period during which icecaps are present on the earth's surface. They can last millions of years and sometimes even more than 10 million years. Between ice ages no icecaps are present. During an ice age variations occur in global temperature and in the amount of ice present in high latitudes and mountainous regions. The colder periods are referred to as glacial stages and the warmer periods between them are called interglacial stages. Glacial stages typically last around 100 000 years and during the last 500 000 years glacial periods have occupied much more time than the interglacial periods. Shorter period cold spells occur that are superimposed on the longer-term glacial and interglacial stages. These shorter cold spells are called stadials and the warmer periods between them are referred to as interstadials.

The magnitude of the surface air temperature changes during the course of most of the earth's existence has been estimated to be about 10°C above and below the normal global surface air temperature, which is estimated to be between 20° and 22°C. The probable mean global surface air temperature during the last ice advance was probably about 9°C; the present mean global surface air temperature is about 15°C.

It is estimated that ice ages have occupied only about 10 per cent of the history of the earth and could be regarded as departures from the normal ice-free state. Even in the grips of the most severe ice age equatorial ocean temperatures have probably only been 2°–3°C lower than at present, increasing to about 2°–3°C warmer than at present during the intervals between the ice ages. Nevertheless, there have been periodic spectacular increases in the size of the continental ice-sheets. During the height of the present ice age, about 18 000 years ago, icesheets covered about 30 per cent of the land surface and had an average thickness of about 2 km, and permafrost and glacial activity covered about another 20 per cent of the land area. (At present about 11 per cent of the land surface is covered by icesheets.) About 50 per cent of the oceans was affected by floating sea ice and icebergs.

Evidence of the nature of early climates is meagre. The oldest rocks contain conglomerates, stones rounded by rolling in streams or along the sea shore. This suggests that water in the liquid state existed about 4000 million years ago with an average temperature between 25° and 50°C. These conglomerates contain compounds that are unstable in an atmosphere containing moisture and oxygen, therefore suggesting that no oxygen was present in the atmosphere. It has been suggested that the atmosphere of this period largely consisted of hydrogen, helium, carbon dioxide, ammonia and methane.

It is beyond the scope of this book to consider the evidence of the evolutionary processes involved that led to the present composition of the atmosphere apart from indicating some of the major stages. It is probable that between 3100 million and 2700 million years ago photosynthetic algae evolved and started to release oxygen into the atmosphere and by about 1600 million years ago the oxygen level had reached about 1 per cent of its present concentration. The strong ultraviolet light then reaching the surface of the earth caused the oxygen molecules to dissociate and recombine to form ozone. This was the beginning of the protective ozone layer that we are in danger of severely damaging today through the use of chlorofluorocarbon compounds.

Evidence exists to suggest the occurrence of ice ages as long ago as the early Proterozoic period (2700 million to 1800 million years ago). There were probably several glacial events with the coldest periods occurring from 2500 million to 2300 million years ago and about 1900 million years ago.

Little can be said of the climate of the Proterozoic period. It was the period of formation of the earliest mountains. Previously the climate was maritime with low continental slabs surrounded by ocean and it is likely no ice ages could have occurred. The mountain-building activity of the Proterozoic period raised land surfaces considerably, allowing glaciation to occur and large icefields to form.

The early Proterozoic period was followed by a relatively warm period up to about 950 million years ago but in the late Precambrian era at least three major ice ages occurred, the first around 940 million years ago and others around 770 million and 615 million years ago. Each lasted about 100 million years.

The remains of animals living up to 570 million years ago suggest an oxygen rich atmosphere with temperatures in the range of 15°±10°C and marine conditions comparable to today. In general climatic conditions between about 570 million and 250 million years ago were relatively warm although there is evidence from the Sahara of a relatively brief ice age about 450 million years ago.

About 250 million years ago at the close of the Palaeozoic era, during the Permo-Carboniferous period, another great ice age occurred which lasted at least 10 million years.

By the early Permian period, about 250 million years ago, giant icesheets covered land areas from South America to Australia and included parts of India. In the early stages glaciation was relatively minor being limited to certain mountain ranges but as the ice age developed the length of glacial periods grew greater and greater. The cyclic glacial periods caused large variations in sea level, drowning great tropical forests and creating the raw material for the coal we use today. Away from the equatorial regions and swampland, climates tended to be extreme with hot summers and cold winters. Sea levels were quite low, and distant from the glaciated regions.

The Palaeozoic era was followed by the Mesozoic era from 225 million to 65 million years ago. The northern continents were mobile and suffered a series of collisions producing a very large Northern Hemisphere landmass with a resulting continental climate. This was the period of the large reptiles and there is no evidence of major glaciation throughout that 160-million-year period. There was a great deal of sea floor spreading activity, which culminated in the sea level being about 500 m higher than its present level. This also reduced the land area to about 15 per cent of the total surface area of the earth.

The period from 60 million years ago to the present is the Cenozoic era. The history of the earth's climate during this period is much better known than that of earlier times and provides some indication of how an ice age may be initiated.

At the start of the Cenozoic era there was essentially a worldwide warm moist semitropical climate. Continental drift and sea floor spreading led to intercontinental collisions from Spain to the Himalayas that, in turn, led to the raising of high mountain barriers and a decrease in the proportion of the earth's surface covered by oceans. Mountains blocked the flow of air and forced moist air to rise vertically. This extracted moisture and latent heat from the atmosphere and led to the formation of dry desert regions and a change in the albedo of the earth. The increased albedo caused more solar energy to be reflected into space at the polar regions and less radiation was available for heating the earth, so disrupting the energy balance. It is postulated that this disruption to the earth's heat regulating system was the dominant factor leading to the present ice age. Minor climatic cycles were superimposed on this longer trend and the glacial periods grew more extensive and severe until about 2 million years ago when the present ice age is thought to have begun in earnest. In this ice age the glacial stages are lasting about 100 000 years and we are now in one of the interglacial stages. In total the interglacial periods have only persisted for about 10 per cent of the life of the existing ice age.

Investigations of cores taken from the seabed of the Pacific Ocean near the equator have given a good indication of the variation in extent of the icecaps during the previous 900 000 years. There have been nine episodes with a global climate similar to the present.

Other methods have been used to examine the climate of the last glacial cycle in more detail. A warm period persisted from about 116 000 years ago to about 60 000 years ago when the last glacial started. Its coldest period lasted only a few thousand years and was followed by a relatively mild interstadial for about 30 000 years. Major cooling then occurred and the glacial maximum persisted for about 10 000 years and was at its severest about 18 000 years ago. Rapid deglaciation followed about 14 000 years ago and led to the relatively mild interstadial of the present time. The warming peaked about 6000 years ago and continued for 1500 years. This period is called the climatic optimum or the hypsithermal and since then temperatures have fallen by an average of 2°–3°C.

Climatic Change Theories

Theories abound on possible causes of climatic change. Some seem to be well corroborated by available evidence; others are not. The formation of ice ages is a complex process involving the interaction of many factors, some of which are discussed below.

Galactic Theory

It is estimated that the dating of the ice ages is in error by no more than ±10 per cent. The episodicity of the ice ages is found to be of the same order as many aspects of the geological record, for example plate tectonic cycles and orogenic revolutions, namely between 200 million and 300 million years. This is remarkably similar to the period of revolution of the solar system around the galaxy.

It has been suggested that some of the variation among the ice ages may be explained by a secondary periodicity in the solar system's orbit around the galaxy, namely its oscillation above and below the principal plane of the galaxy. The solar system encounters high density clouds of intergalactic dust and gas as it moves through the plane of the galaxy with a period of about 32 million years. The dust and gas may have a direct effect on climate by reducing the amount of radiation reaching the earth but the effect is not expected to be sufficient to precipitate an ice age. It is more likely to modify the characteristics of a particular ice age depending on the palaeogeographic features prevailing at the time.

The correspondence between the periodicities in the orbit of the sun around the galaxy and changes in the earth's climate is persuasive. Nevertheless, it does not constitute positive proof and refinement and testing of the theory is required before it can be accepted as an explanation of the observed long-term periodicities in the climate record.

Variable Star Hypothesis

Many stars emit varying amounts of radiation over time. It has been suggested that such variations in the sun may be a possible cause of the onset of ice ages. While short-term variations associated with sun spots are well known there is no known variation that corresponds to the long-term periodicities of the ice ages. This theory is regarded as highly speculative.

Relief Hypothesis

The essential feature of this hypothesis is that physical uplift of mountains would eventually cause the topography to rise above the snow line allowing glaciers to form and, through feedback mechanisms, eventually icesheets. There is much observational evidence that such mountain-building activity has a periodicity of between 200 million and 300 million years. Unfortunately the coincidence of such orogenesis (upheaval) and the ice ages is not perfect. While mountain-building activity clearly is an important factor, the observational evidence suggests that other factors must also be considered to explain the observed palaeoclimate.

Oceanographic Barrier Hypothesis

The various interplate collisions that have occurred since the early Miocene epoch (25 million years ago) saw the transformation of the ocean circulations from largely unhindered east–west flow to the isolated ocean basins of today. It profoundly affected the transport of heat to the polar regions during that period. Barriers to the east–west flow of water forced adjustments to the poleward transfer of heat by the oceans, which in turn fed back into the climate system.

Polar Coincidence Theory

It has been suggested that it is unlikely that an ice age could develop if both poles were located in the open sea. Unlike large expanses of land, the open sea is unlikely to be able to support large expanses of ice long enough to reduce the albedo sufficiently to trigger any ice age. The polar coincidence theory suggests that land areas located at least at one of the poles is a prerequisite for the onset of an ice age. During the Cenozoic era, a narrowing and shallowing of the opening to the Arctic Sea occurred so that it became essentially an inland sea that has been discontinuously ice covered since the Pliocene epoch (13 million years ago). It was suggested by Köppen and Wegener (1974) that the high albedo ice cover at the poles strongly favoured the Quaternary ice age.

Eustatic Hypothesis

The hydrosphere consists of the ice and water of the earth. Its volume is almost constant. However, pulsations in sea floor spreading rates and other plate tectonic dynamics result in a change in the capacity of the ocean basins that leads to large rises and falls in sea level. It is estimated that this process produces changes of about 50 per cent in the land area of the earth and changes in the sea level of between 100 and 200 m.

If the volume of ice covering the land increases, less water is available for the oceans because the total volume of ice and water on the earth is almost constant. This implies that the height of sea level is inversely proportional to the volume of ice on land areas. It is estimated that changing ice volumes on land areas cause changes to the sea level of between 100 and 150 m.

The change in sea level by these two mechanisms would be as great as 350 m, greatly changing the continentality of the earth and forming barriers to both atmospheric flow and ocean currents which would profoundly affect the climate. The eustatic theory of ice ages proposed by Zeuner suggests that increasing continentality and barrier emergence would amplify the effect of decreasing insolation caused by regular variations in the earth's orbit and progressively increase the intensity of glaciation during an ice age.

Atmospheric Effects

The chemical composition of the atmosphere has a profound effect on the absorption of radiation. Of particular importance are water vapour and carbon dioxide. Both are transparent to short-wave radiation but strongly absorb infrared radiation. This is the basis of the 'greenhouse effect'. The role of carbon dioxide in both short-term and long-term climatic fluctuations seems to be that of a powerful feedback mechanism. There are increasing fears amongst the scientific community and the public at large that the large amounts of carbon dioxide being released into the atmosphere as a direct result of humanity's activity may cause significant changes to the present climate in the near future. This problem is discussed below.

Summary of Climatic Change Theories

There is a hierarchy of processes that lead to the cooling of the planet and eventually to ice ages. The revolution of the solar system around the galaxy is probably at the head of this hierarchy. This revolution takes between 200 million and 300 million years. A climatic cycle is also caused by the movement of the solar system above and below the medial plane of the galaxy although this is not believed to be sufficient on its own to account for ice ages. The effect these influences have on the earth depends on the palaeogeographic preparation, which varies through time. Effects that seem to be important are topographic relief, blocking of sea ways, atmospheric composition, the coincidence of land areas with polar regions, the rise and fall of sea level associated with increased glaciation, and the spreading of the ocean floor.

On the shorter time scale of an ice age itself the main variations in the climate appear to be due to variations in the earth's orbit around the sun caused by its eccentricity, by the tilt of the earth's axis and the precession of the earth's axis. These variations cause cycles in the amount of effective radiation reaching the earth with a maximum period of about 100 000 years and secondary cycles with a period of about 20 000 years. Shorter-term variations in the climate are due to various feedback mechanisms such as changing amounts of carbon dioxide in the atmosphere because of the response of the biosphere to variations in temperature.

The Effect of Man's Activity on Climate

Since the Industrial Revolution the activities of humanity have been changing the chemical composition of the atmosphere, causing marked increases in the amounts of various trace gases in the atmosphere such as carbon dioxide, methane, oxides of nitrogen, and chlorofluorocarbons (CFCs). While these gases are still only an extremely small proportion of the atmosphere, their absorption properties have a profound effect on the radiation balance of the earth and this results in the greenhouse effect.

CFCs also upset the balance of chemical reactions that produce a protective ozone layer in the stratosphere which affects the amount of ultraviolet radiation reaching the earth's surface. CFCs have been postulated as the cause of the observed but unexpected ozone depletion over the Antarctic and southern Australia during the spring of 1987.

The Greenhouse Effect

The 'greenhouse gases' exert their influence on the climate through their effect on the energy balance of the atmosphere by selective absorption of radiation. All objects with a temperature greater than absolute zero emit radiation and the wavelength and quantity of radiation emitted is a function of temperature. The sun is much hotter than the earth and emits much shorter wavelength radiation than the earth, which is at a much lower temperature. Figure 9.3 illustrates the spectral distribution of radiation from the sun and the earth. The various chemical components of the atmosphere absorb radiation at different wavelengths. A large fraction of the solar radiation is transmitted through the atmosphere to be absorbed or reflected by the surface. The wavelength of the radiation emitted by the earth is such that this radiation is strongly absorbed by many of the constituent gases and by far the most effective is water vapour. The other strong absorbers are the greenhouse gases. Because the spectral distributions of the earth and sun do not effectively overlap, the net effect is that some of the energy that reaches the earth is trapped. It is converted into heat and contributes to an overall rise in temperature of the atmosphere. While this is often referred to as the 'greenhouse effect' it is somewhat of a misnomer. Most of the warming effect of a greenhouse is the result of the suppression of convection preventing the escape of air warmed by direct contact with the ground.

Figure 9.4 illustrates the heat balance of the atmosphere. The ultimate source of heat for the earth is the sun. Its energy is transmitted as shortwave solar radiation. Of 100 units of energy reaching the upper atmosphere in the form of

Figure 9.3—Spectral distribution of radiation from the sun and the earth.

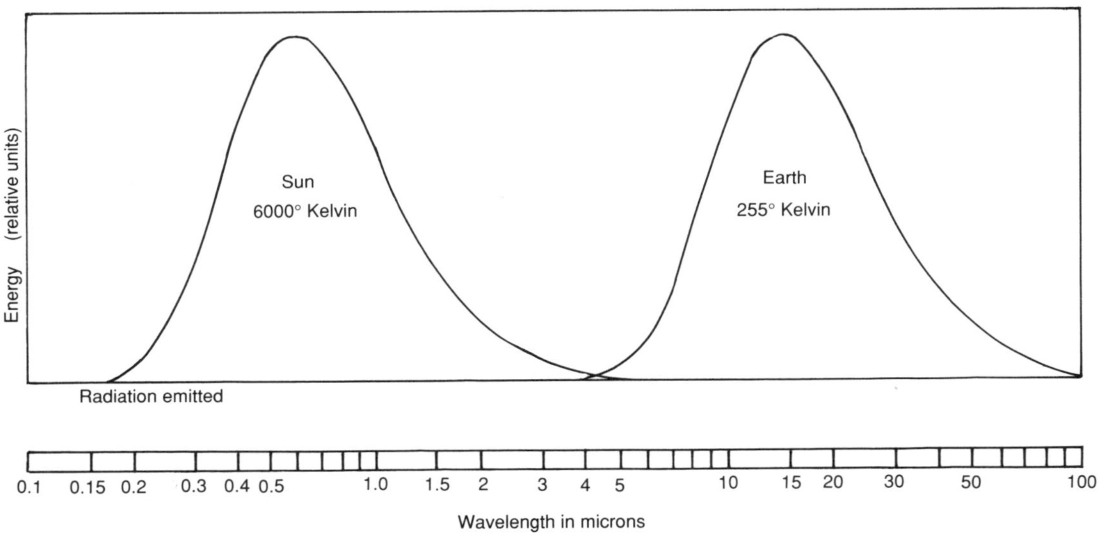

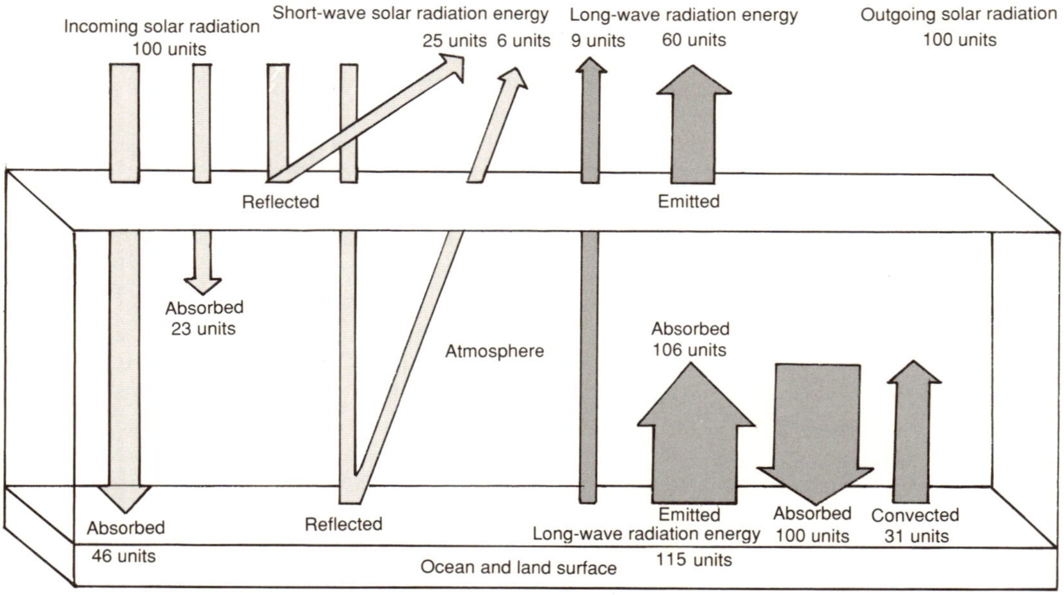

Figure 9.4—Heat balance of the atmosphere.

radiation from the sun, 25 units are reflected back into space by the atmosphere, about 6 units are reflected back into space from the surface of the earth, 23 units are absorbed by the atmosphere and about 46 units are absorbed by the surface of the earth. In summary 31 units of the incident radiation are reflected back into space without participating in the earth's energy balance and 69 units are absorbed. If the earth is not to become continually hotter over a long period the absorption of the incoming energy must exactly match the emission of the outgoing energy in the form of long-wave radiation. This is illustrated by the left side of Figure 9.4. Of 115 units of long-wave energy emitted from the surface of the earth, 106 units are absorbed by the atmosphere and only 9 units escape into space. The 106 units absorbed by the atmosphere are reradiated back to the surface and 100 units are absorbed; the remainder contribute to the heating of the atmosphere. Thirty-one units of heat are also absorbed by the atmosphere from the surface by convection processes. The overall effect of the heating of the atmosphere results in the emission of 60 units of long-wave radiation energy from the top of the atmosphere, exactly balancing the incoming energy of the short-wave solar radiation. Clearly if the long-wave absorption properties of the atmosphere are changed the heat balance illustrated on the right in Figure 9.4 will be altered. Climate models are used to predict the effect on the temperature of the earth and the associated changes to the circulation resulting from such changes to the heat balance.

There is no evidence to suggest that an increase or decrease in carbon dioxide has ever led to the respective end or beginning of an ice age. There is no evidence that runaway heating of the earth has ever occurred from the build-up of carbon dioxide. However, it is a powerful feedback mechanism that does cause shorter-term fluctuations in climate.

There is evidence that previous ice ages have been associated with fluctuations in the amount of carbon dioxide in the atmosphere. This is probably due to the response of the biosphere to the changing temperature conditions.

Since the Industrial Revolution humanity has been burning fossil fuels at a fast rate, releasing much of the carbon (in the form of carbon dioxide) that had been extracted from the atmosphere over millions of years. Deforestation of the tropics has also contributed but carbon dioxide release seems to have been compensated for by increased growth elsewhere. Since AD 1800 the concentration of carbon dioxide has increased from 275 parts per million to 348 parts per million by volume today. Currently carbon dioxide in the atmosphere is increasing at about 0.4 per cent each year. About half the estimated output of carbon dioxide dissolves in the oceans and the remainder stays in the atmosphere. Almost all of the current increase in the atmosphere is due to the burning of fossil fuels.

Methane is also an important greenhouse gas although it constitutes a much smaller proportion of the atmosphere than carbon dioxide. Methane has increased from about 750 parts per billion by volume 200 years ago to about 1650 parts per billion today. It is presently increasing by about 1 per cent per year.

There are various sources of methane. Some enters the atmosphere through losses from coal mines and natural gas fields but by far the greatest sources causing the increase are ruminant animals (cows and sheep) and the increasing acreage of rice paddies. Both of these sources have multiplied because of the growing need for food for the world's burgeoning population.

Nitrous oxide is also an important greenhouse gas. It is generated by various natural means but it is increasing above the natural background level through fertiliser use, caused by the burning of biomass and the combustion of fossil fuels. At present it is increasing by about 0.3 per cent each year.

Recently CFCs have become significant constituents of the atmosphere. These are entirely artificial chemicals that are now known to destroy ozone in the upper atmosphere. This is discussed in a later section. However, they are also a very efficient absorber of long-wave radiation and a strong contributor to the greenhouse effect in the lower atmosphere. These gases have been increasing at the rate of about 5–10 per cent per year over the last 10 years.

If no atmosphere was present and hence no greenhouse effect the average temperature of the earth, with the existing planetary albedo, would be about –18°C. At present the average temperature of the earth is about 15°C and the effect of the greenhouse gases is to raise the average temperature of the earth by 33°C. The effect on the temperature and circulation of the atmosphere of increasing the amount of greenhouse gases has recently been investigated by using global atmospheric models. The results vary according to the model used but there is general agreement that the average temperature at the bottom of the atmosphere would rise between 2° and 4°C by the year AD 2030. These results are based on the assumption that if the present rate of increase of greenhouse gases were to continue, by 2030 there would be an equivalent doubling of carbon dioxide. One result of such warming would be the thermal expansion of the sea causing sea levels to rise. Some melting of temperate glaciers would also contribute to rising sea levels. On average these two effects are predicted to increase sea level between 20 and 140 cm.

It is likely that such changes to the energy balance within the climate system will produce considerable changes in climate at particular locations. However, present global climate models do not have sufficiently fine resolution to predict regional climate changes with any certainty. It is not possible as yet to accurately predict what the likely effects will be on Australia's climate, and reliable regional climate predictions are not expected to be available for several years.

The theory that climatic change will be induced by an increase in greenhouse gases is not based on evidence that changes are already occurring. It is based on the observed changes in the chemical composition of the atmosphere and our physical understanding of the processes that occur within the climate system. The search for evidence of observed changes is complicated by the natural variability of climate that would be expected even in the absence of the greenhouse effect. The present theory predicts that during the last 125 years an average world temperature increase, based on the increase in greenhouse gases, should be about 0.7°C. There is also an observed warming trend averaged over the whole globe of about 0.5°C during that period. While this may be persuasive, it is not conclusive evidence of an enhanced greenhouse effect. Many factors influence global temperature and this makes the problem extremely complex. It is expected that warming of the atmosphere would cause rising sea levels. There is some evidence that the sea level has risen about 10 cm during the past 100 years. However, some scientists have cast doubt on the quality of some of the earlier measurements. It is also very difficult to be sure that the land to which the instruments are attached has not been sinking or rising.

Ozone Depletion in the Upper Atmosphere

In Chapter 3 the formation of ozone in the upper atmosphere by the action of ultraviolet light on oxygen atoms was briefly described. Ozone is both created and destroyed by sunlight in a very complex set of chemical reactions which are still not fully understood. A balance occurs in the rate of destruction and rate of creation of ozone so that the net result is a small but significant concentration of ozone in the stratosphere with a maximum concentration occurring at a level of about 20–28 kilometres. Because ozone strongly absorbs short ultraviolet radiation (UV-B), it forms a screen that filters out such radiation.

A wide range of living organisms are particularly sensitive to ultraviolet light. Exposure to UV-B has been linked to the incidence of non-melanoma skin cancers. There is also evidence that it is linked to the development of cataracts. It has been postulated that in the Australian region each 1 per cent loss in ozone in the stratosphere will lead to a 2 per cent increase in UV-B reaching the ground, which in turn may lead to a 4 per cent increase in skin cancers. It is also known that many agricultural crops are sensitive to UV-B and any increase in its amount may lead to a reduction in crop yields. Many aquatic organisms likewise are known to be very sensitive to UV-B. In particular phytoplankton, which is at the base of the entire aquatic food chain and a key component in the marine ecosystem, is especially sensitive to the levels of UV-B reaching the surface. A change in the intensity of UV-B reaching the surface will have major consequences for the biosphere.

Absorption of ultraviolet radiation by ozone causes warming of the upper atmosphere. It is the process that leads to the characteristic thermal structure and stability of the stratosphere. The thermal structure influences the general circulation of the atmosphere and consequently the climate of the earth. Changes in stratospheric ozone concentration would, through changes in the energy balance of the upper atmosphere, directly affect the local climate.

In addition to having the properties of a greenhouse gas the CFCs are very stable and do not break down easily in the atmosphere. Halons (bromochlorofluorocarbons), which are used as fire suppressors, also have similar properties. It is estimated that they can exist in a stable state for up to one hundred years in the atmosphere. Such gases, through the normal circulation processes of the atmosphere, eventually move into the upper atmosphere where the process of ozone formation and depletion occurs. Because of their chemical nature these compounds react with ozone in a series of complicated chemical reactions and the net result is that the amount of ozone in the upper atmosphere is reduced, which decreases the sun screen effect of the ozone layer. More UV-B reaches the ground and increases the potential to damage living tissue.

Recently, evidence has been accumulating that the ozone concentration in the stratosphere has been reduced by the activity of trace gases such as CFCs. There is a natural variability in the concentration of ozone in the stratosphere related to such factors as the eleven-year solar sunspot cycle. Sunspots are associated with changes in the strength of certain wavelength radiation emitted from the sun which in turn affect the chemical reactions which produce ozone in the stratosphere. After the removal of these effects, ground-based observations of ozone taken from 1969 to 1986 between latitudes 30°N and 64°N indicate a reduction in concentration between 1.7 and 3 per cent, depending on latitude. Ground-based observations for other latitudes are not sufficiently accurate to detect any changes. However, it has been possible by using a combination of ground-based and satellite-based observations taken between 1978 and 1987 to obtain sufficient accuracy to show that the total atmospheric ozone between latitudes 53°N and 53°S has, after removal of solar cycle effects, decreased on average by about 1.1 per cent. Satellite data indicate that over Australian latitudes (from the equator to 39°S) there has also been about a 1.1 per cent depletion in ozone concentration.

These observations are consistent with numerical models that simulate the effect of CFCs on the ozone layer. They suggest a reduction in concentration between 0.7 and 1.5 per cent depending on the details of the models. However, while the general predictions are consistent with observations, the seasonal decrease in mid-to-high latitudes of winter concentrations were underestimated by these models.

Since the late 1970s there have been large and unexpected depletions in ozone concentration over the Antarctic during spring. This is the so-called Antarctic ozone hole. It is not so much a hole but rather a severe reduction in the concentration of ozone. In the spring of 1987 the lowest recorded ozone concentrations were observed over the Antarctic with a concentration 50 per cent below normal spring values. Recent observational evidence suggests that the spring depletion is due to a combination of the winter–spring Antarctic stratospheric circulation and the presence of CFCs. During winter and spring a regional circulation sets up an isolated air-mass over the Antarctic. The air flows around the South Pole and this circulation is known as the polar vortex. Because the air-mass remains in the darkness of the Antarctic winter during the whole season there is no heating by the sun to replace heat lost by long-wave radiation and very low stratospheric temperatures occur. This causes the formation of stratospheric clouds consisting of ice and frozen inorganic acid particles that, in the presence of CFCs, interact, when the sun returns to the Antarctic in spring, to cause a series of chemical reactions that severely deplete the ozone concentration over the Antarctic.

Over Arctic regions the isolation of the air-mass during winter is much less marked and the dramatic reduction in ozone concentrations does not seem to occur during the northern spring.

In 1987 various nations of the world agreed to limit the production of CFCs by 50 per cent during the next decade. This agreement is known as the Montreal Protocol. Present models predict that such a reduction will result in a further overall depletion of atmospheric ozone of a few per cent during the next fifty years and this will then be followed by a slow recovery to pre-1980 levels. In 1989 various nations agreed to further restrict the production and release of CFCs into the atmosphere following the severe depletion of ozone over the Antarctic during the spring of 1988. In June 1990, ninety-three countries met in London and agreed to completely phase out CFCs in the industrialised countries by the year

2000 and in developing countries by the year 2010. The EEC, Canada, Australia and New Zealand plan to phase out CFCs by 1997.

While the present Protocol will eventually allow the return to the overall pre-1980 ozone concentrations, it will not help the situation over the Antarctic. A 50 per cent reduction in the emission of CFCs in the next decade would still result in a doubling of chloride levels by 2075. Based on the present understanding of atmospheric chemistry and meteorology over the Antarctic, an 85 per cent reduction in CFC release would be required to stop the Antarctic hole becoming worse. It is not at present clear what effects the Antarctic hole may have on the Southern Hemisphere biosphere, particularly the phytoplankton.

Summary

The climate system is the result of a complex set of interactions of many influences with the atmosphere. Evidence exists that there have been major fluctuations in the earth's climate since its formation over 4700 million years ago. Possible causes of past fluctuations range from galactic influences to internal planetary rearrangements of the earth's surface but it appears that now human influence is becoming increasingly important. In the context of past climate history and the ability of life forms to adapt to new climates, the increase of carbon dioxide, CFCs and other gases because of human activity are predicted to cause an extremely rapid change in climate. Such a rapid change would have catastophic effects not ony for humanity but for the whole biosphere. There is still considerable uncertainty about some aspects of these predictions and continuing research directed towards a better understanding of weather and climate and improved monitoring of the atmosphere is essential if unplanned catastrophic changes are to be avoided.

Ripples of altocumulus, West Macdonnell Ranges, NT. *(See Chapter 6.)*

Distant showers over the Three Sisters, Blue Mountains, NSW. *(See Chapter 2.)*

Glossary of Terms

Air-mass A large body of air that has almost uniform temperature and humidity across its horizontal extent.

Albedo The reflectivity of the earth.

Biometeorology The effect of weather on living organisms, particularly human beings.

Buys-Ballot's Law An observer facing the wind has low pressure to the left in the Southern Hemisphere and to the right in the Northern Hemisphere.

Cloud types Classification of clouds into groups based on altitude and method of generation.

Coriolis force A force caused by the rotation of the earth. It acts perpendicular to the direction of the movement of an object and its magnitude is proportional to the speed of movement. In the Southern Hemisphere it pushes moving objects to the left and in the Northern Hemisphere it pushes to the right.

Cryosphere The total ice on the earth's surface. It is a combination of the polar icecaps, the sea ice and glacial ice.

Effective temperature The temperature of saturated air giving the same thermal sensation as any given combination of temperature and humidity.

El Niño Refers to an exceptionally warm ocean current that flows down the west coast of southern America and may extend as far as 12°S.

Equatorial trough The shallow area of low pressure where the trade winds of both hemispheres meet. If the trades meet at a large angle and considerable convergence and vertical motion occurs it is called the intertropic convergence zone.

Evaporation Liquid water at the surface reverting back to gaseous form.

Front A narrow boundary or zone separating air-masses of different temperatures.

Frost Basically, frozen dew. Widespread over Australia during the winter months.

Geostrophic wind The wind which results when the only two forces acting on a parcel of air are the pressure force and the Coriolis force.

Gradient wind The wind which results when the only forces acting on a parcel of air are the pressure force, the Coriolis force and the centrifugal force.

Greenhouse effect The heating of the atmosphere by the absorption of impaired radiation by certain gases such as carbon dioxide, methane and others.

Hail Accretions of frozen rain associated with strong updrafts in thunderstorm cells.

High An area of high pressure around which the winds blow anti-clockwise in the Southern Hemisphere and clockwise in the Northern Hemisphere.

Humidity A measure of the amount of water vapour in the surrounding air-mass.

Hyperthermia Extreme heat discomfort, which can lead to collapse and tissue damage.

Hypothermia Extreme cold discomfort. Can cause collapse because of reduced body core temperature.

Insolation Incident solar radiation.

Instruments, meteorological Various devices for measuring the 'weather elements' such as temperature, humidity, wind, sunshine, etc.

Jet stream A narrow ribbon of strong winds (greater than 110 km/hr) usually in the upper atmosphere. Normally a jet stream is thousands of kilometres in length, hundreds of kilometres in width and some kilometres in depth. The two major westerly jet streams are the polar front jet stream and the subtropical jet stream.

Latent heat The quantity of heat required to change a unit mass of substance from the solid to the liquid state (latent heat of fusion) or the liquid to vapour state (latent heat of vaporisation) without a change in temperature. Latent heat is released when water vapour condenses into droplets and when water droplets freeze.

Low A low-pressure area around which winds blow clockwise in the Southern Hemisphere and anticlockwise in the Northern Hemisphere.

Meteorology The study of the weather. From the Greek *meteoros* and *logos*, meaning a discourse of things high in the air.

Monsoon A seasonal wind which is caused by the seasonal difference in temperature between the land and sea. The winter monsoon is a cool dry wind that blows from the land to the sea and the summer monsoon is a warm moist wind which blows from the sea to the land and often results in widespread heavy rain.

Ozone layer The layer of maximum concentration of ozone in the stratosphere between 15 and 30 km above the surface of the earth.

Recurvature The change in direction of movement of a tropical cyclone from a general westward drift to an eastward movement caused by its capture in the upper-level westerly wind flow of higher latitudes.

Sensible heat Perceptible heat. Unlike latent heat, the gain or loss of sensible heat causes an increase or decrease in temperature.

Stratosphere The layer of the atmosphere immediately above the troposphere where the temperature generally increases with height.

Subsidence Sinking air in the atmosphere.

Temperature Measure of the warmth of shaded, free-flowing air, usually as read by a thermometer.

Thunderstorm Giant cumulonimbus clouds produced by powerful vertical motion currents in the air. Produces lightning and thunder and, on occasion, hail.

Tropical cyclone A cyclonic, low-pressure system of tropical origin which rotates clockwise in the Southern Hemisphere.

Tropopause The boundary between the troposphere and the stratosphere.

Troposphere The lowest layer of the atmosphere where the temperature generally decreases with height. It is the layer in which the weather occurs.

Vapour pressure A measure of humidity. It is the pressure exerted by the water vapour in the surrounding air-mass.

Walker circulation A convective cycle that is the result of the gradient of sea-surface temperature along the equator in the Pacific Ocean. Sea-surface temperatures over the western Pacific are generally warmer than those in the eastern Pacific resulting in general rising air in the western Pacific and sinking air in the east.

Wind Air in motion. Caused basically by the heating of the earth by the sun and the rotation of the earth.

Further Reading

Ashton, H. J., *Meteorological Data for Air Conditioning in Australia*, Bureau of Meteorology, 1964.

Asnani, G. C., 'The Equatorial Cell in the General Circulation', *Journal of the Atmospheric Sciences*, vol. 25, pp. 133–4, Boston, 1968.

Australian Co-operative Observers' Guide, Bureau of Meteorology, 1973.

Bureau of Meteorology, *Climate of Australia*, Australian Government Publishing Service, 1983.

Bureau of Meteorology, *Climatic Atlas of Australia*, map sets 1–8, Australian Government Publishing Service, 1974.

Bureau of Meteorology, *Manual of Meteorology*, Part 1—'General Meteorology', Australian Government Publishing Service, 1975.

Clarke, R. H., Smith, R. K., and Reid, D. G., 'The Morning Glory of the Gulf of Carpentaria: An atmospheric undular bore', *Monthly Weather Review*, vol. 109, pp. 1726–50, Boston, 1981.

Colquhoun, J. R., Shepherd, D. J., Coulman, C. E., and McInnes, K., 'The Southerly Buster of South-Eastern Australia: An orographically forced cold front', *Monthly Weather Review*, vol. 113, pp. 2090–107, Boston, 1985.

Director of Meteorology, *Brisbane Floods, January 1974*, Bureau of Meteorology.

Downey, W. K., Tsuchiya, T., and Schreiner, A. J., 'Some Aspects of a North-Western Australian Cloud Band', *Australian Meteorological Magazine*, vol. 29, pp. 99–113, 1981.

Drosdowsky, W., and Holland, G. J., 'North Australian Cloud Lines', *Monthly Weather Review*, vol. 115, pp. 2645–59, Boston, 1987.

Foley, J. C., *Frosts in Australia*, Bureau of Meteorology, 1945.

Garratt, J. R., Physick, R. K., Smith, R. K., and Troup, A. J., 'The Australian Summertime Cool Change. Part II—Mesoscale Aspects', *Monthly Weather Review*, vol. 113, pp. 202–23, Boston, 1985.

Gedzelman, S. D., *The Science and Wonders of the Atmosphere*, John Wiley and Sons, New York, 1980.

Gibbs, W. J., and Maher, J. V., *Rainfall Deciles as Drought Indicators*, Bureau of Meteorology, 1967.

Grace, W., and Holton, I., 'A Mechanism for Downslope Winds with Special Reference to the Adelaide Gully Wind', *Meteorological Note 179*, 1988.

Haltiner, G. J., and Martin, F. L., *Dynamical and Physical Meteorology*, McGraw-Hill, New York, 1957.

Henderson-Sellers, A., and Blong, R., *The Greenhouse Effect—Living in a Warmer Australia*, New South Wales University Press, 1989.

Holland, G. J., Lynch, A. H., and Leslie, L. M., 'Australian East-Coast Cyclones', Part 1—'Synoptic Overview and Case Study', *Monthly Weather Review*, vol. 115, pp. 3024–26, Boston, 1987.

Hounan, C. E., *Evaporation in Australia*, Bureau of Meteorology, 1961.

Hughes, P., 'American Weather Services', *Weatherwise*, vol. 33, no. 3, Washington, 1980.

Kidd, D. A., 'Weather Lore in Aratus' *Phaenomena*', *Weather and Climate*, vol. 4, pp. 32–5, 1984.

Landsberg, H. E., 'Drought, A Recurrent Element of Climate', *Special Environment Report No. 5*, pp. 41–90, World Meteorological Organization, Geneva, 1975.

Landsberg, H. E., 'Weather, Climate and You',

Weatherwise, Washington, October, 1986.
Landsberg, H. E. (ed.), *World Survey of Climatology* (15 vols), Elsevier, Amsterdam, 1985.
Letestu, S., *International Meteorological Tables*, World Meteorological Organisation, Geneva, 1966.
Linacre, E., and Hobbs, J., *The Australian Climatic Environment*, John Wiley and Sons, 1977.
Lorenz, E. N., *The Nature and Theory of the General Circulation of the Atmosphere*, World Meteorological Organisation, Geneva, 1967.
Oliver, J. E., and Fairbridge, R. W. (eds), 'Encyclopedia of Climatology', Part XI of *Encyclopedia of Earth Sciences*, Von Nostram of Reinhold, New York, 1987.
Peach, B., *Australia Wide*, Australian Broadcasting Commission, 1977.
Pearl, C., *Our Yesterdays*, Angus & Robertson, 1954.
Pearman, G. I. (ed.), *Proceedings of the conference—Greenhouse '87: Planning for Climate Change*, CSIRO Publications, 1987.
Physiological Principles in Heating, Ventilating and Air Conditioning Guide, American Society of Heating, Refrigeration and Air Conditioning Engineers, vol. 38, 1960.
Pittock, A. B., Frakes, L. A., Jenssen, D., Peterson, J. A., and Zillman, J. W. (eds), *Climatic Change and Variability—A southern perspective*, Cambridge University Press, Cambridge, 1978.
Roberts, A., and Roberts, M. J., *Dreamtime Heritage*, Rigby, 1975.
Ryan, B. F., and Meadows, J., 'A Relative Flow Isentropic Analysis of a Cut-off Low', *Australian Meteorological Magazine*, vol. 27, pp. 42–57, 1979.
Ryan, B. F., and Wilson, K. J., 'The Australian Summertime Cool Change', Part III—'Subsynoptic and Mesoscale Model', *Monthly Weather Review*, vol. 113, pp. 224–40, Boston, 1985.
Spillane, K. T., 'Atmospheric Characteristics on High Oxident Days in Melbourne', *Clean Air*, vol. 12, no. 4, pp. 50–6, 1978.
Taljaard, J. J., van Loon, H., Crutcher, H. L., and Jenne, R. L., *Climate of the Upper Air*, Part 1—'Southern Hemisphere', vol. 1—'Temperatures, Dew Points and Heights at Selected Pressure Levels', Naval Weather Service Command, Washington DC, 1969.
Tapp, R. G., and Barrell, S. L., 'The North-West Australian Cloud Band: Climatology, characteristics and factors associated with development', *Journal of Climatology*, vol. 4, pp. 411–24, Royal Meteorological Society, 1984.
Toup, A. J., 'The Southern Oscillation', *Quarterly Journal of the Royal Meteorological Society*, vol. 91, pp. 490–506, Berkshire, 1965.
Whittingham, H. E., *Extreme Wind Gusts in Australia*, Bureau of Meteorology.
Wiin-Nielsen, A., *Compendium of Meteorology for Use by Class 1 and Class 2 Meteorological Personnel*, vol. 1, parts 1, 2, and 3, World Meteorological Organisation, Geneva, 1978.
World Meteorological Organization, *The Global Climate System—A critical review of the climate system during 1982-1984*, World Meteorological Organization.

List of Abbreviations

m	metres
km	kilometres
hPa	hectopascals
°C	degrees Celsius
°K	degrees Kelvin
kg/cm^2	kilograms per square centimetre

Index

Numerals in **bold** type denote maps, tables, diagrams, etc.; those in *italic* type denote photographs.